Poets on Place

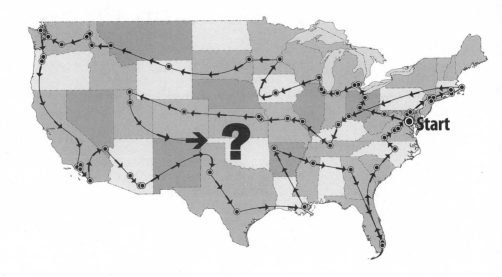

Poets on Place *Route Map*
September 2003–May 2004

Poets on Place

Tales and Interviews from the Road

by

W. T. Pfefferle

with a foreword by

David St. John

UTAH STATE UNIVERSITY PRESS
Logan, Utah

Utah State University Press
Logan, UT 84322-7800

Manufactured in the United States of America
Printed on acid-free, recycled paper

Library of Congress Cataloging-in-Publication Data

Poets on place : tales and interviews from the road / [compiled] by
W.T. Pfefferle ; with a foreword by David St. John.
    p. cm.
  Includes index.
  ISBN 0-87421-597-8 (pbk. : alk. paper)
  1. American poetry--20th century--History and criticism--Theory, etc.
2. American poetry--21st century--History and criticism--Theory, etc. 3.
Poets, American--20th century--Interviews. 4. Poets, American--21st
century--Interviews. 5. Pfefferle, W. T.--Travel--United States. 6.
United States--Description and travel. 7. Place (Philosophy) in
literature. 8. United States--In literature. 9. Regionalism in
literature. 10. Local color in literature. 11. Setting (Literature)
I. Pfefferle, W. T.
  PS325.P634 2005
  811'.540932--dc22
                                        2004028467

For Tucker Satellite
who would have loved the trip

Acknowledgments

I want to offer my sincere thanks to the sixty-two poets who let me into their places and poetry. Their kindness was remarkable, and I am forever in their debt.

Thanks to Bonnie and G.O. for meals and fellowship during the final months of the book. I want to thank my mother, who taught me the lifelong value of reading and who always stuck up for me when English teachers gave me any lip.

I'd like to thank Jim Cummins of the Elliston Poetry Room at the University of Cincinnati for his kindness and resources. And, at a time when the project was winded and spent, David St. John's encouragement kept us on the road and searching.

Some of the interviews appeared in slightly different forms in *Poets & Writers*. My thanks to the editors of that magazine and especially to Kevin Larimer for his excellent guidance. A few of the interviews in this book appear out of their actual sequence.

I've been lucky to have John Alley as an editor. His advice is always measured, insightful, and reasonable, and I've known from his first contact that the book would be in good hands. Kyle Sessions has been terrific in helping us all realize a unique and pleasant look for the book, and Rebecca Marsh's copyediting saved me from the punctuation junk heap many times.

Finally, it's impossible for me to express how integral my beautiful wife Beth was in the planning and execution of this book. Her unwavering support and endless help on all matters, large and small, made this project as much hers as mine.

- James Harms's "Landscape as the Latest Diet (Southern California)" was published in *Tar River Poetry* (fall 2003). It is reprinted by permission of the author.
- David Citino's "Through a Glass, Darkly" is published here by permission of the author.
- Richard Tillinghast's "Wake Me in South Galway" was published in *Six Mile Mountain* (Story Line Press 2000). It is reprinted by permission of the publisher.
- Mark Strand's "A Morning" was published in *Selected Poems* (Random House 1990). It is reprinted by permission of the author.
- Marvin Bell's "Port Townsend, Washington, Waterside" is published here by permission of the author.
- An excerpt from Michael Dennis Browne's "At the Cabin,"

published in *Great River Review*, is reprinted by permission of the author.

- David Romtvedt's "With Caitlin, Age 8, Building a Qhuinzee for a Winter Night" is published here by permission of the author.
- Sandra Alcosser's "Mare Frigoris" is published here by permission of the author.
- Robert Wrigley's "Ordinary Magic" is published here by permission of the author.
- Nance Van Winckel's "Awaiting the Return Ferry" is published here by permission of the author.
- Mark Halperin's "Accident" is published here by permission of the author.
- Jana Harris's "Mr. Elija Welch, First Planting" was published in *The Dust of Everyday Life* (Sasquatch Books 1997). It is reprinted by permission of the publisher and the author.
- An excerpt from Barbara Drake's "The Man from the Past Visits the Present" is published here by permission of the author.
- Floyd Skloot's "A Warming Trend" is published here by permission of the author.
- Carol Muske-Dukes's "Twin Cities" was published in *Hunger Mountain* (fall 2003) and is reprinted by permission of the author.
- David St. John's "Dijon" is published here by permission of the author.
- Donald Revell's "A Parish in the Bronx" was published in *New Dark Ages* (Wesleyan University Press 1990) and is reprinted by permission of the publisher and the author.
- Richard Shelton's "Local Knowledge" was published in *Selected Poems 1969–1981* (University of Pittsburgh Press 1982) and is reprinted by permission of the publisher.
- Jane Miller's "#15" comes from *A Palace of Pearls* (Copper Canyon 2004) and is reprinted by permission of the author.
- William Wenthe's "Alien" is published here by permission of the author.
- Naomi Shihab Nye's "Pause" was published in *Fuel* (BOA Editions 1998) and is reprinted by permission of the author.
- An excerpt from Beth Ann Fennelly's "The Kudzu Chronicles" is published here by permission of the author.
- Natasha Trethewey's "South" was published in *Shenandoah* (spring 2004). It is reprinted here by permission of the author.
- Denise Duhamel's "Valentines, Hollywood Beach" is published here by permission of the author.
- Terrance Hayes's "Threshold" was published in *Swink* (2004). It is reprinted by permission of the author.

- Alan Shapiro's "Bower" is published here by permission of the author.
- Charles Wright's "High Country Spring" is published here by permission of the author.
- Rita Dove's "The House on Bishop Street" was published in *Thomas and Beulah* (Carnegie Mellon Press 1986) and is reprinted by permission of the author.
- Henry Taylor's "Harvest" was published in *The Horse Show at Midnight* and *An Afternoon of Pocket Billiards* (University of Utah Press 1975, 1992) and is reprinted by permission of the author.
- Dave Smith's "Gaines Mill Battlefield" is published here by permission of the author.
- Nicole Cooley's "Unfinished Sketch: Green Sandbox Winter Sky" is published here by permission of the author.
- David Lehman's "April 9" was published in the *The Daily Mirror* (Scribner 2000) and is reprinted by permission of the publisher.
- The excerpt from C. D. Wright's "The Ozark Odes" was first published in *String Light* (University of Georgia Press 1991) and subsequently in *Steal Away, Selected and New Poems* (Copper Canyon Press 2002, 2003). It is reprinted by permission of the publisher.
- James Cummins's "Spring Comes to Hamilton Avenue" is published here by permission of the author.
- Frederick Smock's "Heron" is published here by permission of the author.
- Mark Jarman's "Nashville Moon" was published in *Unholy Sonnets* (Storyline Press 2000) and is reprinted by permission of the publisher.
- Scott Cairns's "Mud Trail" was published in *Philokalia* (Zoo Press 2002) and is reprinted by permission of the publisher.
- Elizabeth Dodd's "Sonnet, Almost" is published here by permission of the author.
- Paisley Rekdal's "Ode" was published in *Colorado Review* (summer 2004) and is reprinted by permission of the author.

Contents

Foreword

Poets on Place is an extraordinary and unique collection of interviews with American poets. Collected with intelligence and wit by W. T. Pfefferle on his cross-country travels, these interviews on the importance of place and landscape in poetry—better than any anthology of poetry or prose I can think of—exhibit the profound richness and dazzling diversity of American poetry and its poets.

W. T. Pfefferle is always careful to locate the urgencies of American poetry—indeed, he does this repeatedly, poet by poet—against the backdrop of real places, actual landscapes, all the while allowing his poets to reflect upon the landscapes of childhood or the vistas of a particular past, especially those made resonant by memory and reflection. He also has found poets who live comfortably in the fiercely imagined landscapes of their interior lives, their personal desires and hopes, and shows the way these more private and internal tensions are mirrored in a poem's more literal, external landscape.

Whether charting a sense of personal history or the many courses of their futures by summoning the coordinates of a place from the past (often a private landscape of childhood inflected by the imagination) or by reckoning the precise physical details of their immediate surroundings or by describing the shifting verbal star fields—those more mercurial landscapes—of their own poetic language, these poets reflect with humor, brilliance, and candor the crucial and constant necessity of place in the making of poetry, in their pursuit of the poetic art.

Physical space and spiritual grace have long been connected in poetry, and the invisible maps of these poets' experiences stand as the templates of their own poems. Whether a poet's poems echo above the summits of the Colorado mountains or along the canyons of office buildings in Manhattan, the backdrop of place—the insistent particularity and resonance of the physical world in which they live and dream—remains the recognizable point of reference by which they are able to join us to their own poetic paths.

We all live in a world that is constantly in movement, perpetually fragmenting and reassembling itself. Those places from which we come and those to which we've moved provide the ground against which the figures of our lives themselves move, change, depart. Poetry is forever looking to discover and then describe what we mean by a sense of "home." Is such a place located in an actual place, in the imagination, in albums of memory, or in some combination of them all? We all fear from the time we are young that loss of home, of place, of belonging. In this collection of interviews, each poet struggles with the details of his or her own biography, of the complexities of residence and movement, in order to speak with the voice of place, the voice of landscape, within the poetic voice. Whether gypsy-nomad, confirmed homebody, or reluctant exile, the poets in this collection know that the poetry of the human heart and the living mind always seeks residence in the available landscapes of the lived world. The poetry of American solace is the poetry of place.

Often, the summoning of place is an almost incantatory act against loss. In the same way that we tell stories of those who have died as an attempt in some measure to keep them alive, so do many of the poets in this collection tell—in their poems—the stories of landscapes they fear may be lost to memory or to progress or to any of those many erasures we gather under the rubric of "time." So, too, we recognize the intrinsic social and political natures of these poems of place, however personal they may at first seem, however overtly their authors foreground their environmental or ecological concerns.

We begin to see in the course of these interviews in *Poets on Place* that, although collected individually, these voices weave together into a fabric that exhibits a profound sense of American poetic community. It is truly both comforting and consoling. We carry place both with us and within us. Certainly our most powerful memories are those fixed in specific landscapes, those that we then bring with us to our newly chosen homes. As those places and landscapes quietly begin to emerge in our poetry, we are rewarded with a profound sense of arrival, of homecoming. It is what Donald Revell suggests when he says, "Place uses me." And as the poets here repeatedly make clear, we are constantly paying back those debts we owe to the landscapes of our childhoods. Every poem of place, every poem of landscape continues to enact a complex and subtle rescue of our (wildly various) pasts. In so doing, these poems and these places make possible the experience that we are, however briefly, fixed upon this earth. It is an incalculable gift to be able to feel this, and *Poets on Place* and the voices of these poets remind us of the magnitude of that gift. This collection is a movable feast, a portable homecoming you can carry with you everywhere that you care to travel.

—*David St. John*

Introduction

All books start as ideas, but *Poets on Place* started as a choice to leave one life behind and to go in search of another. My wife and I had great careers. We had worked hard for them, had been busted and broke during our early years, but now I was a writing program administrator, and she was a sales executive for a network-owned TV station. We had worked hard for almost twenty years, and we loved our jobs and the life we led. But we lived in ten different places during that time, and when we both eased into our forties, we started wondering about another move, one not predicated on a job. We thought about taking a look around the country and seeing everything we could.

We had the fantasy of drifting around and starting a business in a pretty little town on the water. A bed and breakfast, maybe. I wanted a place where you could have poetry readings and live music. My wife wanted to make soup (but not salad) and cookies (but not cakes). I thought maybe a Laundromat would be easy to own, but my wife wanted to know who'd fix the dryers. I wanted to open a radio station, play all my favorite songs, and hire college kids for pennies to run it when I wanted to sleep. My wife wanted to know who was going to clean the bathrooms. We kept the fantasies to ourselves. There was always something a little secretive and naughty about our desire to break from the real world.

A move from Texas took us to a suburban community outside Baltimore, Maryland. When house prices began to skyrocket and our neighborhood boomed, the fantasies gained new life. A neighbor sold his three-year-old house for twice what he bought it for, and we began to do calculations in our heads. How much time and space would that money buy us?

We liked where we were; it was a nice bustling suburb, near two big cities (I worked in Baltimore and my wife commuted to D.C.), but it wasn't really home. We had never found that place. We were visitors wherever we went, never afraid to go on to the next stop. In some ways, home for us was always somewhere else. Home could be anywhere we slept that night. Home, really, was just with each other.

We don't have kids; our dear fourteen-year-old Boston terrier had recently died, and so we just thought we'd go and see what there was to see. It became a real thing, this fantasy. We could investigate the red and black and "blue highways" of the big country and see if we'd stumble across a place that held a deeper magnetic resonance for us than all the other places we'd lived in in the past.

But we couldn't just sneak off in the night. We told our families and friends. People told us we were brave. We liked that at first. But after a while, "brave" started to sound like "stupid." People said "brave" with their voices lifting at the end, like a question. Like "brave" really meant "Are you both insane?" And we got nervous.

We had sleepless nights. No jobs meant no money. Sure, there'd be money at the beginning; the house sale would solve that problem. But it wasn't a lot of money. It was a year's worth, if we kept things simple. If we bought the generic macaroni and cheese. If we did laundry on a rock in a river.

But it still was in our heads, so we started planning. None of it was as romantic as I hoped. I started thinking about mail. Where would our bills go? How would we get health insurance? We started thinking of things we could do with our stuff, and then—like a switch getting thrown—things just moved forward. We quit our jobs. Over the phone, we bought a small investment house near my wife's folks, and then we gave our furniture and boxes to burly men in a moving van and prayed that they would be willing to take it there.

We bought an RV. A motor home. A Class C. A giant cab-over with a slick interior, a tiny stove, a tiny bathroom, a tiny bed, and giant tanks for gasoline and water. It was a great big rolling tin can, a moving version of our home. In went the smallest version of our stuff that we could imagine. We piled in clothes and cans of soup, paper towels, hoses, wrenches, flashlights. My Swiss Army knife. It was a mini-everything-we-owned; it got only eight miles to the gallon, but it was our ticket to the highway.

Suddenly, twelve months stretched ahead of us like a long, straight line. We wondered what in the world we were going to do for all that time. We knew that the first days would be delicious and long. No work. No clocks. Nobody waiting at school for me or at the office for my wife. We didn't have deadlines or reports that were due. No students were waiting in a classroom. We imagined the bliss would be overwhelming.

Until the second week. Then what? My wife had longed for more time in the natural world than her career afforded. For years she had stolen the occasional three-day trip to go rafting or camping. She'd come back hungry for more, more trees, more land, but would settle for more reports and more paperwork instead. So the immediate future was intoxicating for her. She shed her old self like it was a coat she had outgrown. She was ready for new places, new experiences, and was going to eat them up no matter how they came to us.

I'm considerably more trouble, however. I have to have something to do. I have to have something to finish. So we talked projects. I'm a writer, a poet, and the thought came to me that I could do something with that. For as long as I've written, my own work has been grounded in place, steeped in the sensibility that where we live and work matters. Shortly after we got married, we lived for a dozen years in Texas. I felt that state's effect on everything in my work, from the content of a poem to the length of the line. The endless vista of west Texas, the scrubby desert outside Van Horn. I wrote what the wind sounded like. In the places of Texas I found my own voice as a writer. Texas taught me patience. It taught me that what was in between the towns was more important than the towns themselves. And though Texas continued to work on me after I left, the new places added their own colors and textures. So Florida added something, and then Maryland. I wondered about the rush my poetry got from a new place, a new setting, and I thought about how the places of my life were a part of what I wrote, how I wrote.

And I wondered about other poets. How does a poet go from Chicago to Montana, and how is her life different? What happens when a writer from the mountains ends up in a prairie state surrounded by grasslands? How is the art different for someone living on a mountain in Idaho and someone in a 300-square-foot apartment in Greenwich Village?

Poetry is a rich collection of things, people, ideas, language, and places. And it rocketed through my head that the greatest poetry of all, for me, was always somewhere else. The greatest poem ever written is that stretch of highway on the way to a town you've never heard of before. The wondrous discovery of every turn.

Each state, another poem. Each town, its own stanza. There was poetry in every bump on the interstate, through every corner of every tiny road. It was all poetry, every place I'd lived. A poetry of places that stretched for endless miles in every direction, under tree-lined streets in Ohio, and under the ominous skies of the Pacific Northwest, and under the perfect blue canopy of the Florida Gulf Coast.

I wanted to know what other writers thought of it. How did their work spring from the places of their lives? And there was only one way to find all of this. We'd have to go to them.

Wherein We Begin Life on the Road

We leave our old home in suburban Baltimore behind at 5:30 a.m., making our way west through the dewy morning. We move carefully through the Maryland panhandle, passing working farms, one time waving at a father and son on a tractor coming the wrong way up the interstate's shoulder. We cross into West Virginia, and by 8:00 a.m. the sun is up behind us, diffuse, but lighting our way.

Yesterday we watched several men put our furniture and boxes in a large truck. They left late in the day, headed this direction; and every time I come over a hill, I half expect to see the truck in a ditch somewhere, our couch upside down in a creek.

By 9:30 we're in Morgantown, too early for the interview. We hit Wal-Mart and get a longer water hose and some animal crackers. We pull up at a small park and open all the windows. I drink orange juice and eat a big donut, while my wife looks outside and listens to whatever kind of bird is going to town on the trees there. A woman and a surging black lab go past the front of the motor home, disappearing down a dark wooded trail.

James Harms
Morgantown, West Virginia

Jim Harms couldn't be a more amiable fellow. He lets me in the front door of his neat, white bungalow. I step over his sneakers on the front porch, but leave mine on. We sit across a small coffee table from each other, and I see he's a music fan; the Elvis Costello box set gives that away. His laptop rests between us, as if at any moment it might be needed. The warm breeze comes in the open windows, mixing with the downward draft of a single, lazy ceiling fan. Harms wears a T-shirt and shorts, loose white socks. He moves his hands around when he talks, but it's all relaxed. He tells me about his youth in California and his now decade-long stay in West Virginia.

~ ~ ~ ~ ~ ~

Are the places in your poetry based in California, or have you been in West Virginia long enough for it to have taken over?

Most of the places in my poems are the places of childhood, the places of dreams. For some reason, California seems to be the most pervasive landscape in my work: it's the default landscape.

So when I sit down, it's less a matter of what's outside the window, as it is the feeling of locating the calm in this wilderness of constancy, the constancy being memory, the past. I grew up in California. And when I remember the California of my youth, it's the foothills I see— that particular type of wild grass, the sage, the chaparral. Now that I haven't lived there in so long, other residue of place is starting to filter in. And it's only been in the last three years that West Virginia has begun to materialize. And I'm excited by that because it's such an amazing state for so many reasons—not just its physical beauty, but its unique history. It's a tragic state in many ways because of the history of exploitation. It was essentially a state owned by people who didn't live here, and that legacy has been difficult to resolve for many native West Virginians.

In many ways the landscape of West Virginia is caught up in the politics and the social conditions of West Virginia. And that's how it's been entering into my poems, very politically. I'm writing a lot about the destruction of landscape, the lack of concern for place, all the time being very conscious of its beauty. So there's a lot of tension in these newer poems.

I've also learned over the years to let the present place, the place where I'm working right now, leak into the poems. If we were talking about issues of time, they'd be anachronistic poems. The past would be contiguous with the present. In my poems, California and wherever I'm sitting at the time sort of meld, sometimes very obviously. There are a lot of disconnects, and instead of trying to massage them out of the poems, I've allowed them to remain in all their disruptive glory. To me, poetry is all about simultaneity of time and place. I'm really wanting and encouraging that kind of disconnect, a disconnection that is ultimately rather healing in that the normal rupturing of space and time that feels real—if rather alarming—to the rational mind is mended in the poem.

My book *(Freeways and Aqueducts)* is ultimately a book about leaving one place and finding another. So the book is organized to foreground that notion. The first section is called "West," the third section is called "East," and the middle section is a sequence of poems that acts as a reinvention of the myth of Los Angeles. The collection ends up being about physical and emotional movement: here's memory, here's my sense of coming to terms with the past, and here's an attempt to reconcile myself to the new place.

I knew I had to find a way of coming to terms with a new landscape, a way that wasn't naive, that wasn't simply a glorification of that landscape, or a too surface-y consideration of it. And what came to me was the old cliché of "Home is where the heart is." Family, ultimately, ended up being my way of coming to rest. To say, my home now is with people within a landscape. My kids were born here in West Virginia. I started my family here. So the third section of this new book is very much about the presence of family taking over any other concern with landscape.

Place ended up being connected to my children, to settling down.

But do you still think of yourself as a California poet?

I certainly still do. It's not something I feel I have to exorcise. Although there is a sense that it's important to feel at home in the world, so if you're always feeling displaced that it could work against other factors. One of my teachers, one of my good friends, David Wojahn, always said that it was the condition of twentieth-century American poets to be in exile. Because most of us teach, we tend to move away. We follow jobs, et cetera. That ends up being something about the way the American poem has evolved. And I think that's right. There is that sense of displacement in American poems. But I feel a lot less anxiety about that displacement now. I really wouldn't want to live in California again. I love California, and my family and most of my good friends are there. And I visit as regularly as I can. But it no longer seems like an ideal. Because it's the landscape of childhood, the landscape of dreams, I'll probably always write about it.

Landscape as the Latest Diet
(Southern California)

Instead of butter, the ten a.m. light of June
   on Little Island, masts blending the mist
      until it clarifies into nothing.

Instead of salt, the sand beneath
   Balboa pier, cool even in July, trimmed
   with wrack and empty cans, the blue haze of spray
      and breeze between the pilings.

Instead of bread, the violet stains
   on the sidewalks of South Pasadena, the jacarandas,
      their small cry tuned to rhyme the sky.

Instead of eggs, the foothills under smog, the sage
   and scrub oak browned by drought
   and the tick of ozone in the air.

Instead of meat, the arroyo at sunrise, the gray
   inside gray of tulle fog and
   coyote, coyote bouncing down
   the deer trail, a pigeon in its mouth.

Instead of sugar, the date palms along
   the dry wash gathering wind
   in their fronds for the hourly reprimand,
   an endless hush.

Instead of wine, the smell of oranges
   and ocean water, the smoke
   of smudge pots before dawn.

Instead of supper, the song of bells
   in the harbor, the seals draped
   over buoys like fat uncles on the furniture.

And everyone at ease in the middle distance, in repose.
   And the meal, like memory, a cure
   for nothing but hunger, but forgetting.

—James Harms

David Citino
Columbus, Ohio

My wife parks the motor home alongside a large metal fence outside the edge of the Ohio State campus. The campus is ungodly large, yet construction continues to flourish everywhere. We pass work trucks, guys getting out with metal lunch pails, helmets, and other gear, and make our way across to a two-story McDonald's. The place is fantastic inside, clean, empty. Nobody there but Janet behind the counter. We give our order and then head over to a corner of the room. This feels like a vacation to us, like it's a school day and we're playing hooky. We laugh while we eat, wonder if—as is planned—our furniture is arriving in Arkansas this morning.

After we eat, my wife heads back to the motor home, and I sling the big equipment bag of cameras and recorders over my shoulder and start stumbling through campus looking for Denney Hall.

When I find the building, I'm a few minutes early so I sit down on a bench. I notice a first-floor office with lights on. Inside I recognize David Citino. He's moving around his office, pulling a book off a shelf, going back to his desk.

He's talking with a colleague when I go inside and knock on his open door, but he waves me in. He has one of those offices every professor wants, full of books, spacious, well lit from inside and out. I've played racquetball in smaller spaces.

~ ~ ~ ~ ~ ~

In what way has place impacted your own writing?

Well, first of all, I think it's done so in immeasurable ways. I've always been of the belief that every poem happens somewhere. That there is a place, even in that love lyric or that expression from the heart of despair that doesn't mention Cincinnati, Ohio, or Rome, Italy. That the poet is in a place—his or her head and soul are in places—and that place helps to inform the poet and the poem. Many of my poems are obviously poems in places. They happen in Ohio, or they happen in other places I happen to be, like Italy. And they use the lay of the land. They are very obviously somewhere.

But I think of place as internal as well as external. I'm from Cleveland. I'm living in Columbus. The where I'm from is a template. If I'm in Dublin, or Rome, or Florence, I seem to relate to cities by what I know. That

6

city I was born and raised in, Cleveland, was gritty and industrial, wonderfully ethnic. It had its neighborhoods of Slovaks and Slovenes and Italians, and black and white—often with their own newspapers, their own grocery stores, bakeries. Cleveland then was divided east and west by a crooked, viscous river that sometimes caught on fire. That's my city, that internalized place. I tell my students that each of us seems to have some ur-place within—some place we know better than the back of our hand. It might be a neighborhood. It might be those four or five houses where we played as kids. We remember our playmates. We remember  what their mothers and dads looked like. We remember the way their houses smelled. It might be a city block. But it's a magical place, and in our writing we go back there, over and over again. You know the joke that you sometimes hear is "Every poet just has one poem. He or she just writes it over and over again." I think that in some real sense, every poet has one place. And he or she is able to go there or to see new places always in terms of that original one.

I know you've lived here all of your life, but do you feel like an Ohio poet?

There's no doubt about that. I've been here for fifty-six years. Ohio poet is what I am. And I'm very proud of it. Having been here so long, I know the place. I know Ohio, the magazines and the poets, in addition to the towns, valleys, lakes, and rivers. The idea of being an Ohio poet might be to some very limiting. "You're an Ohio poet? But what about America, the world?" But I believe that so many poets draw strength from that place, from their roots. Think of Faulkner, who is so popular in Japan. Think of Hemingway and those early Hemingway stories from up in Michigan, still read in Russia. There is something about paying attention to one's specific place that enables us to touch the universal.

You talked earlier about traveling. What happens in your poetry when you travel?

So many writers are energized by dislocation. Especially those that are so ensconced in one place. You think of what exile did for James Joyce. He, in *Ulysses*, recreates this city that he knew. But he was elsewhere, in other cities in Europe, to do that. I've been electrified by travel. I start writing like a maniac, and I still can work on poems that started twenty to twenty-five years ago somewhere else; but you bring them home, bring them back to your place, and you begin to see them better, see better what you're trying to do and say.

Because of my ethnic background, traveling to Italy is going back to my roots at the same time. So it's someplace that's terribly different and exotic, and yet it's a place that feels familiar, as my name might indicate. My grandparents came from the toe of the Italian boot, Calabria, between Naples and Sicily. They came to America because they were peasants and ended up in Cleveland. They met in Cleveland, even though they'd lived in adjacent villages, adjacent mountain tops, really, in Calabria. He worked on the B&O railroad for fifty-four years. I grew up listening to them, my other relatives, and their friends, speaking in Calabrese dialect in a Cleveland accent.

That's another thing. We carry inside us this magical place I've been talking about. But what about the places of our parents, and their parents, even the places of our children? We can't be in only one place. In the old days in Cleveland, you lived on the same street, in the same house, and all your relatives lived around you. But even then you had other places. I often think about one of my father's places. A young man just out of high school gets sent to Guadalcanal. It's a world war. And we have all the photographs of him. He was a second lieutenant. With his men, tents, palm trees, rifles, and, of course, fighting. What a dislocation that must have been. But he was still Cleveland Giovanni, Cleveland Johnny, who just happened to be in the Solomon Islands, fighting the Japanese, writing moony letters back to his wife in Cleveland. I feel that I can appropriate some of his place because blood gives me that right.

Do some places, just by their singular qualities, ever force their way into your work?

I taught once at Marion Correctional Institution here in Ohio. In the first two quarters I taught Remedial Writing I and Remedial Writing II. I didn't think much about it at first. I thought the students—their place—would be so foreign to me that I'd just be this kind of separate entity, not touched by the place, and leaving each day to go back where I belong. But I was amazed to find out that I had a lot in common with my students, as I always do. They were Ohioans, after all. Some were from my own neighborhood in Cleveland. And we had incredible things in common. They had so much to write about. I was touched by their place very much. In my book *The House of Memory* is a poem called "Marion Correctional, Basic Writing," that I wrote from that experience. That place became my place. Of course, I was there two hours a day, three days a week, for one year only, whereas some of them were there twenty, thirty years, more. I'd get in there with my briefcase, and I'd be frisked. There was one guard who'd joke, "Got anything in there but poems, Doc?" I was moved by that place. Terribly new, and yet somehow familiar.

Through a Glass, Darkly

—for the students, who put me in my place

I'm all mouth, mustache, cane, grandiose Italian nose.
I squeak, speak in tongues, Cleveland, Little Italy.

But for you, these fevered weeks, I'm cuckoo,
vireo and finch, redbird, nighthawk, jay—

a squawk, a call at the windows of this stanza
called The Writing Room. *Poetry,* I try to say,

I crow, I swear. *Poetry poetry poetry poetry.*

—David Citino

Martha Collins
Oberlin, Ohio

As we move through Ohio, roads are closed everywhere we go. We're detouring through towns we've never heard of. I imagine dreamy shortcuts that will save us, but more than once we turn down another hopeful street only to bump up against the "No Outlet" sign. My wife and I perfect a thumb movement, a jerking toward the back that says, "Back it up." We use it for a laugh even when we're on a straightaway.

The small towns in this part of the state are about the prettiest I've ever seen. Each is full of endless green lawns and 1880 houses, bright white with crisp green or black roofs. Nobody is scurrying; traffic is light and friendly. Even the town bank is an architectural beauty. A little girl sitting on a chair waves at us when we go by her house, her mom behind her twisting the little girl's hair into two stubby pigtails.

In Norwalk, we get caught in the wrong lane. Momentarily we stop traffic in every direction while I work the steering wheel to find the right path. Nobody honks. Nobody flips me the bird. When I pick a direction, we all start moving again; and we push down yet another street with perfect houses, red flower planters on porches, a fat kid bouncing a ball, and a fire station done up in American flags with a banner announcing: "Pancake Breakfast, every Sunday."

We get where we're going in the late afternoon of the first day of the semester at Oberlin College. The campus is bustling, but beautiful. A middle quad of enormous relative size is ringed by benches, large painted rocks, and students of every variety walking back to dorms.

Martha Collins has given me directions to her Rice Hall office, but I stagger around campus awhile first, cursing the bag of equipment. Two girls wearing red "Lifeguard" sweatshirts are talking to a young man with a blank look on his face. He's holding a crumpled piece of paper and is actually scratching his head.

When I find Martha in her office, she's cheery. I'm tired from driving and have a head full of allergies to some of these gorgeous trees, but Martha's smile is big and welcoming and we get to work. During the conversation she laughs easily. It's clear she's tickled by the discoveries my questions have brought. She talks about her work with real care. She doesn't have a casual relationship to it. I get the feeling from the precision of her comments that her poems were written by an exacting woman, and even talking about them years later, she's affording them the same kind of attention.

~ ~ ~ ~ ~ ~

How has place impacted your poetry?

I probably couldn't have answered that until fairly recently when I began to spend half the year in Ohio.

I grew up in the Midwest, in Des Moines, Iowa. I haven't lived there since I graduated from high school, but there's a poem in my first book called "The Farm." It's the most autobiographical poem I ever wrote; and although I didn't in fact grow up on a farm, it's about Iowa. "The Farm" takes on the question of place in a number of ways. It starts out negatively. I didn't grow up on a farm. And then it says, "When you think about Iowa, you think about certain things, but you're wrong." The poem moves to Germany, where I spent some time. It moves to California, where I went to college. It ends up in New England, where I was at the time when I wrote the poem.

The poem, in retrospect, seems significant to me in terms of what I often do with place. Very often there is more than one place in a poem. I very rarely sit down and write about this place or that place. There's always a little tension between "Here I am" and "There I was." Here are the bare hills of New England; there were those lush cornfields in Iowa.

Can you think of a single physical space that influenced a piece very specifically?

My next book is made up of three sequences of poems, and one of them is called "A Book of Days." It was written during a yearlong fellowship at the Bunting Institute at Radcliffe. The Institute was then located in Radcliffe Yard, which is very Ivy League-y, with a lot of brick buildings, a lot of trees, and grass. I thought I was going to write a book-length poem about some people traveling all the way across the country, and the first sequence of the book is in fact the beginning of that. It's called "Images of Women in American Literature, Part One." Well, the characters only get past Niagara Falls into Canada, because I stopped. And the reason that I stopped was that I was sitting in an office in Radcliffe Yard for the entire year. I started writing out of the experience of sitting there and staring out the window, and what resulted was a thirty-part sequence called "A Book of Days." The poems are not descriptions of what I'm looking at thirty times around. But what I'm seeing is often the basis or starting point for a poem. I think that's most frequently true for me, that place is one of several starting points.

You don't live in Oberlin full time. Does it feel like home to you?

I think that being in a place that is not my home tends to make me think about place more than being in my home. Getting away from my usual place makes me conscious of place, not only the place where I am, but also the places I've been. Strange places evoke familiar and different places.

The opening poem in my third book is called "The Border." I've been thinking about borders for a long time. I'm obsessed with the idea of borders. The poem is a collage. It starts with a kind of "tourist Spanish" that might be heard on a Mexican-American border. But then it moves across a lot of different borders—geographical, psychological, social. That poem seems to define who I am. That I'm never content to sit anyplace: I'm always on a border between here and there.

Linda Gregerson
Ann Arbor, Michigan

Linda Gregerson lives in an idyllic setting north and west of Ann Arbor. It's impossible to imagine that there are towns or cities anywhere near this place, set amidst barns, pumpkin fields, and endless trees. The only thing I can think of this morning more beautiful than this spot are Linda's poems themselves.

Linda's home opens into a wooded area. A brook awaits a hundred feet away, and deer and woodchuck often come to peruse her self-described "suburban" garden. We sit on white chairs on a porch and let the warm breeze blow through our conversation.

She shows me around the yard a bit, pointing out plants given to her by some dear friends. I'm looking for a woodchuck, however. The plants can wait. Ever since she said woodchuck, I've been singing that childhood song in my head.

~ ~ ~ ~ ~ ~

What roles have the places you've lived and the natural world had on your work?

Huge and incalculable. One spends a certain amount of time sitting at the desk, or the kitchen table, or out on the screened porch, staring as one works. And I'm sure that space and material place have consequences far beyond my conscious awareness. I mean, in some of the obvious ways it lends itself thematically.

There's a little creek that runs out there *(pointing into the area that bounds her backyard)*. The road is called Hidden Brook Lane, and there's actually a hidden brook that eventually makes its way toward the Huron River.

And this place, the trees, the snow, the deer, the woodchucks have big consequences, as well as the hum of the refrigerator and the chance to go out and weed in my garden.

But I'm sure there are other things. I'm sure the proportion of the room, the height of the ceiling, whether or not one can have some air coming in the window eventually influences the shapes of stanzas or the breath units in a poem. I'm confident of that. The realm of the aesthetic is not some extracted realm of theorized beauty. Aesthetic just means feeling, and the realm of the aesthetic has both wealth of components and all kinds of ways of occurring under the radar. Poetry relies so much on the material properties of language.

Some of the poets I've spoken with have admitted a great debt to the landscape of their childhood. Where did yours take place and how do you think it's affected your work?

I grew up in the Midwest—northern Illinois, and Wisconsin. My grandparents and other members of the family farm there to this day. So the logic of a certain kind of upper midwestern small town makes a lot of sense to me. The logic of American upper Midwest farm fields, the layout of them, the scrub oak that's in between, the way there will be a grouping of farm buildings in a certain way. It's not only the case in other climates, the Southwest, or the mountains, or the Southeast, but even in comparable climates it's not the same idiom, say, in a European country. It's about proportion, about how much space the buildings take up compared to the crops. It's all that sort of stuff, and there's also a vernacular architecture that's very warm.

There's a really rich sense of nature in your work, especially the work in Waterborne. *What are you trying to do with those elements?*

My body's relationship to the natural world has largely been one of hostility. I'm terribly asthmatic. I have terrible allergies. Almost everything lovely, interesting, and living makes me sick, makes me sick in a literal way. I was always terribly sickly as a child. I was never good for anything useful. I could never mow the lawn. And indeed, as an adult, when I was in graduate school in California and stuff didn't get killed off by winter, I got progressively sicker and sicker until my life was almost not livable.

So it's not just the usual, standard-issue oblivion that characterizes some youth, but it was also this medical, this invalid, plastic shell that augmented it. Really, the living—the free breathing in a world of grasses and trees and the local woodchuck—is a phenomenon of middle age. It's a blessing; it's quite belated. I'm now the gardener, which is hilarious, because I'm quite inept at it. But I'm out there, enthusiastically, with my mulch, with my soil enrichers. It's very new. I'm learning, primer level, ABCs. Remedial living in the growing world. And, it's thrilling.

But clearly this life—my bit of digging around in the dirt and planting bulbs, studying up on woody perennials—is exceedingly suburban. I can't pretend it's got anything of the wilderness about it. It really is about this tiny little margin where America of a certain wealth and leisure gets to allow the claims of a wilder, nonhuman universe to make claims or assert its presence on a certain scale. It's about how people—who entirely need the world—and the world, which doesn't remotely need us at all, find little patches of intersection where we can accommodate one another. Where we gain some purchase, and understanding, and competence, and leverage, and, of course, a sense of wonder.

It seems to me that a lot of your work springs from physical places rather than events.

In some ways physical place is most keenly for me the place of daily habit. So, for instance, a poem called the "History Play" began because I was finally trying to catch up with some filing—I save playbills from when we go to the theater—and there were some bits of gold foil that I had saved. My husband is also a Shakespearean, and he and the girls and I spend summers in England when we're able to and go to lots of plays. We'd gone to a production in Stratford of *Henry VIII,* and in the final scene when there's the celebration of Elizabeth's christening, they dropped all sorts of little shapes, flowers—basically bits of daub made out of gold foil from the ceiling—and I saved some of it as a remembrance. And they have a very strong evocative power for me. It was really about the bit of domestication that we as a family enact in the places we return to. I used the scene of that play as the occasion, and used some language from that, and also used the problem of history. It's called a history play, not so much because it's about kings and queens, but about the whole notion of history and reenacting it and what that does for human imagination.

I think time eludes us so much. We're here so briefly, you know, the kids are little and the next minute they're leaving us—our elder daughter went off to college this year. But it's also a way of trying to rescue a little moment. It's partly elegy. It's celebration of the family we are, and elegy to the family we were, and our way of trying to stave off the dissipation of ongoing time. And so much more important than that particular evening at the theatre was the little routine we had around going to the play. There's a little walking route that we take to the theatre at night and back to the hotel afterward, and it goes over a bridge. And because it's Stratford, there are swans on the river below. And so it was emphatically about place and the way one can be given some friendliness on the part of place, simply by returning to it and savoring it in memory. It's about the intersection of physical place and habits. That connectedness is both very dear and very fragile.

Richard Tillinghast
Ann Arbor, Michigan

Writers work everywhere. Poets can scribble on notebooks in planes and in hotel rooms. Some use every part of their homes: the study, the bedroom, even backyard sheds.

But Richard Tillinghast is the winner of the porch sweepstakes. While rain threatens from the southern skies, Richard and I sit out on his porch on either end of a large, bulky sofa. The sofa is pinned in by books, notepads, and a set of homemade flash cards, from which Richard is learning Turkish grammar for an upcoming trip to his beloved Istanbul.

He shows me some great photos from his travels, and we go through how his geographical wanderings have informed his writing over a long and productive career. While we talk, his neighbors go by out front, and it seems everyone has a dog or two. We're in the middle of Ann Arbor, a college town where professors and students live near each other and their shared home—the university.

But Richard is on leave right now. He's just come back from upstate New York, where he was a featured instructor at a conference. Soon he'll be back in Istanbul, where he will meet and talk with Turkish writers—and use his improving language skills.

I wonder about this porch. Who will keep it running in his absence?

~ ~ ~ ~ ~ ~

How has place impacted your work?

Hugely. I don't know where I got this idea—something in some book about Native American thought, perhaps. I remember getting the idea that they feel that it isn't just *what* you are thinking or perceiving, but it's you in combination with *where* you are thinking and feeling. There's no such thing as separating the individual from the place.

But when I think about writers and a sense of place, I always think of writers who have stayed in the same place. William Faulkner in Mississippi and Marcel Proust in Paris, to pick two really different examples. But the way my life has turned out, I've lived so many different places; and every place I've gone has been reflected in my poetry, whether it be the South, California, New England, Ireland.

Has your work always reflected your interest in place?

I've kept that interest in place all the way through. What really made an impact on me were three Southern writers that I discovered in high school: John Crowe Ransom, Robert Penn Warren, and Faulkner. Oxford, Mississippi, is only eighty miles from Memphis. It's a straight shot, and I used to remember the number of the highway. The fact that those writers wrote about a landscape that was familiar to me was really empowering. That gave me the sense that this was a landscape I knew. And I think that the poet who influenced me the most when I first started writing was Ransom.

One of the things I learned when I was writing *The Stonecutter's Hand,* when I was writing the poems based in Ireland, is I think you can write more effectively about place if you're not always naming the place. If you're always naming the place, you run the risk of having it sound like tourist poetry. I think the trick that I've learned now is to write about the place without saying what place it is.

But my position on that, traditionally, would be a hard position to defend, because there is in Irish writing, in *dinnseanchas*, a kind of a charting of all the different places in Ireland through poetry. Seamus Heaney does that very consciously, and the old poets writing in Irish did that. And if you think of Southern music, "Tulsa Queen" and all the songs, "Memphis Blues" and all that. And that's a very strong tradition too.

What are your thoughts about regionalism in poetry?

Well, you're talking to a Tennessee boy, who hasn't lived in Tennessee—with the exception of one year—since 1962. That's a long time ago. I still consider myself a Tennessean. I think I would like to have been a regional poet, but the circumstances in my life have made it impossible. I've always been a traveler. I've lived in Massachusetts for a very good chunk of time. And I've lived in California for a dozen years, and now I've been living in Michigan for twenty years. We bought this house in 1984, and my youngest child was two weeks old. I would be flattered if Southern poets thought of me as a Southern poet, but I don't know whether they do or not. Just think of all the great writing that has come from poets we think of as regional poets. I guess it's worked out for me that I'm a poet of several regions. And I feel bound to each of these regions. It took me a long time to relate to Michigan, because the landscape—on the surface of it—doesn't appeal to me, I guess because it's so flat. I'm a fly fisherman, and I now spend a lot of time up in northern Michigan every summer, so now I feel that connect. So I guess if I lived long enough, I'd become a Michigan poet.

Do you think you've captured a place in that way, turning a real place into a sort of mythic or poetic place?

Istanbul. That's a place. Certainly it's one of the oldest cities in the world. All the layers of history. I think I've done pretty well. That's my latest infatuation, with that city. And talking to Turkish writers or anyone who loves that city. They seem to enjoy reading my poems about that city. But the difference between going to someplace that you don't know at all and experiencing it fresh without any background, that's great. But then going someplace where you know all the history. I like to experience a place in a multilayered way.

Wake Me in South Galway

Wake me in South Galway, or better yet
In Clare. You'll know the pub I have in mind.
Improvise a hearse—one of those decrepit
Postal vans would suit me down to the ground—
A rust-addled Renault, Kelly green with a splash
Of Oscar Wilde yellow stirred in to clash
With the dazzling perfect meadows and limestone
On the coast road from Kinvara down toward Ballyvaughan.

Once you've got in off the road at Newquay
Push aside some barstools and situate me
Up in front by the door where the musicians sit,
Their table crowded with pints and a blue teapot,
A pouch of Drum, some rolling papers and tin
Whistles. Ask Charlie Piggott to play a tune
That sounds like loss and Guinness, turf smoke and rain,
While Brenda dips in among the punters like a hedge-wren.

Will I hear it? Maybe not. But I hear it now.
The smoke of the music fills my nostrils, I feel the attuned
Box and fiddle in harness, pulling the plough
Of the melody, turning the bog-dark, root-tangled ground.
Even the ceramic collie on the windowsill
Cocks an ear as the tune lifts and the taut sail
Of the Galway hooker trills wildly in its frame on the wall,
Rippling to the salt pulse and seabreeze of a West Clare reel.

Many a night, two octaves of one tune,
We sat here side by side, your body awake
To a jig or slide, me mending the drift of a line
As the music found a path to my notebook.
Lost in its lilt and plunge I would disappear
Into the heathery freedom of a slow air
Or walk out under the powerful stars to clear
My head of thought and breathe their cooled-down fire.

When my own session ends, let me leave like that,
Porous to the wind that blows off the ocean.
Goodbye to the company and step into the night
Completed and one-off, like a well-played tune—
Beyond the purified essence of hearth fires
Rising from the life of the parish, past smoke and stars,
Released from everything I've done and known.
I won't go willingly, it's true, but I'll be gone.

—Richard Tillinghast

Winnie Cooper

On I-94 the wind pushes us from the side as we go and makes the steering harder than it has to be. The motor home is top-heavy. It's twelve feet high and twenty-nine feet long; but any breeze threatens to tip us, and any slick pavement makes it feel as though we're going to slide into a yawning ditch. At any speed over 5 mph, the steering wheel pushes and pulls back and forth. The whole experience in the driver's seat is like wrestling a big angry hog, slick as snot. Twenty miles can feel like a hundred. Forty miles an hour on a turn pins me against the groaning driver's door.

We call this big rolling tin can Winnie Cooper. It's bigger than some apartments we've lived in. It's clean and new, but it already feels cozy and homey.

We drive most days, stopping on the side of the road for lunch or searching another town for a poet's house. The stops are always short—there are many miles to go. Soon we're out on the highway again, the wind from eighteen-wheelers buffeting us from both sides, the coach drifting from the white center line to the warning marks on the shoulder.

It's early in the trip. Months still stretch in front of us, and as I drive I am wracked with nerves. What is it that I'm writing? What am I going to do with these interviews? What happens if I lose all of these tapes? What is that clanging noise?

But my wife is peaceful. Her face is bright and unlined, and she smiles up at the sun and the sun back at her. She reads the paper in the morning, does the crossword. She writes email to our pals and shoots photos out the window of sunrises, planes, or odd little stores.

Sometimes after a long day of steering, I turn the wheel over to her. I throw up my hands, turn over the maps, and slump down. The driving doesn't seem to bother her. She puts the cruise control on, her hand limply on the steering wheel. She listens to "Rhythm Is the Dancer" on the CD player and hums along. She looks over and smiles.

I want to scare her. I hope that a large badger will race in front of the vehicle to make her swerve. I want to see some of the wild grim fear I've been feeling.

"Look," she says, pointing up ahead. "That guy's selling fresh tomatoes."

What is wrong with her?

Orlando Ricardo Menes
South Bend, Indiana

Orlando's beautiful wife Ivis is eight months, three weeks pregnant when we arrive in South Bend. This has been on my mind for days. I'm very grateful for the chance to meet and interview Orlando, but do not want my hurried and cacophonous visit to initiate childbirth. Should I somehow induce contractions, I can only hope we will be on the highway miles away when it happens.

The house is bustling with their daughter, Ivis's mother, and a sweet dog.

I visit over rich, dark coffee, cookies, and cakes, then Orlando and I go down to the basement to his study. Books line both long walls on black bookshelves. Two lamps and a tiny ceiling-height window provide the lighting. His laptop sits on a wide desk, and it's blinking throughout the conversation, information coming in or going out.

While we talk, Orlando points out paintings by the Cuban-born, nineteenth-century painter Valentin Sanz Carta and a book of photos called Havana 1933 *by the photographer Walker Evans (famous for his depression-era photos of American farm workers). These are among some of the sources that have inspired poems in the past.*

~ ~ ~ ~ ~ ~

Am I right to suggest that you use your poetry to examine your cultural heritage?

Well, when did I begin to explore my Cuban-ness as a poet? I'd have to say the summer of 1993 when I began to do research into Santeria, one of the syncretic religions of Cuba. It was an aspect of Cuba I knew little about, yet I was soon drawn to its beauty. And what developed was a body of work that created hybrid worlds of my own imagining; that is, worlds that combined Santeria myths and rituals, other elements of the magical and the surreal, as well as the Catholic religion with which I was raised.

I remember that summer vividly. I was living in this hotel on Miami Beach; and I would walk through the beach, and all these images, these floods of images, would come into my head. However, I never saw nature by itself. I saw nature refracted through the prism of myth. And all this material started to well up. And I took this material back with me to Chicago, and I started to draft the poems that would make up *Rumba*

Atop the Stones: "Fish Heads," "Doña Flora's Hothouse," et cetera. And these poems were extremely important because they set up this book, this book of magical places that bring together all these different strands of my poetic identity, my cultural identity.

You mentioned your Cuban heritage. Is that something you carry with you like a landscape?

This Cuban-ness is so complicated because I never lived in Cuba. I grew up with Cubans who remembered Cuba. It's that mythic Cuba that I connect with. I don't connect with the real Cuba. It's a terrible thing to say. I traveled to Cuba twice, first in 1998, then December of 2002; but neither time did I actually experience any recognition of returning home. More likely a disquieting sense of alienation. It's the mythic Cuba that I feel passionate about, that I feel close to. Stories about sugar cane. Stories about the war of independence. Stories about poverty. Stories, too, about the many social and racial injustices.

The poems were also based on stories that my parents had told me, my mother, my father, about the racial divisions in Cuba, that people don't seem to know or have any sense of, but they were very real in the '30s and '40s. My dad told me that in the Cuban countryside, at town dances, there would sometimes be a rope strung to separate the blacks from the whites. The blacks and mulattoes would be on one side, and the whites on the other. And this was Cuba in the '30s and '40s. It's real. And the Cubans in Miami don't like to talk about this. They don't like to deal with this history at all. I think the white Cubans in Miami would rather pretend it didn't exist, or it happened a long time ago, or it has nothing to do with us now. So there's this recurrent denial of the injustices dealt to black people. And it was also this silence, this denial that created this urgent rage in me, which proved so conducive to writing morally centered poetry.

Some of the poets I've spoken to have talked about being regional poets and, therefore, in some small way, responsible for chronicling that region. Does that notion fit you?

I'm a son of exiles who lives in exile in Indiana. My Cuba is not a Cuba that can be accessed by everyone who goes there. It's a very particular version of Cuba. I like to write poems that have embedded in them some distance between the actual experience and the memory of it. In other words, memory allows me to transmute the world, rather than to be imprisoned by the world. I see myself as a Cuban American poet, as a Latino poet. And though this identity does not necessarily entail any social obligation, I do feel that I wouldn't be true to myself if I were writing about topics that were more general and that I have no personal investment with.

For so many years I felt separated from my cultural heritage because I wanted to fit in, I wanted to be an "American." Then I married Ivis, who was born in Cuba but raised in Spain. Ivis is very Spanish indeed, and she wasn't going to put up with my Cuban-American confusion. She made it possible for me to go back to those roots.

At the time I was growing up in Miami in the early '60s and early '70s, America had this effect of pushing me away from my roots. I was too ethnic. And America, at least at that time, didn't really like the ethnic person. There were certain ethnic identities that America valued at that point. I mean, Americans have this tendency to value certain ethnicities over others. And how it values those changes over time. So it's very capricious. Now, being Italian is wonderful. Well, a hundred years ago Italians were deemed inferior by the Anglo majority. And now they're part of the mainstream. They're in the club now. Maybe a hundred years from now Cuban Americans will be in the club, and people from somewhere else will be the outsiders. It's one grand comedy, which is only comic after a certain historical distance.

Mark Strand
Chicago, Illinois

On a bright Sunday morning, I'm sitting with Mark Strand in his apartment, about ten floors up and looking out over Lake Shore Drive. The 70-degree weather pours in through a bank of open windows. The blinds flutter sometimes, and the sound of weekend construction floats up to us as we talk. From my chair I can see the water, and I think about heading over there after the interview to walk alongside the lake, watch the joggers and dogs. Peer up the lakeside all the way to whatever is north of here.

We're just on the edge of the University of Chicago, where Strand has been teaching for the past several years. He is a revered and monumental American poet of this or any generation. His work is frankly astonishing in its breadth. His early work virtually reinvented what we understand to be the contemporary poem, his later work consisting of clear-eyed and unflinching poems about age, love, beauty, and light.

Strand, now unthinkably seventy, is tall, lanky, and still the handsome rake. It is not unusual to see the word "swoon" in any retelling of a meeting with him. He's soft-spoken, erudite, and he puts me at ease.

We sit opposite each other across a low table cluttered with thick and glossy art magazines. The room is a perfect square, with hallways on both ends, the door to one side of us and the huge windows on the other. Strand rarely moves while he talks, choosing to sit back, one leg crossed over the other.

~ ~ ~ ~ ~ ~

As I thought about this interview and this project, I had trouble envisioning what I'd ask you about. But suddenly it struck me that your poems are about place, but not necessarily about the world outdoors. Your poems are full of rooms, people in rooms. Is the room the landscape for your work?

It's interesting you bring it up. As soon as you mention rooms, I realize that it is the dominant space in my work. I haven't formulated any notions of why I use rooms, but they are an enclosed space in which I can arrange things as I want. As long as I'm arranging the space, I'm in control. It's more my world than anyone else's or anything else's. The space of my poems is the space of the rooms in the poems.

How does that work with you, someone who has spent such a lot of time in the out of doors, both Canada and Utah, for example?

Utah offered me a change of décor. The out of doors is not the basis on which I order my poems. The seascape of my childhood in Nova Scotia—many summers spent in Nova Scotia—was a convenient landscape for me for years. Later on, Utah and the mountains and the valleys of the intermountain West became an inescapable reality that I incorporated in my poems—but largely as background.

I don't ask people to imagine the details of the world in my poems. I just want them to know that there's something there. I don't think we do that when we read, imagine every little thing that is written down. But I enjoy trying to write about the light in the mountains, the spaciousness one experiences in the West that one has no access to in the cities of the East or the hilliness of New England. The airy texture of everything. The air seems lighter and less thick, especially when you're elevated like you are in Salt Lake City.

That must have affected you in a number of ways, given that you're a painter as well. Do you see any connection between your work as a painter and poet?

I do think in terms of organizing space. There's something consistent about the space in my poems. Some things are behind others—you can only see half of them. The light comes from one direction. It's part of my makeup. But I see the same attention to arrangement in the poems of Elizabeth Bishop, who had an eye for painting, who made charming little watercolors. But when I'm drawing or painting, I don't feel any connection to writing. Whenever I draw, I feel it's an escape from writing.

A number of poets have told me that there is often a dominant landscape in their work, a sort of default landscape that exists in the background of their work.

It's true.

What is it for you?

If it's a landscape, it's Nova Scotia, and then it became Utah. Right now it's anything I want it to be. It can be the desert, but it's very often—like you noted—a room. But it's also a composite. It's the landscape you need for a particular poem. It's not necessarily a constant landscape. But because my poems are limited—meaning they're all written by me—what I think of as different landscapes may have a lot more in common than I recognize.

When I wrote *The Continuous Life* and *Dark Harbor* out in Utah, clearly the background was a western background. Even *Blizzard of One* had that. But now it will be different. Now I'm in Chicago.

There's a line of yours from Blizzard of One that goes, "Life should be more than the body's weight working itself from room to room. A turn to the forest would do us good." I think that so neatly points to a dilemma of a poet who writes about rooms, who recognizes that rooms sometimes aren't enough. What are some of the things in the natural world that  *work on you the most, the things that act as triggers for you?*

The endlessness of space, the horrific, terrifying vision of the night sky. The endlessness of space is unimaginable. Because it's unimaginable, I find it terrifying. There's no way to domesticate it. I'm powerless before it. I feel a little like Wallace Stevens did before *Auroras of Autumn.* I want to run inside, get under the covers. That's the most powerful experience of being outside. And now we have these new photographs from space, and to see those stars—and so many of those stars we see are actually galaxies, with billions of stars in them—only creates a feeling of more intense vulnerability and upset. If I thought about outer space all the time, I'd be absolutely bananas. But fortunately, I'm not constructed intellectually to deal with that. Emotionally, I'm a coward.

Like you, I was born in Canada, and despite being many years removed from that place, I find elements of it still are very important to me. Are there elements of Canada that still work on you?

Yeah, I still say "eh?" *(Laughs.)* "Are we going to the store, eh?"

I still think of Nova Scotia. My parents are buried in Halifax. I still think of being on the water, near the water, picking blueberries. St. Margaret's Bay. Sailing. Going out with Albert the fisherman, dropping a line, and catching a cod. I don't know if you can still do that or if it's all been fished out.

My summers in Nova Scotia were very happy. I remember having to go indoors at five every afternoon because the mosquitoes got so bad. I can still remember my aunt and my mother making blueberry pie. The adventure of being able to take the boat out by myself, walk in the woods. Picking up cigarette butts outside the general store and smoking when I was six or seven. This was a childhood of incredible freedom. Now, children spend more times in camps, sports camps. Their parents have designed vacations for them. My childhood was great. I associated Canada with freedom.

Do you think poets have any obligation to write about the places of their lives?

No. Because place is not an audience. Place is not what you're writing for. Poets have an obligation to the language they use and the language of which their poems will be a part. But poets don't owe anything to place because place is just geography. It's accidental. But we choose the language that becomes identified with ourselves. Our identity is in the way we use language, not necessarily the place from which we come.

In other words, you read Robert Frost because you want to hear the voice of Robert Frost. You're not going to learn anything about New England. Or Wallace Stevens. How much are you going to learn about Connecticut? It's the way he puts words together. It's true of any good poet.

Then what role does place have?

It's a grounding element. It's a place in which you set the action of the poem. We don't imagine places as we read a poem. Words are signifiers, but they suggest an imaginary world, not an actual world. Even if the poem is set in a particular place, the particular place is erased by the imaginary place that is suggested by the poem. The poem takes the place of the actual world. The poem is the experience *of* the experience of being in the natural world.

A Morning

I have carried it with me each day: that morning I took
my uncle's boat from the brown water cove
and headed for Mosher Island.
Small waves splashed against the hull
and the hollow creek of oarlock and oar
rose into the woods of black pine crusted with lichen.
I moved like a dark star, drifting over the drowned
other half of the world until, by a distant prompting,
I looked over the gunwale and saw beneath the surface
a luminous room, a light-filled grave, saw for the first time
the one clear place given to us when we are alone.

—Mark Strand

Karen Volkman
Chicago, Illinois

At the Rainbow Restaurant in Elmhurst, Illinois—a crowded and cheery Formica fantasyland—I receive the following food when I order the Cattleman's Special: three-egg omelet stuffed with sausage, hash browns, two pieces of toast, four strips of bacon, and a large chopped steak smothered with cheddar cheese.

I stare down in disbelief and look up again only when the waitress brings me what she couldn't carry the first time—two pancakes the exact size of the hubcaps off a Ford Crown Victoria. My wife swirls her oatmeal and sort of rolls her eyes at the dishes piled in front of me. I grin back and begin with gusto.

Gusto. That's a good word for Chicagoland, a town full of big people, all smiling, half of them smoking, virtually all of them red-faced and ready to give a visitor directions to the nearest place to get a Polish sausage.

I don't finish all of my breakfast, but come close—close enough that I imagine they should put my photo up somewhere.

We're due back in Chicago for another interview. We drive down Highway 290, steer through Ukrainian Village, a close-knit urban neighborhood just a little north and west of downtown, and pull up to a three-story apartment building to meet with Karen Volkman, a wonderful nomadic young poet. She buzzes me in, and I go up a set of narrow stairs to her apartment. Karen's place is done up grad-school-funky, books on plain wood shelves, a futon, and a majestic thrift store desk.

Her work is surprising and intense. The prose poems are riveting, "relentless" in the words of one reviewer, and a reader can't help but go through them unblinking and silent.

In person she's friendly. She laughs easily and often as she talks. She remembers the stunning temperature shift of moving from her childhood home of Florida to Syracuse, where suddenly she saw winter, spring, and fall. She sits on a futon, and I'm across on a straight-backed chair.

~ ~ ~ ~ ~ ~

There is certainly the tradition of wandering academic poets. You are one, obviously. How does one get settled and back to work after so many moves, so many new spaces.

I wonder about that, too. I guess you have to improvise, use whatever works. My books always come with me, or at least a healthy selection. That's a centering thing. And projects extend through the relocations—*Spar,* my second book, followed me to a lot of places, so the work becomes a means of continuity.

And that enormous desk in the other room—which I got for $25 at the Salvation Army on Twenty-third Street in Chelsea—that damn thing has come with me on every move *(laughs).* A lot of this stuff *(motioning at furniture in room)* I've had since I was an undergrad. Things probably have a role in keeping me stabilized through all the transitions.

What role have all these different places played on your work as a poet?

I'm still tracking those changes—at this point I'm still a youngish poet, with two books and one nearing completion. In parts of *Crash's Law* I was treating place more directly. The opening poem deals with Miami—but what's interesting is that poem wasn't written in Florida at all; it was written in New England during a blizzard. I just happened to be thinking for some reason about Miami, where I hadn't been for four years, while the external circumstances could not have been more different. A few months after writing that poem I took a trip to Miami and realized I had succeeded in capturing some of its strangeness—the intensity of color and light, the car culture and leisure culture, the whole pleasure industry. I don't generally think of my poems in these terms, but I think "Infernal" captured something from an imaginative remove that I probably could not have captured while in that landscape. I needed the distance.

Spar is very different. It's a more fragmentary book, so place comes in by way of sensory information in flashing, intermittent ways. There was an important period for *Spar* when I was living in the south of France—I had a residency at the Camargo Foundation and spent a few months in Cassis, a town on the coast of the Mediterranean with the most stunningly beautiful landscape I've ever seen. The amazing blue of the Mediterranean and red cliffs jutting over it. A little port. And in the other direction, almost a desertscape with bone-white cliffs. These amazing contrasts between the dry, arid landscape and the ocean. Strange sharp bristly plants and scree. I had never experienced anything like it.

Are there particular natural elements that help trigger things for you?

Light and space, which may seem obvious, but they affect me very powerfully. Since I grew up in south Florida, I encountered searing sunlight as the norm—the uncanny norm. It's truly relentless. There's almost a disturbing quality about it, that relentlessness, and the brilliant blue sky day after day. So when I first went to gray, upstate New York, I was deeply unsettled by the lack of sun. I didn't stop writing though. The disturbance was very productive for me. Not necessarily for my psychic health but certainly for my writing.

Cassis, when I first got there—because I came after four years in New York City—was a huge shift in the experience of space, space as a phenomenon that resonates in your consciousness. In New York, space is regimented by the linearity of streets and the height of the buildings—your sightlines are very controlled. So to suddenly get to a landscape of vast openness and this insane blue sky, the huge expanse of the ocean, was actually terrifying. The poem I just mentioned, "There comes a time to rusticate the numbers," was definitely written out of the shock experience of my first couple of weeks there. A holy fear of the void opening. Those poems to me feel very torn open.

Do you think poets have any obligation to write about the places of their lives?

No. I'm tempted to say poets have no obligations at all, but that's a hedonistic answer. And as soon as I think that, there's part of me that says, "Oh, of course they do." I think poets feel their way through what their obligations are. As I've gotten older and read and thought more about poetry, my idea of what experience is has changed. Even my idea of place has evolved. The prose poem I mentioned is a rendering of how I experienced that place. But it can't communicate what I consider the experience through a narrative account. It doesn't have a speaker saying, "I walked along the pier of the port of Cassis," and go on from there, which may be the way another poet might frame their account. For me, a discursive narrative is a way of structuring the experience by making it linear and logical, which cancels the most interesting aspects of it. I see the poem as a way of renewing that complex experience and communicating it intensely and viscerally to a reader. So, "what happened" in the experience is the sensual/sensuous effect on the mind and psyche, a kind of compression of intensities at the level of language and sound—so the poem embodies an experience rather than describing it.

Lisa Samuels
Milwaukee, Wisconsin

We travel north out of Chicago at such a time that we've hit rush hour both there and then in Milwaukee. As we inch along, we get a phone call from my wife's parents, who have just come from seeing the "tornado of boxes" that the movers have delivered to our tiny house in Arkansas. I shrug. Too late now, I think.

We push on—as if there were any choice—and we find Lisa Samuels's 1927 house on a busy road north of Milwaukee. I discovered her poetry recently. It is varied and exciting, seeming not to be tied to one or another type of method or approach. She's comfortable with long and short poems, even concrete and prose poems. And the language is always careful, literate. Dense one moment, then revealing in the next.

Her house is gorgeous. Long driveway to the back. Porch. She lets me in the front, and we talk houses and Milwaukee for a bit. We sit in a beautiful living room, all dark woods. A welcome and late afternoon shower is taking place, and the room has a gray but pleasant feel. The room is huge. How many boxes could I fit in here?

~ ~ ~ ~ ~ ~

What role has place played in your work?

I've moved around a great deal in my life, particularly while growing up. This is the fifteenth state I've lived in, as well as four countries overseas. It isn't really a sense of displacement I feel, but non-placement, un-placement, something like that. It's had a couple of effects. I have tended to feel a strong sense of socioeconomic contingency, a kind of structural and allegorical legibility in the places I've lived. Things are replaceable. The trees are recurrent. The people are recurrent. They inhabit certain kinds of postures. I think this sense of contingency has given me a lot of freedom, but, of course, in social and emotional terms it can mean adaptation is quirky. Not thinking anything is permanent— not just in the shaping of relationships, but in being a member of a productive or continuous economy, in a large sense—meant that a sense of commitment to a "real" was hard for me to develop.

Another way to look at this question of place in poetry is quite site-specific. I lived for six years in the Middle East—four years in Israel and two in Yemen. I was a teenager during the Israel years and in my midtwenties in Yemen. Those kinds of landscapes, landscapes of otherness, have a strong appeal to me. I also lived for two years in Utah, with its own otherness landscapes. I love the desert and mountains and things that are empty. You can go from that geography to an interior sense—a Buddhist emptiness or via negativa, something like that. That sense of ontological or spiritual placedness being activated by the resolute sublimity and emptiness of a particular quarter, like the Maze in Utah, or the Empty Quarter in Saudi Arabia.

I put on the cover of my latest chapbook, "War Holdings," a photograph that I took in Yemen of an ancient remnant of a moon temple, which is two thousand seven hundred years old. The image of the ruins is framed by a barbed-wire fence. I know that such images come back to me in writing.

I remember reading a poet who said his imagination was locked into place by the Vietnam War. I think my imagination was locked into place by these kinds of desert scenes of solitary otherness and ruin.

By otherness, I mean predominantly this: things that are other than me. Being in places where I am cognizant of not fitting, as a puzzle piece fits in a puzzle. I like that unresolved feeling. I recognize it. Maybe that's why I like it.

You've been here in Wisconsin for a few years now. Do you feel glad to be in one place, or do you feel a bit like it's time to get going again?

I feel—by default—that it's time to go. But I tend to feel that way after two years anywhere. Part of it is that I know how to be new in a new place.

Your question is a loaded one, in a good way, because even though I know it's my default setting to go, I also know that when I was at Virginia I actually started—because I stayed there for so long—to cycle back through myself the energy I'd usually use for adapting to a new situation. And that's when I agreed, as it were, to become a member of the world. To say, I'm going to produce things. What are we on earth for? Arguably, to love and to make beautiful things. Okay, I said to myself, I haven't yet made things; I've gone around and seen and experienced interesting things. That's when I seriously started to write. I'd scribbled and dabbled but didn't really write until graduate school. And that was wonderful. It's hard to imagine producing as much when you're moving around.

What's your connection like with the natural world?

I like taking walks. And I think of two things: one is that the absence of visitation from without, the absence of forced input, is very desirable to my mind, my imagination, and my body. Being out in nature, especially when there aren't too many people around, you feel that there are things around and you are taking them in. It partly has to do with bodily knowledge. By contrast, if you're reading—even if you're reading for pleasure, not being too teleological about it—you're still being forced to a particular kind of attention, which is more strictly, abstractly, neural than when you're walking through a park.

The second thing that happens is looking at configurations of lines and light. It often happens with trees. There's suddenly something about the structure of lines and light that gives me this kind of miniorgasmic thrill. You don't want to stare at it too long, because you just want it to come. I don't necessarily associate this thrill strictly with nature; I can also get it with some architecture or at museums in a similar fashion. And that response to forms and space is a crucial part of my pleasure in being out of doors and crucial to my pleasure of being in the desert.

Marvin Bell
Iowa City, Iowa

We're lucky to find Marvin Bell at home. He and his wife are geographical champions. They live in three different places during the year, a peninsula in Washington State, on far eastern Long Island, and in this home I'm visiting in Iowa City. And Marvin has traveled, lived, and written in a score of other countries.

His rich understanding of these places—and their distinctive characters—is deep. He grew up on Long Island but finds himself "home" in the others as well. He's been a part of the famed Iowa Writers' Workshop for thirty-five years, although now he spends only half a year or so here.

We sit at a dining-room table stacked with books, CDs, and a big bowl of fruit, from which Marvin pulls out a banana to steel himself for the interview. Behind him are windows that are partially obscured by some hanging plants, vinelike, falling in green waterfalls. On the wall facing me are Japanese fans and painted masks.

We talk a bit about work habits, and he volunteers to show me a tiny nine-by-twelve shed in the backyard, where he wrote much of his early work. It's exactly the size someone would need for the task. A small single mattress, two circa 1940 Royal typewriters, a desk lamp, and a buzzer that served as a sort of intercom in prewireless days. Marvin doesn't tell me if the buzzer was used for him to let his wife Dorothy know something, or vice versa. As a married man, I can only guess.

In the shed is a stack of paper, ready to go in one of the typewriters, but yellowed and covered with spider webs. The paper is almost comically aged. It couldn't be new; you couldn't fake the authenticity of this old paper. Marvin rolls a sheet into the machine and then sits there, the gentleman poet.

We go back into the house and up the stairs to his study, where an Apple laptop waits for him. This is where he works now. He sits at the desk in the same manner as he had in the shed, but I must confess he looked more natural in front of the manual machine. Marvin, I think, looks like a typewriter guy to me. And his poetry, long lines spilling out often beyond the margin of the page and looping back, feels like it should be made on a machine that makes a little noise. Something that presses ink into paper.

~ ~ ~ ~ ~ ~

Having a background in all of these different regions, do you have any thoughts about what it means to be a regional poet, and have the places of your childhood or youth stayed with you in your poetry as you've written?

I suspect that most poets feel that a sense of place is a sense of all places at once, as well as of the local. Everyone is regional to an extent. W. H. Auden spoke of coming from England to this country and being amazed because a young man here can stick out his thumb and go three thousand miles. And we move around so easily now, that many of us have lived more than one place for substantial periods. So I think there's a sense of place that is bigger than one place. There's no denying that place pushes its way into one's poems. My poem "Long Island" is largely a catalog of those Long Island things that made me what I am. Fire Island, for example, across the bay, where they practiced strafing during the war. You'd find shell casings with your feet in the sand. And the boats: crab boats, clam boats, home-built fishing boats, speed boats with sand bags hung from the prows to keep the bows down as they sped up. The stuff you grow up with is what you are. The gist of "Long Island" is that I learned about big things by means of little things. Three times, the poem changes midstream from first to third person because that earlier self is not me but someone I used to know well. My older self contains many places at once.

And every place is visible in the poems. "White Clover" is an Iowa poem. Those clover blossoms pop up in backyards because they were farms where cows grazed. The long poem "Initial Conditions" starts in a coffee shop in Port Townsend and stays in the region. The poem "After a Line by Theodore Roethke" begins in the minus-tide we see there.

I've said before that I like ideas to have a little dirt on their shoes. It's what (William Carlos) Williams says in "Tract" when he's telling people how to perform a funeral. He says, "You can do it; you have the ground sense necessary."

And I take physical reality as it is. I rarely fret over the distance between a thing and the word for it. Life is impure. Language is impure. Language is subjective and relative. Language has slippage. Fine. Those are givens. Get on with it.

Do you think your work belongs to any of these places more directly than the others?

When I'm in the Northwest, which I dearly love, and I am writing, I feel as if the Northwest itself wants to be in the poem. But I resist it. I resist it because I feel I haven't earned it. I'm not from the Northwest, even if I have lived there parts of nineteen years. I haven't earned it because there are many Northwest writers who are decidedly regional in their outlook and verbally aware of their place in their writing. I want to be careful that I don't appear to be one of them, because I can't be. Oh, sometimes I am—there are poems. But I resist till it overtakes me.

I taught in Iowa City for many years before I realized I was an Iowan. People would ask where I was from, and I'd say, "I teach in Iowa, but I'm from Long Island." And eventually I realized that the answer to that question was, "I'm from Iowa." Even today, there's a part of me that feels that, while Iowa is a natural part of my poetry, I still have to resist it a bit, just enough to be sure that it deserves to be there, or that I deserve it. But I never have that feeling on Long Island.

When I'm on Long Island, I feel it's all mine, and I can use any part of it. In fact, the Long Island that was mine is rapidly disappearing. You can't escape these feelings though. You come from somewhere. And even if that somewhere is rapidly being erased, it still exists within you, the way people who have died are still alive in your mind. I know lots of people—more and more—who have died. Their names come up in conversation. I tell stories about them. John Logan, Richard Hugo, William Matthews, William Stafford—poets, friends, relatives, even some former students. To me, they are alive.

Port Townsend, Washington, Waterside

The log they use as a loveseat
rode here on the tide, alumnus of a boom
when forests were thick as Iowa soybeans
and stately as Kansas wheat shocks.
Pitted now, splintery on its way to driftwood,
it's a perch for locals who watch the ferries
ply the channel to Whidbey, barges of sawdust,
kayaks and subs, trawlers putting out to sea,
and in the foreground hoppity plovers,
eagles harassed by gulls, a slivery heron,
and a light that painted Maine and Manhattan,
coated Illinois, spotted Arizona canyons,
and erased the stars from east to west
to arrive unbroken at the Strait of Juan de Fuca
where it slowly bent toward the Pacific,
leaving the mountain ash, the hawthorn,
and the monkey puzzle tree to droop a bit,
sensing north, in air that smells of cedar,
near beached logs akimbo in time.

—*Marvin Bell*

Dust, Corn, and Popcorn People

Before continuing on the trip, we take a southern detour to visit my brother-in-law in a corner of Iowa. He's taught high school for almost twenty-five years, and he's my wife's only brother. He's a funny and brilliant guy, who knows enough about history and baseball to keep you talking all night. He's the first person we see on the trip whom we really know, who knows us from our old lives. I find myself chattering about the trip like it was a religious quest. I inflate the journey, the project, the travel. At one point he says, "Well, as long as you're having fun."

My wife's family is from Iowa, and she was born just about twenty miles from here. One of our stops this weekend is that little town, but we also have plans to see a two hundred-square-mile area that covers six counties tucked in this corner of the state.

Most folks have no concept of the Midwest. To them, it's just a flyover area of blank spaces, a green patch in a road atlas, a place they've never been. There is some sense of cold. If you say "Iowa," some folks imagine corn.

But there's so much corn you can't even fully describe it. As we drive the highways, dirt roads, and gravel roads (all brilliantly straight north and south or east and west), we are always bordering corn or soybean fields. The corn stalks are dead, harvested, but still straight and standing and whistling a bit in any breeze. Up close they make a rustling sound, like cardboard against paper, dead leaves against a window. Field after field, and nothing but that on the horizon. Trees intrude only inside towns or around river bottoms. The fields themselves are uncluttered, rows and endless rows, sometimes a shocking group of silver silos, a single combine or harvester, a row of gigantic power lines escaping toward Nebraska, two cows looking through a fence.

On a blue and sunny Saturday my brother-in-law drives us around. We roll in his giant Buick on dusty roads, the dust pouring in vents or half-closed windows. Dust so thick it makes a fog around you. Think Pigpen. Think Cary Grant and that crop duster. Dust so heavy you can feel it on your tongue. You sneeze. You blow your nose, then take another deep breath of dust. The car is full of dust, but how could it not be? It's been a drought year, and dust is what you get from that.

41

Every town we see has a population of about eight hundred. My brother-in-law tells us which towns are dying out, which ones are hanging on. They all look much the same, with old prairie-style homes from the turn of the last century, a tiny post office, one or two restaurants (one's always a buffet). Farmers push into town in pickups or congregate on benches or by the feed stores.

Everyone waves, smiles. The sun beats down. The crop for corn was okay this year; the soy beans won't be quite as good. But it's a beautiful place, even with the dust.

We roll into Hamburg, Iowa, where my wife has not been since the day she was born there. It's like most of the other towns we've seen, but a little larger, a little more prosperous. "These are all popcorn," my brother-in-law says, pointing at over a hundred squatty silos, about forty feet high, about forty feet across. A banner hangs on one announcing the yearly popcorn festival.

We go through town and then head up a narrow hillside road that goes by some homes. "These are all popcorn people up here," my brother-in-law says, as we wind up in the driveway of a nice brick house, sprawling green lawn. A kid on a lawn mower nods at us and keeps going. We get out for a minute and peer over the back of their backyard—fields, a distant Interstate, dust rising off a county road, and a single green pickup.

We go by another town, where my wife graduated, and another where my brother-in-law's high school volleyball team is going to play that week. One of his players is sick, his best player. She has mono or West Nile or something. She missed the last couple of games. The phones in the area have been buzzing about her: will she get well? Will she be back to play Malvern? We have to have her back to beat Malvern!

We head up another gravel road. It's big enough for one and a half cars of this size, so we're right in the middle. Dust roars in both windows. I'm smiling, holding my breath. Suddenly, a giant red combine appears ahead of us, moving in the same direction, but slower. My brother-in-law is pointing out the window on his side. "One of my players lives there," he says, as he motions at a small farmhouse down a dirt road. We fly past the combine, two wheels half in the ditch, the combine's massive red arm right at eye level on my side.

When the day is over, we get out of the Buick, and the dust settles on me, my clothes. I can't see anything.

Michael Dennis Browne
Minneapolis, Minnesota

I've met Michael Dennis Browne before. He came to the campus of Southern Mississippi in 1985. At the time I was a boorish grad student, sure of myself, sure I was right about everything. I'd even developed a little phobia about contemporary poetry. "Give me some Keats, but take anything modern and get out of my way."

But as a student in the program I got drafted to go to Michael's reading. His voice, a sturdy mixture of his boyhood England and his adulthood Minnesota, worked the poems in the best way. Not caressing the words, not inflating the language, not inspiring anything into them that wasn't already there. And the poems were worth the effort it took to read and hear them.

He finished with one of his most well-known pieces, a gorgeous one called "Hide and Go Seek," which uses the childhood game as an extended metaphor for the growth, happiness, and safety of his nieces and nephews. The monster the speaker plays in the waning daylight hours mirrors the monsters of the contemporary world. The poem ends as the speaker cries a plaintive, "All in. All in." It was simple and beautiful. I bought one of his books the next day.

I tell Michael about this as he gets lunch together for me. Ahead of my visit he's walked to a local co-op to fetch tomato basil soup and a fine salad with giant garbanzos in the bottom. He puts some bread in the oven as he gets the meal ready and we talk about the project. Like many of the folks I've met, Michael is envious of the trip and of the time I've got to do it. This is one thing all the poets I've met seem to share, a sort of wanderlust. New places mean new ideas, new poems, new worlds.

Once we're done eating, we go out in the backyard to Michael's shed, a wooden structure, no bigger than four by seven. A big window opens to the southern sky, and a hand-hewn desk falls out of the wall on little hinges. The wood is all fence lumber. Michael's glad to sit in the shed for me, and I get a few pictures. It was built for three hundred dollars, and it's one of two places where Michael does most of his work.

The other place, the dream place, is a house up in the north woods of Minnesota, a cedar house with a screened porch and a twenty-four-foot peak. It's instructive to tell you that Michael shows me two pictures during my visit. One of his kids. One of his cabin.

~ ~ ~ ~ ~ ~

What role has place played in your work?

It's a huge fascination, topic, obsession for me, place. I call myself an Anglo-Sotan, half Anglo-Saxon, half Minnesotan, not quite belonging either place. I was born in England, but I left at twenty-five to come to Iowa. Started a whole new life in a whole new landscape. But England is my native soil, my holy ground. My parents are buried there; my sister's buried there. And it was Ireland before that. Three of my four grandparents were born in Ireland. So when I went there, I thought, "These are my people, my tribe." I saw the family face. So much of my temperament, background is Irish. And I love those rocky coasts, those moors, and fens. Ireland, England, and now Minnesota, where I raised my family. The north woods where we have a cabin. My own little private phrase is "Holding the holy places." Which means, as I walk around, I have a little constellation of places *(pointing at chest)* inside me. I think it's important to be fully present where you are, to be there and not somewhere else.

I tell my students this: if you want to be imaginative, figurative, and analogical, you start by being completely attentive and present to where you are at the time. And that attentiveness to me is like a hard surface. If I want to bounce a ball a long way, I'll bounce it off the tabletop like this, rather than the grass out there, because there's more reverberation in a surface like this *(hitting table)*. As you attend to the present moment, the movement of something, you're far more likely to suddenly go somewhere a thousand miles away or thirty years away if you're fully *here* first.

So it is with the imagination. Fully present to this landscape, which is the landscape of my maturity. I've lived here longer than I lived in England. This is where my children were raised; I love the north woods. But I carry England with me, always. And I carry Ireland with me. And there's certainly an imaginative tension there. When I'm writing well, the times it happens, stuff comes out of the archives that's unbelievable. And often it's place related. But I can never predict where I'm going to go. But I always try to start with a fully attentive Minnesota-based experience and see where it takes me.

I have a great love of place. Also, in terms of my own religious belief, I do see the physical universe as what someone called the body of God. God's self-expression. So I do find nature of infinite fascination, especially trees that I revere. And I know there's an old tradition of tree worship in pre-Christian times. Trees, water, birds, the movement of the wind in the leaves.

I find it, moment by moment, of profound fascination. Where one is, where one was, where one could be.

Do you seem to write better or differently in any of the places where you write?

I tend not to like to come back from the woods. I have a little studio building, somewhat larger than that little shed there *(pointing into the backyard)*. I find it is womb-like. Picture window, the trees; I can hear the loons. I think I can focus. There's more stasis there, and I don't mean I'm stuck. So I think I've done a lot of my best work up at the studio, up in the woods, two hundred miles north. I can work anywhere. I like to work here *(kitchen table)*; I like to work there *(backyard shed)*. I work on planes and buses. I work in a little study in the library. But I do save the studio to finish a project.

I always want to surprise myself. I always hope the blank page will take me somewhere I don't know how to go to until I go there. There's a Randall Jarrell quote, "If I know what it is, it's not what I want." So the basic principle is you don't want to know. I've learned by going where I have to go. In most poems I write, however, I would think at some point an element of the natural world would suggest itself. Because the natural world is that profound repository, just something that I gravitate toward. I do find real correspondence between what's happening here and what's happening there. I'm really quoting (Rainer Maria) Rilke there. Rilke says, "Images are equivalents of the real world seen inwardly."

Did something happen to you and your work when you moved to America?

I arrived in Davenport, Iowa, thirty-eight years ago, and it was a hot, tropical night. There was heat lightning all along the horizon, like a distant war with no sound. I thought I was in this exotic world. I was living on a farm in my second year, and it was like going west; it's like the big sky. And I thought of (Walt) Whitman: "Unscrew the doors from their jambs." Yes, the physical enlargement of the place exhilarated me. It was a correspondence between the opening going on inside at twenty-five—I was just wild at twenty-five in my imagination. I was in a landscape that was Whitmanesque, so it totally supported the expansiveness happening inside. I was bursting open, and the landscape was bursting open.

The expansiveness of the American landscape came at the perfect time. It was brilliant timing. I tend to write in open forms, and I come into these. It's been a constant wonder to me.

from At the Cabin

LATE MARCH

fell asleep
   as I'd wanted to
      on the wind

became the branches
   leaping about
      I'd dreamed to be

flew by myself
   too fast
      for myself to see

LATE MARCH

I hear old winter hanged himself;
I heard it from three crows going over.
Not that they were telling it to me
personally; any fool could receive
such news in that echoing landscape.

CABIN, CRY

startled at the squeal
   of brakes in the driveway—
somebody's here!—
   but no, just some
harsh bird back there
   in the yellowing woods,
its mechanical cry

In August

                as if one afternoon
           the summer begins
        to accept her age
the lines in
her face ease
       and yellowjackets
           begin to wander
                out of the crevices

September

now smoke begins to flower
   above the cosmos
that are past their prime

dry sticks
  fit only
for the fires

and little melons
   that will never
reach a mouth

When the Deer Reminds Me of My Son

when I go out and he is there
   (the storm door bangs behind)

when he startles in the clearing
   begins to run

when he bounds off through the brush

when he is gone

Balcony, Evening

watching the leaves shiver
letting the little leaves go

sounds of our neighbor Lou
still mowing below

no way to say
to the shadows: no

—Michael Dennis Browne

David Allan Evans
Brookings, South Dakota

We head west out of Minnesota toward South Dakota to see Dave Evans. Evans's poetry was pretty new to me when I started working on this book. But I took to it immediately because it was so rich in the physical world. An accomplished athlete all of his life, Evans fills his poems with concrete details. His poems are about the corporal world, bullfrogs, bars of soap, an aging racquetball player.

We're an hour or so early, and I have the corporal world on my mind as well. When we are low on supplies, we steer toward the outskirts of almost any town and look for the familiar Wal-Mart sign. We pull Winnie Cooper into two nose-to-nose spaces in the far reaches of a gigantic parking lot. We stroll inside, buy some new RV antifreeze, some tiny cans of soup, a magazine or two. After long, quiet nights in the motor home and long driving days, it's fun to just stand in the dazzling hum of enterprise.

When it's time, we drive wide, quiet streets, following another rudimentary map. I go to the house, and Evans meets me at the door. We walk through his sprawling home and go out into the backyard to look around. It's sunny today. Crisp. It's already the time for occasional snows in South Dakota. But today it's brilliant and pretty.

We go down to his basement to chat. Like other basements I've seen on this trip, this one is full of books. It's well lit, and his computer rests in the far corner. We sit on comfortable chairs and start talking about poems from his upcoming book, a personal best collection of his work from over thirty years.

I ask him about the poems written for Sioux City, Iowa, and despite the fact that he's been in South Dakota now for thirty-five years, he talks fondly and in detail about the alleys and streets of his hometown.

He leans toward me when I ask a question and then leans back to answer. As we go along, it feels as though we're pulling and pushing the words into shape.

~ ~ ~ ~ ~ ~

What role has place played in your poetry?

First of all, I consider myself a writer who is very much concerned with the physical world. Having been a physical person much of my life, with sports, I'm not a poet who writes a lot of poems that are subjective

50

or highly cerebral. I tend to write about literal things that I see, that I've observed, that I've actually done.

I grew up in Sioux City, Iowa, and a good percentage of my poems contain images and experiences that come out of the landscapes of that city, especially a neighborhood on a railroad bluff where I lived as a teenager. Teenagers go through a lot of changes and turmoil, so it's not surprising that I would remember very vividly many experiences of that period of time. Even in my sixties, a number of my new poems go back to Sioux City, especially to that one neighborhood.

I think that the early physical environment is important to any writer or artist, if only because those early experiences tend to stay in one's memory. As Stanley Kunitz said, "Poets are always revisiting the place of their innocence." I think there's a lot to that. At least for me there is. But, I've moved around a bit. I've lived in Brookings, South Dakota, for the last thirty-five years and been aware of small-town and country landscapes and the flat prairie environment, where you can look out and see—as they say around here—"as far as the eye can see." I've been out there as a hunter, somewhat, so that my writing over the years has been influenced by a variety of environments—urban, small-town, and country. All these are in my poems.

But I like to think of myself as a poet who has written out of a very literal sense of where I've lived.

Since you've lived your whole life in Iowa and South Dakota, do you consider yourself a regional poet?

Because I was born in Iowa and have lived most of my life in the upper Midwest, I can't help but write out of that context. William Stafford said that all art is local. Art comes out of local landscapes or, in other words, the near at hand. I have no problem with being labeled a regionalist. The word "regionalism" is quite often used in a pejorative way—it gets a lot of negative knocks—but I have no problem with identifying with a particular landscape. William Faulkner identified strongly with a little piece of ground in rural Mississippi, and I'm proud to be connected to a particular landscape in Iowa or South Dakota. I think this strong identification has been a strength in my writing over the years. Poets and other artists have to go on the assumption that there is really nothing but the near at hand. They have to believe that they can make art out of the place or places they have lived in.

What do you think poets miss if they're not plugged in to their physical space?

When you think about it, place is very much a biological matter and not just a cultural one. The most basic rule in biology is that you have an organism and a particular place that it inhabits. The human brain, according to Steven Pinker, the brain scientist and evolutionary psychologist at MIT, "equips us to thrive in a world of objects, living things, and other humans." In other words, a sense of place is wired into our brain. It's quite natural, then, for a poet, or any artist, to respond to and describe actual physical settings, to stay aware of where they are located at any given time. Some poets are more keyed to specific locales than others, of course. I've always been taken by poetry that has a strong feel for the local in it. And I'm very much opposed to the postmodern, blank-slate, arrogant assumption that has been around for some time now that the physical world is not physical or tangible, but rather is culturally or socially constructed by human beings. The world that we inhabit was here long before our species evolved and will probably be here long after we're gone. We don't construct it; we adapt to it, just like all other living things.

Wallace Stevens said that "the greatest poverty is to not live in the physical world." What Stevens said is surely true of writers and other artists. Their productions are enriched when they have definite settings and roots in them. I think poetry and fiction become rather airy and subjective if they lack a convincing sense of locale. Much of the power of the poetry comes from the reality of the locales described and celebrated in it.

David Romtvedt
Buffalo, Wyoming

In one long day we travel the stark and beautiful stretch across South Dakota into Wyoming. In a light rain, we push past miles and miles of badlands and high prairie grasses. But the land changes near Buffalo. The trees begin to crowd the highway, and the Bighorn Mountains loom in the west. There's every indication that the driving and the travel will get tougher.

Downtown Buffalo is packed with coffee shops, old hotels, and art galleries. Friendly folks in front of their stores sweep brooms and talk to one another.

The weather is unseasonable, warm, headed to the eighties, and everyone's making use of it. At the Catholic Church, a maintenance man rakes and then scoops up some leaves that are slowly deserting the confused trees. The long and warm autumn has everything a little off-kilter.

I find David Romtvedt hollering to me from behind the fence to his backyard. I've been looking forward to today for a while. Romtvedt's work is packed with this town. He lets the "prairie, mountain, and sky" of the place into his work frequently, and seeing the area in person makes me realize how richly the poems are arrayed.

We say hello, and he spies our motor home. He, like many of the poets I've met, is intrigued by the practical elements of this project. How does one get to Wyoming, Washington, Wisconsin, Iowa, Idaho, Indiana, and back? David's leaping and happy dog Leo is up for the adventure so we go open the door to Winnie Cooper.

Leo is the first to bound in. My wife is just sitting down to check email but is glad to see us all. David looks around. I try to explain that the place is bigger when the slide-outs are fully extended, but he likes it anyway. Leo is up front by the driver's seat, and I'm thinking that he looks pretty comfortable. Does he know we're going into Montana now? Does he want to go? Does he know the way?

~ ~ ~ ~ ~ ~

How do you think places, the places you've lived and worked, have had an impact on your poetry?

I believe that my work has been strongly influenced not so much by the particular landscape of the northern Rockies where I live as by the

53

presence of the natural world. And by "natural," I mean the nonhuman. I have found myself drawn again and again to wondering about the human relationship to plants and animals, to the rivers and oceans, to the sky.

My work is shaped very deeply by what the meaning of place is more than it is by a particular place. It wouldn't matter to me as a writer if I was living in Kentucky or Arizona or Wyoming. I would still be drawn by what it is to be in a place. It isn't as though there's some magical specific connection to only one place.

People often distinguish nature from human beings. When they say "nature," they mean every single thing in the universe but human beings. By separating the human from the natural we are able to discuss certain issues. Of course, it's also true that human beings are a part of the natural world and the natural world includes human activity, human thoughts, and feelings. So I've tried to think about my writing as dealing with sky, leaves, autumn, but in relation to people doing things. I think my work is driven by what is the meaning of our lives, both within a natural world and as part of it.

Your poem "Implacable America" has an ominous tone about it. These deer are in a gorgeous woodland, but modern America—citified America—is roaring toward them. The poem makes it seem inevitable.

Yeah, there's something coming closer. What is it? There are a bunch of really obvious sensibilities. Like when you build a Wal-Mart in Sheridan, Wyoming, you change the entire business community of Buffalo, Wyoming, forty miles away. Not to mention that half of Sheridan's businesses go bankrupt. And the business that drove them all out, it's not just that it's a better business, it's also a globalized business. So you change labor relations. You change the kinds of products people own. You change their relationship to the making of things. Now I don't know if you can take all of that from my poem, in which deer are watching pickup trucks drive by on the road. That's a very physical and real poem. I hike out here, right near where I live, where there's a creek that comes down out of these mountains and runs right through the center of town. This creek is the water supply for town. I hike there all the time, and there's an oxbow, a big deep bend that forms a little spit of land—almost like an island. It's so beautiful to lie there in the rocks and the leaves. I was doing that one day, and, of course, the deer love to be in lowland, wooded areas. We call them "parks" here—open areas where the trees are not very dense and where there are rather level grassy areas marked by widely dispersed boulders.

I'm sitting there with the deer and the water and the mountain mahogany—that's tight and hard, and you don't want to lie on that—and off in the distance I hear pickup trucks. The poem's very real in that way, and I'm thinking, "Here we have this tiny little road and here's this sound of this motor roaring, and there is no stopping it."

Do you feel you have a responsibility to speak for your region or area?

I actually do think that's true. First of all, I have the privilege, the opportunity, to have become a writer. Whatever my small failings as a human being, I actually do have a responsibility to what I would call the highest level of my ability to have social and intellectual honesty in my writing. And I hope that doesn't sound stupid or inflated.

But more than that, it's a pleasure to get to speak for a place that I have such deep feelings for. I live in Wyoming because I came here as a resident at an artist's colony, fell in love with a woman who is now my wife, and never left. I never planned to live here, and I never liked the social fabric of the place. My home is marked by the height of the western idea of independence, the self-made person, the individual against nature. And at the same time the reality of these rural places is cooperation. These places don't work on individual tough-guy-isms. They work because people have cooperated. They have been physically harsh places.

I want to speak for my home's beauty as a place and our association with it in a way that doesn't destroy it. Right now we're seeing our current U.S. administration—through the Domenici bill—do everything possible to define the primary use of public lands in the northern Rockies as mineral exploitation. It would counteract to some degree the multiple-use policy that has been in effect throughout the twentieth century. Which is one that some people argued wasn't good enough anyway. Multiple use meant rape and exploitation, but it also allowed us to protect some lands.

So I've got a responsibility to say something, but I don't want to just give lectures. As a poet, I believe in poetry that wanders around and speculates and dreams and speaks out of love and passion, and not necessarily out of some great insightful intellectual political skill. Some poets don't have that skill and don't want it.

With Caitlin, Age 8, Building a Qhuinzee
for a Winter Night

Early in the day we shovel snow
into a mound six feet high and fifteen feet around.
In the afternoon we dig, shaping a doorway.
Then, on our backs, we hollow out a room,
the snow falling onto our faces.

We lay out ground pads and sleeping bags,
push a spoon into the domed snow wall and set
a candle in the spoon. By glow of candlelight
we lie in our sleeping bags and I read aloud
the first book of *The Chronicles of Narnia,*
the one in which four children stumble
into a wardrobe and emerge in a world
of perpetual winter. Warm in our bags,
we soon grow tired and sleep.

In the night, I wake, needing to pee.
I wriggle out of my bag and on my back
slide through the doorway. The cold hammers
the top of my head, then my forehead and eyes.
The stars come into sight, the blue black sky,
the moon, nearly full. I stick my head back in
and call my daughter, "Come quick." She wakes
and, like me, wriggles out on her back.
As her head emerges she blinks
and her mouth opens. "Oh," she says.
"Oh."

We hold hands and jump around but I can't
jump for long as I still have to pee. So I walk away.
When I come back I look at the thermometer
on my coat. "Well?" Caitlin asks. "26 below," I tell her.

In the morning we slide out and stand once more
in the frozen air, ice crystals hovering around us,
remembering stars. "26 below," my daughter says.
"Yes, not many eight year olds have slept out like that."
"But we built a qhuinzee," she says, and throws herself
down on the snow, starts slapping at it while grinning
up at the pale blue sky.

—*David Romtvedt*

The West

I've often told people in the East that I thought of myself as a westerner. I love the West, I'd say. I'd tell them about going to college in Arizona, my love of the Oregon coast, and some story about smoking a cigar on a car hood in Coeur d'Alene, Idaho.

I never had to say much more than that. That was always strange enough for most people. In the circles I've lived in for many years now, the West is like one of the moons of Jupiter. There are pictures, but nobody's been there.

In the past week we've traveled far from the Midwest, through South Dakota, Wyoming, and now into Montana. Big empty states. Beautiful empty highways that are always snaking through badlands or hills, pastures, wheat fields, and then mountains. Twenty-four Black Angus cows, steers, whatever, all lined up by a lone tree. Actual cowboys moving a herd of cattle down the side of the highway outside Aladdin, Wyoming—population fifteen. Endless and stoic power lines disappearing into the horizon in Crawford County, South Dakota.

As we left behind badlands and high prairie grasslands, we started to get into hills through eastern Wyoming, and by the time we got to Buffalo, in the north central part of the state, we could see parts of the Rocky Mountains looming ahead of us.

From Buffalo to Butte, Montana, we climbed from 3,000 feet to nearly 6,500. It's not the easiest thing in the world to encourage a twenty-nine-foot motor home up to 6,500 feet. But we mashed on the gas, hugged the right-hand lane with some semis and moving vans, and ended up crossing the Continental Divide at a brisk 35 mph.

And every mile over the past few days has been stunning. The land out here just eats you up. In South Dakota, it's the horizon that kills you. It's everywhere. You look any direction and see the earth moving away from you. But now in Montana, there are hills and mountains on every side, the highest of them snowcapped, despite the fact that we're in our third or fourth seventy-plus-degree day in late autumn, breaking records all over.

We spent the day in Missoula, a sparkling western college town with art galleries, ranchers, college students, artisans, and hippies. We spent some time at a Kinko's, doing work for this book, and darted out for lunch at one of a hundred quaint cafes.

One thing that has really struck me since being here this time is the very real and important role nature has in the lives of westerners. In the East, the lack of rain or snow in a normal winter is weather talk. Here, it's different. The environment is not just an abstract topic of discussion. The health and well-being of the land, the watershed, the trees—all of it is crucial to the simple survival of the people, their homes, and the way of life. While talking with an old-timer on a bench outside the café, I asked about the snow the past couple of winters. It's been down, I know, and I was really asking just for something to say. In my head, I sort of expected something like, "Yeah, nice warm winters. It's been great." But instead, the old guy says, "Yeah, it's been terrible. Not enough snow, so no runoff. The lakes are down; the rivers are down. The forests are dry and brittle. We had 400,000 acres of fires this summer." They lost firefighters out here, right from Missoula. Lost homes. Lost animals. The beautiful and living land was scorched. Trees that have stood for a hundred years or more lost in a flash.

We wandered back to a small car we had rented in order to get around and do some errands, but I kept thinking about the conversation and all the things I'd seen in the past few days.

People are tougher in the West. You see houses and farms up mountains, perched on cliffs or just butted at the end of long dirt roads. It gets cold out here, and the snow does come, and these folks are cut off from the world for a while. Ranch after ranch we passed with hundreds of hay bales already saved, covered, put aside for animals all winter. These haystacks tower above the fields, some covered with tarps or wood. Each house has a wall of firewood at least six feet tall, sometimes forty feet long. Firewood for a nice fire, perhaps, but usually for heat and sometimes to get them through a hard stretch.

Sandra Alcosser
Lolo, Montana

At 10 a.m. Sandra Alcosser pulls up beside our motor home. We've parked at a small park-and-ride on a highway south of Missoula, about five miles from Sandra's home in the mountains between Florence and Lolo. She warmly greets us both, and we pack our stuff into her wagon. This is the first of the interviews that my wife has been a part of. I suspect ahead of time that a cabin in the mountains is too enticing for her to miss.

We head up a gravel road, then a dirt road, and then squeeze halfway between the trees and the ditch to let a neighbor go by. "That's Harve," Sandra says, waving at her neighbor's pickup truck. We press on. There are only six houses on this stretch, and Sandra's is at the end.

We turn in to the tiny driveway and see her new dog, the lively Rio. Rio is spectacularly glad to see us all. To the south, the land and the trees slope away, back down to where we started. Behind us, the mountains climb, but not so far. We're a long way up. Pine trees pop up everywhere. The sky is a collection of colors, dark clouds to the north and west but above us blue, and the sun's coming through and warming up the ground around the cabin. We hike along a small path behind Sandra's house, a path that literally could take us all through the rest of Montana and into Idaho. The air is thin, and we start to feel the cold. Sandra leads us inside the cabin.

It's gorgeous. The wood is warm, the furniture heavy and old—some of it from an old drugstore in Missoula. Sandra uses some of the furniture to hold books, but one piece is still mostly empty, waiting to be filled. The shelves once held a collection of amber bottles of strychnine and belladonna.

Sandra seats us around her table with cookies, fruit, coffee, and delicious and cold blueberry-banana smoothies.

It feels odd setting up my equipment with my wife there. It's always been clear that the project was mine. We travel together, spend the days and nights exploring America together, but this book was always my thing.

Our work selves have always had their own space, and suddenly she's watching me, and it's disorienting. What must she think of this talk of poems and place? How many times have my eyes glassed over at one of her work functions when she and her colleagues talked about advertising, network TV sales, the demographics—my God, the 18–49 demographics? At how many English department parties have we exchanged comical glances when I'd be locked in a life-or-death discussion about Ginsberg or Stevens while my wife would be motioning like she was starting the car and driving us home? We know couples who work together, who have the same work pals. But that's not us. When we're not working, we like to check right out. There's no chance of a spontaneous chat about the upcoming NBC sitcoms, nor are we likely to discuss whether or not we think Robert Frost could be excised painlessly from the canon. We talk about dinner. Movies. The last Grisham. Our pals, families. It's not better or worse; it's just us.

But today it feels okay, partly because Sandra makes us both feel so at home. My wife gets started on the muffins, and I get started on the interview.

Sandra feels strongly about place, the energy of New York versus Montana or San Diego (where she still runs the poetry program at San Diego State, a program she started). She's passionate about her work and about poetry in general. Over the years she's logged tens of thousands of miles working for the NEA, teaching drug addicts, running the Poets in the Park *program in New York City, teaching and reading around the country.*

She talks easily about her work and her role in its creation. I pose some sticky questions that have come up in my earlier interviews, and Sandra thinks about each question and answers them assuredly, deftly, with force and clarity.

~ ~ ~ ~ ~ ~

Why is place important to you?

I come from a state, a region, where a sense of place is easy: 146,000 square miles and 900,000 people or about six people per square mile. Mountains, though some formations are relatively new, are between 30 million and 600 million years old. It is as easy to live in geologic time as sidereal or star time. One walks out the door and is surrounded by so much space, so much uplifted granite, it is impossible not to feel a communion between self and landscape.

As a poet, are you responsible in any way to write about where you live?

The landscape may not need us or our poems—spicebush existed twenty million years before a human came along to taste it—but we need its stories. A good poem might protect or restore a place, and one grows that poem walking every day over the shifting plates of the planet.

Montana has an amazing community of readers and writers. I've only lived here for twenty-eight years. Some writers have Montana stories gathered from four generations of family. Much longer, of course, for Native Americans. That in itself gives one a sense of place. Humility. Though there is always much to be humbled by.

What about your connection with the natural world? You live in this beautiful place. Do you find that the trees, the mountains, and the sky filter into your work?

Absolutely. It's everywhere in my work. Robert Duncan talks about the answering intensity of the imagination: "The mountains speak to me; I speak back." I like to spend enough time in a place for it to stain me. When I went to Louisiana, I felt as though I lost the landscape that I knew, but I mean the language for that landscape. I could take you out *(pointing out her window)* and name the rock formations. What each tree is. What plant it is and when it flowers. Over time, you just come to know this, because you watch through the seasons. And you begin naming, and that language becomes the language of the poems.

Your experiences in New York City in the mid-1970s must have been quite different from your home on a mountain.

Both places encourage quixotic, risk-taking behavior. In the Bitterroots you might spot a tawny ribbon pulled through green and realize that a mountain lion is running parallel to you. Or have a bear lean up against the plate glass of your living-room window and wonder about the tensile strength of glass.

Phillip *(her husband)* and I met in the Green Guerillas in New York, an open-space greening coalition. When government came in and tore down buildings, we'd ask the neighborhood, "What do you want here?" I was working with drug addicts planting gardens in Needle Park. I was twenty-seven. I had gone to New York because of a *Mademoiselle* guest editorship and worked there a couple of years. But I didn't want to be in an office, so I started teaching poetry in drug rehab, to emotionally disturbed patients and so forth. It got so hot in those places that people became restless, so I'd say, "Let's get out and garden," but we had no gardening tools or implements. We used broken wine bottles.

At night I'd go back and clean up what we'd done that day. There were many people in the neighborhood from the Dominican Republic and from Puerto Rico. They would come and stand around the fence and serenade me. They'd say, "quibombo," pointing to a row of okra, and be as pleased to see their island's red-throated flowers as I was to hand-pollinate tomato blossoms with a Q-tip the way my Uncle Paul had taught me in Indiana.

You have a couple of prose poems in your last book that seem to really capture that time when you were growing up in Indiana.

My elders were first-generation eastern Europeans. Every Wednesday was soup night, and anyone and everyone knew about it. My grandmother baked potato bread and made vats of soup, and our entire family—plus the workers at the body shop and anyone passing through—found a seat and a bowl of soup. That land was paradise, with a stone fishpond, a marble-floored grape arbor, bird yards, and orchards, all built and tended by my grandparents. It was a safe place, thicketed, and high-pitched enough to shape an imagination.

Mare Frigoris

Coming home late spring night, stars a foreign
Language above me, I thought I would know

The moons like family, their dark plains—sea of
Crises, sea of nectar, serpent sea.

How quickly a century passes,
Minerals crystallize at different speeds,

Limestone dissolves, rivers sneak through its absence.
This morning I learned painted turtles

Sleeping inches below the streambank
Freeze and do not die. Fifteen degrees

Mare Frigoris, sea of cold, second
Quadrant of the moon's face. I slide toward

The cabin, arms full of brown bags, one light
Syrups over drifts of snow. Night rubs her

Icy skin against me and I warm
Small delicates—cilantro, primrose—

Close to the body. A hundred million
Impulses race three hundred miles an hour

Through seventeen square feet of skin and
Gravity that collapses stars, lifts earth's

Watery dress from her body, touches me
With such tenderness I hardly breathe.

—Sandra Alcosser

Robert Wrigley
Moscow, Idaho

Robert Wrigley lives a few miles outside of Moscow, Idaho, a rugged college town near the Washington border. Winnie Cooper squeezes up a combination of gravel and dirt roads, through severe switchbacks to the top of a towering hill that looks south and back toward town. The view is extraordinary, three mountain ranges, one more than 100 miles away on the horizon. On a clear day you can see all the way to Oregon.

Wrigley greets us and shows us his studio, a twelve-by-fifteen building he built himself. Inside it's full of books, pictures, and a gleaming white Fender Stratocaster that Wrigley won in a raffle. Wrigley played as a kid around St. Louis but now just uses the guitar to help delay the inevitable work that awaits him at his desk, where his hard-backed journal and mechanical pencil await.

He sits in a high-backed office chair, and I'm on the couch-futon and we talk easily. It's not hard to see how the natural world that populates Wrigley's work ended up there; we're in the midst of a mountain forest that teems with animal and plant life. He tells me about moose, coyotes, owls, snakes, and bear.

~ ~ ~ ~ ~ ~

How would you say place has played a role in your work?

The fact of the matter is I came of age as a man and as a poet in this part of the country. I didn't think that I would wind up living in the West. I was born in the Midwest. I had visited the West and visited the Rocky Mountains as a kid, and I thought, "Wow, that was really great." But it never dawned on me that I'd live here.

I wound up going to graduate school at the University of Montana, and in my two years in Montana I got absolutely hooked on living in the mountains. I became convinced from that time, nearly thirty years ago, that I couldn't be happy living anywhere else. I don't think my first book, which I wrote mostly in Montana and Idaho, has a lot of western images in it, nor does it have a lot of poems generated by what I was living in the midst of. But now I have to say that this landscape, this place, the animals who live here, and the things I find myself doing here have become the theater of my poetic operations. This is where I get most of my images. My new book is called *Lives of the Animals,* and the principal animal in that book is the human. But the book is filled with this absolute bestiary of critters that I run into daily. They're not all big romantic western animals *(laughs)*. There's the occasional mosquito, grasshopper.

The larger context of my work is the search for the idea of the soul. I want to believe there is a soul, but I am not guided to it and not made to understand how it might exist, where it might exist, or how I might reach it via traditional, organized religion. I get my religion, I get my spiritual self regenerated in the woods, in nature. Wild country is my church. You combine those things—the idea of spiritual regeneration or communion and this boundless source of images that I get from the wild world—and it's everything about what I do as a poet.

Your poems, as you've just noted, are full of animals. I think of the owl in your poem "Explanatory," for example. What is it that you see in the animal kingdom that makes you want to bring them into your poetry?

It might well be envy. There was one review of my book *Reign of Snakes* where the reviewer said something like "Part of Wrigley's enterprise is this envy for what animals have that human beings can never have." That's also connected to the spiritual stuff. Animals don't want to die; they'll run from danger. They will fight if they are cornered. But at the same time they won't exhaust themselves fretting about what's going to happen to them after they die. They are absolutely alive in the moment in a way that human beings don't often get a chance to be. And I think that's what I like about poetry. There's a way in which poems enter into that sort of animal experience. That we are more in the presence of a poem that's got us by the aorta, or whatever it gets us by. That we are as alive in the moment as we are capable of.

There's that wonderful passage in *Song of Myself* where (Walt) Whitman says, "I think I could turn and live with animals, they are so placid and self-contain'd." None of them prays to anything that's dead or worries about what's going to happen to them after they die. They are just there. And I love them.

This is a sparsely populated part of the world. Is there something about the emptiness of it that makes it a good place for you to write?

Not really. I mean, I can look out the window here and see Moscow, Idaho, six miles off. I can see the university where I teach. There are things, civilized things, to do and see here. It's not that empty, in other words. And I write in the midst of my family's life, too.

The emptiness—the woods, the canyons, the undeveloped land—is what I have come to value as a human being. No doubt that's something valuable to me as a writer, but it's not lack of population that drives my poems.

But I have to say, when I come home from teaching, I love to listen to what I listen to when I'm here. This is a ponderosa pine forest, and ponderosa pine forests make a kind of a wind sound that no other forest makes. It's a very specific sort of sound, and I will come home sometimes, early in the fall semester, and my wife and I will sit out on the deck and the sun will be almost down and we'll hear coyotes. And that's just a much better place for me to be; those coyotes and that wind song are a much better sound for me than an ambulance, a siren, or horn. This is where I have to be. Maybe just to regenerate the soul, or whatever engine it is that drives the poems. It may be that my imagination just needs that kind of silence to start processing.

A number of poets I've spoken with like being called regional poets, but, of course, others don't like the limitations of that term. What about you? Are you a regional poet?

I'm one of those people who is uncomfortable with labels. I get described pretty regularly as a nature poet. I've gotten over being irritated by that. It used to make my flesh crawl. There's a way in which some of these labels become ghettoes, but I'm happy to live in this ghetto. I guess I'm comfortable being a western poet. And it's probably true that all poets are regional poets in some way or another. There is, as you say, that default landscape that provides us our poetic vocabulary, that gives us our stage of poetic concerns.

Ordinary Magic

The dog doesn't notice the bucket's scummed
surface. Or doesn't care. Nor does she see
that her snout must descend through seven
or more concentric rings of pine pollen dry
along the sides just to lap and take in
the gold dust of forest fecundity
as well as the water. And when I shoo
her off and take the bucket up, the dark
circle left there—like a cold sun the world
shines a wide shimmering penumbra around—
she doesn't see that either, and therefore,

for as long as it takes to clean and fill
the bucket, I feel for her something like
pity, almost, or sadness, this poor dog
I love, who cannot see the things I see
as clearly as I: ordinary magic,
I think—trope, symbol, signifier, thing
in itself more than it is. Except that
now is when I notice she's taken off,
running a crazy circuitous path
through the woods below the house, on the scent
of what I simply cannot imagine.

—Robert Wrigley

Nance Van Winckel
Liberty Lake, Washington

Nance Van Winckel lives outside of Spokane, Washington, in an airy and beautifully appointed second-floor condo that looks over Liberty Lake, a small but gorgeous body of water surrounded by trees.

She shows me her writing studio first. The large high-ceilinged room faces the lake and is lit by a floor-to-ceiling window nearly five feet across. She tells me she has plans to add another window in the same room, and I picture the room with one entire wall of windows. It will be spectacular.

We go out to the living room. Nance sits on the couch, and I face her in a rocking chair. We cover some general questions first, then begin to discuss some new things for me. Because Van Winckel is also an accomplished fiction writer, my questions about place generate some new angles.

~ ~ ~ ~ ~ ~

What thoughts do you have about how place has impacted your poetry?

I think about it in two ways: the way place has affected my process of writing and the way place becomes part of the subject matter of my poetry. In terms of place as subject matter, I think that poems often need to have some sort of stage to play themselves out on. This is the eighteenth place I've lived. My dad moved us every year or two when I was growing up, so I've lived all over the U.S. But places where I've lived, especially the Midwest, where I spent most of my coming-of-age, kind of return to me. Memories of things that happened are triggered in my poems, and the place itself comes back.

It's the whole feeling of the place that memory evokes—not just the physical space.

As regards how place affects the process of writing, what happens for me is that what I want to do is erase the glass window between me and the mountains, the lake, and sky, and just sort of fool myself into thinking that I'm not in this physical body, that I've somehow thrust myself out of this enclosed place and am in a place where the mind can loosen and unleash itself from its confines. For me, everything that is physical is associated with consciousness. And escaping that strict adherence to consciousness for the unconscious is what I want to do.

Have there been places that have been more conducive for poetry?
The last book I published was called *Beside Ourselves,* and those poems were set in Czechoslovakia and Bulgaria. I spent some time there in the mid 1980s, when those countries were still part of the communist machine. I took some notes while I was there. A lot of the notes had to do with the physical surroundings, and then fifteen years later I started writing these poems. That's often how poems operate for me. There needs to be this time gap from when I'm experiencing things to when my imagination can take possession of them. I sort of like when a memory comes back as a surprise. It floods back in on me. And it was interesting for me when I was working on those poems set in Eastern Europe that I never did look at those notes again. I think it was probably because I had already written them down, though, and so imprinted them. I didn't need to go back and look at what I'd written. I was working on poems about a torrid love affair, and those poems kept calling up that physical place I had visited. In reality, though, this nutty, wild, illicit love affair had occurred in a completely different time and space than the world of Eastern Europe. But I realized as I began to revise and arrange these poems into the book that my imagination had seen these things as "together" because of their shared chaos—the chaos and devastation of much of Eastern Europe at that time. That physical chaos matched the emotional chaos in the poems. But as I was initially writing the poems, I had no sense of why or how that event-world and that physical world were connected.

I think the imagination has to have something to do. And that's what it wanted to do in these poems, to sort of forge those two things— the temporal-spatial world and the emotional terrain. Chaos was the linkage.

I know you've published three books of short stories as well. Would you say that place figures more prominently in the fiction than in the poetry?
Yes. Because the fiction is intrinsically narrative, it has to have that physical plane for the drama to be acted out on. This last collection of stories *(Curtain Creek Farm)* I worked on is set on a commune in northeastern Washington. It's a purely fictional place, but I could drive you exactly to where it is up on the Pend Oreille River. And, of course, there'd be nothing there but a wheat field. But I've driven up that way

often, and I knew I wanted the stories set there. There are specific physical and geographical things I wanted to have in those stories. I wanted to have an osprey. Because there's a story with a big flood in it, I wanted to have the river. I wanted to have a canyon and certain little towns that are close by on the river up there. That was a really important kind of beginning place for me for those stories, to know the physical environment in which they were situated.

Would you say poetry doesn't require that to the same extent?

I would say it doesn't. It may have to do with how narrative a poem it is you're working with. It may be that this narrativity connects to how much of a stage it really needs to act itself out on. I sometimes talk to my students about this: do poems need to be grounded in the physical world at all? Can they just live as, say, many of Emily Dickinson's do? As pure lyric, as the voice disembodied from the physical? And for my own poems, I don't want to have any sort of rule that I'm held to. Increasingly I've been moving back and forth between fairly narrative poems and more lyric ones. And I like that. That ranging about.

I sort of take the place wherever I go. As I was saying about those Bulgarian poems, it may have to do with my notion of having that larger temporal distance. Maybe I'm writing now about events from college days in Milwaukee. Or maybe I'm writing now about something from my first teaching job in Kansas in the late 1970s. I have a feeling that this place, my lovely little lake here in Washington, might figure more in my poems ten years from now. The subconscious needs to chew on it first. The place, like everything, probably has to go down and get processed by something other than the conscious mind. It must somehow be transformed; it must feel a little different or be seen anew. I rarely write about anything that's going on right now in this year, in this time.

Awaiting the Return Ferry

(Balfour, British Columbia)

Ghostly echoes of old guffaws from a crowd
who's wise-cracked out. Late morning,
we watch the day get darker, not lighter.
Perched on pilings, gulls bring
few peaceful tidings to shore.

Clear last night but for one snowflake
that fell into our old horse's eye—black pupil
that blinked and took me in, where the cold
had blown open a gold spaciousness. High above
was a lofty dome and dangling from its apogee
what could only be a soul before it's met up
with the body it'll wear to shreds, to rags
around an old shoe on a step.

I stepped at dawn onto this rickety dock.
I'd been trying to read. From the morning's
earliest scrawls on my notebook pages, all the *O*s
loomed up, shimmering with silver inside.

Now I board with the walk-ons.
We move silently. We've heard about
the storm, and we have an idea
how rough the crossing will be.

—Nance Van Winckel

Christopher Howell
Spokane, Washington

The light is going down quickly in Spokane. It's only 5:00 p.m., but it looks like 8:00 or 9:00 anywhere else. We park in a quiet neighborhood next to a gigantic pile of fallen leaves that are carefully raked and just waiting for a kid to jump in.

Christopher Howell greets me at the door and shows me around. We go out into the bricked patio area off the back door of his house. We talk a bit about a new book of his that's coming out. He walks me into the house, through the kitchen, and into his small and homey office.

We sit across a heavy wooden desk to talk, while drinking coffee. Howell is a quiet man with a studied nature. He answers my questions in complete and precise sentences. He works the phrases slowly, and they are elegant and well wrought.

I can tell instantly whether or not my questions are good. A good question elicits a solid nod, an intake of breath, and the beginning of an answer. When I ask a question poorly, he's able to draw an angle from it that's interesting and more in line with what I wanted all along.

He's so good at this that I try a brand new question. It sounds garbled as I say it, but Howell sees an area of light in it. He gives me an answer I'll be able to simply type into the book. No edits. Sentences with punctuation.

~ ~ ~ ~ ~ ~

Do the places of your life end up in your poetry?
I think there's a good deal of subjective literal reference, that is to say, unnamed reference. The quality of light in a particular yard or a particular room. The pattern of interaction with neighbors or people I knew. I think that my experience growing up on a small farm outside Portland probably has influenced a lot of my writing, just in terms of promulgating a kind of emotional context that I think of as utterly sustaining, into which I can return by means of the imagination or by means of the combination of imagination and memory. And I think at times it's not all that easy to tell which is which. I think that our attachment to places keeps on growing, just like our relationships with people keep on growing even after they're gone. By means of memory, imagination, and by means of our own yearning, by means of a sort of comparative sensibility for what we have and what we have experienced or what we yearn for.

74

I've spoken with other writers and listened to them talk about the poetry of place, and it always seemed to me that the notion of place as discussed in public discourse is much more literally geographical than it is in fact for the writer of poetry. It's not a matter, generally, of reportage, or even of description. But of invocation. So what you are invoking is never the literal thing; it is always this amalgam of the things I was talking about, memory and longing and imagination. What one wishes had happened, for instance.

Some poets I've spoken to who teach note that younger writers are less inclined to being poets of place—that is, their place is more virtual than that of an older generation of writers. Do you see any of that in your own writers?

I taught all those years in Kansas, and Kansas is still a place people feel themselves, actually, to exist. As opposed to kind of inhabiting a putative potential geography, which can change at any minute, which is the destruction of distance and, therefore, of distinction. My students there wrote freely or from a particular sense of place.

And when I came here, there's something similar. I teach mostly graduate students and the graduate students, for the most part, are not as susceptible to the technological erosion of their actual being and the actual presence, actual things, and the actual distances between one thing or another. But I think it's a real thing that's happened in our culture, and it's bound to have an effect on our literature; and perhaps that's part of what's already happening in terms of the language poets and so forth, whose work has basically no locus beyond the intellectual. Who basically consider a physical locus passé. Along with narrative of any sort.

In fact, I have felt that poetry, at least the poetry that means the most to me, is an antidote to that placelessness. People who live here in the Pacific Northwest, who were born or grew up here, almost have a sense of grounding. I think it may be something similar to New England, where I also spent many years. But it's surprising how few poems you come across are really about salmon, or mountains, or Douglas fir, or the coastline. It's really assumed. Frankly, it's even assumed in (Robert) Frost. Not even the landscape, but the tradition, the kind of culture that has gone along with New England, is assumed in the poems. I think that's true if you look at William Stafford's writing, who lived here for fifty or sixty years. Although it's interesting that some of his best poems are really about Kansas. I mean he grew up there and came out of that very powerful geographical particularity, which he carried with him.

Wherein the Author Ruminates on RV Life

The cab is great, CD player, weather-band radio. The seats are comfy. They tilt. They've got the big captain's arms. I'm Kirk on the *Enterprise*. We have a handheld GPS unit that tells us where we are and, more importantly, which upcoming exits have a gas station or a Taco Bell. We have a twenty-six-inch TV with DVD and VCR and an automated dish that pivots and twirls until it locks on a giant satellite that floats above the Texas Gulf Coast.

We have the microwave, a nice refrigerator, three burners, and an oven. The bedroom in back has a queen-size bed with room to walk around both sides. Storage is good. The living room has a four-seater dining-room table and a full-length couch. When the sun's up, we have all the windows open, and the views are almost always pretty spectacular, given where we've been traveling.

The shower is located about halfway back and to one side. It's an efficient space. Imagine a phone booth. Then think of something smaller than that. With running water. The toilet is across the hall from the shower and includes a stool, washbasin, and enough storage for two toothbrushes, some soap, some towels, and the medium-size tube of Crest. If your belly wasn't as big as mine, you'd think you were in a phone booth. Or something that would fit inside a phone booth. With a little chair.

By day we drive, stopping absolutely whenever we want, making sandwiches at rest areas or scenic overlooks. Sometimes I take a cigar out and stand there, like today, staring out at the swelling Columbia River at a roadside stop outside Vantage, Washington, as we pushed west on I-90. Sometimes we just sit inside, slurp our soup, make phone calls on one of the cell phones, marvel at the gas receipts, count semis as they pass on the highway.

Mark Halperin
Ellensburg, Washington

Mark Halperin is a delightful guy, who greets me on a chilly but sunny day. He and Dasha, his sweet half-Husky, half-Malamute, are walking through a light dusting of snow as we arrive. We start by going around the house and through the backyard to see one of Mark's writing areas, this one in part of a finished shed. I meet his wife, Bobbie Halperin, a painter. Bobbie spots my wife sitting out in the driveway—paying bills online—and brings her in to see her own studio. The four of us and Dasha stand around a bit and chat like we're all pals.

Our wives disappear with Dasha, and Mark takes me to the warmest room in their long, charming house, his study.

We talk about the standard items from this project but also get around to Mark's love of fishing. He's a serious fisherman, a fly fisherman, who can see the edge of his beloved Yakima River from any of a number of windows on the south side of the house. When fishing doesn't take up his time—and he fishes all summer in lieu of writing—he can reach over and pick up one of his treasured banjos or acoustic guitars. He has a Gibson acoustic, an L series from 1913. He picks it up at one point and fingerpicks a sort of Leadbelly-style country-blues.

He's a great interview. He listens to the questions, recognizes the answer I'm probably looking for, then spins his answer a couple of ways. He says he doesn't mean to be contrary, but it lights him up to do it. He is animated and fun to listen to. We fill one side of a tape, and I pop another in and keep going.

~ ~ ~ ~ ~ ~

How has place affected your poetry?

It's a big question. On the one hand, when I write, I look out the window, and it has an effect. If I lived in the South, I'd have one kind of climate. I remember living in Tucson for one year. The weather didn't change much, whereas here, that changing is part of your sense of time. In the summer I fish, and in the winter I ski, different activities at different times. So maybe in a place with four seasons you're more aware of the passage of time.

In the summer I fish a lot and don't write much. The river is right here *(pointing across the road)*. I've gotten to the point of tying flies, making rods, the whole thing. But I doubt I'd fish the way I do if I lived somewhere else. If you're interested in listening to classical music, there isn't a lot for you here: the university, Seattle, which is a long drive and far from a classical music capital. But fishing? Where I live is a great place to fish.

During the numerous times I lived in St. Petersburg (Russia), I'd go to Shostakovich Concert Hall weekly. Tickets were inexpensive, and the music was great. I think in a city you should do city things. In the country you should do country things. When I moved here, I asked myself, "What should I do? What's here?" I wanted to see if I meshed with any of them.

How does fishing mesh with your work?

Well, I write about it, so it becomes part of my subject matter. Then too, it's a way to divert myself. People who write probably have noise going on in their heads continuously. You follow out thoughts. You track things. It's a pursuit occupation. You don't write things that you know. You write in order to know things, as many people have said. I've come across the idea in so many variations that I'm pretty sure it's true.

I'm a fly fisherman, which is a complicated pursuit. That means it takes you out of yourself; it's another form of being, like speaking Russian, which has also taken me a long time to learn—and I'm not done. When I talk Russian, I'm a different person—or have an opportunity to be a different person. Different assumptions begin to operate. I have to use different approaches because the language is constructed differently. On the water it's like that, too. You can't outthink fish because fish don't think. You have to move into a different mode. It has a physical aspect too, how you hold your mouth when you speak another language, the rhythm to casting, to observing, to picking things out. You have to adapt, which is very exciting. And it's exciting when, in writing, you stumble across things you don't know or didn't know you did. Even at the level of words, even making them work together. Like when you get the right fly and fish start taking it, or when you don't know if you can land a fish because you've got a number twenty fly in its lip.

Here, something about fall starts me off writing. Place has that kind of influence. Whatever window you look from, the view is never the same. The colors change all the time; the trees look different. Imagine what happened when I looked out of the window of my room in Moscow at the sixteenth-century church across the street.

There's a widely held belief that place is reflected in writing, that you have to be tied to place in some way. And I understand that and believe it's true in some respects. But I also reject it. When Jews were persecuted in the Soviet Union, they were often accused of being "rootless cosmopolitans," which became a code term for being Jews. Connections and loyalties were being questioned. Russians have an idea of nationality, which differs from ours and is independent of citizenship. It has to do with "coming from a place" and being a part of its history, religion, et cetera. Everyone, supposedly, has a nationality, and if you're not "us," you're "them." I'm sensitive to that, being Jewish. There's a part of me that says, "Yes, isn't that nice, but everybody writes his or her own poems." What's nationality then?

Or to take it in another direction, when I'm in Russia, I tend to write about here. And when I'm here, I frequently write about Russia. In both cases, you might say, I'm drawn to the exotic. Don't people write as much about the past as the present? When you're calm, don't you rummage about in what you've been through, and when you're at loose ends, don't you write about the present?

Someone recently told me you have to write about blue herons to be a Northwest poet. And I said, "I've got one!" But I didn't really believe he was right. I've lived here for thirty-five years, more than half my life. If I'm not from here, where am I from? It's a consciousness that some people cultivate, and some fall into: being an outsider. Writing poems is being an outsider; so is being a Jew. It can be uncomfortable at times, but the view's great.

Accident

Are you okay? When I answered *yes,* adding
I'd already called it in and was waiting for
the tow-truck, she blessed me from the cab,
then Jesus for preserving me, then got down.
You've no idea when the tow truck will show up;
you might stand in the cold for hours, she said,
moving beside the truck, which, like her,
had been around, rummaging in her sacks
of groceries and pulled a bagel out. *No*
thanks, I said. She insisted. It was easier
to accept than fight with her, and beside,
there was something so natural, so direct,
for all the bless Jesus-es, the bagel, so
soft, topped with burnt onions, garlic chips,
so bereft of any *yiddishkeit* . . . I took it,
like her benediction, with a nod, a Jew,
ankle-deep in snow on a rural road in
eastern Washington, car down the steep
embankment, cradled by cattails. How
had I come to be there, hand around a roll
as much a bagel as I was a Jew, I wondered?
Only a deity who delighted in far-fetched
scenarios could have concocted a delivery
like that. Before I took a bite, rather than
a *motsi,* I peered at my precariously balanced
car, then into the shimmering distance
from whence the wrecker would come.
Hat on, I blessed her and my good fortune.

—*Mark Halperin*

Jana Harris
Sultan, Washington

With cold temperatures threatening the finicky plastic plumbing, we've been without running water in Winnie Cooper for a few days. We've been lugging water back and forth from campground bathrooms in big pots. But this morning the sun shines brightly, we turn the water on, fire up Winnie Cooper, and get back on the road.

As we have traveled outside of the urban areas of Washington State, we've found the towns a little tougher, a little more wild. People are more independent here, especially when compared to the reserved folks we know from our time in the northeast U.S. Hippies and rednecks live happily next to ranchers, methamphetamine entrepreneurs, the ever-present militia folks in their cammo outfits, loggers, and fruit growers.

We wind through some narrow roads outside Sultan, Washington, and up into some pretty ranchland. Mountains crowd the sky, and we drive between orchards and pastures until we get to Jana Harris's farm on a spacious and quiet piece of land with a barn, a long house, and a pond.

Harris lives on a working farm, and before we see the house, we see four beautiful horses in separate paddocks on a clear and sunny chilly late morning. Jana welcomes both of us into the house. She is whipping up some food in the kitchen. She talks about her land and horses while she cooks, and we drink in the smells.

After a feast of food and conversation, we go with Jana outside as she brings the horses in from the fields for some hay and carrots. The horses are gigantic, but Jana hooks them and hauls them in easily, all the time talking to them, catching them up on these new visitors who are suddenly in their barn.

~ ~ ~ ~ ~ ~

How have the places of your life had an impact on the work you do?

I've lived and worked in New Jersey and New York, where there was very high energy. That was great. As far as the West, I've lived and worked in California, Washington, Oregon, and Wyoming. I get a tremendous sense of place. I write a lot about pioneers, primarily women and children, who came some distance on the trails to get here. Lately, I've been writing about the women and children who didn't make it all the way to the Pacific, but who got stranded along or settled by the

81

trail. Between here and, say, Missouri, you can still see the ruts of their wagon wheels. And this is a trail that I have a hard time traveling along in a car with air conditioning. In some places in Wyoming you can still see teepee rings.

When you're writing about these places—Wyoming, Idaho, Oregon, and Washington—does simply going to the place energize you? What is it about the ruts in the road that inspire your work?

Absolutely. I am always stunned by the vast expanse and emptiness of the terrain, the clean clear air, the visible heavens, the silence—especially the silence—the color of the earth, the flora and fauna. It's about the miles covered on foot in hard leather, usually handmade shoes—and hand-knit socks if they had socks. The rocks in the road. The little hills, those ups and downs we don't notice in a car. The wind in your face, the rain in your face. The heat, the cold, the smell of rabbit grass and sage grass. The trying to stay clean. Water—how much to save for the cattle? The minute I'm there, I'm there.

I guess one of my themes is survival. And when I first started doing research on these people, it was because I moved to a farm and I take care of horses. You can read about horse husbandry endlessly and go to vet school, but a lot of it is just intuitive. And a lot of the really good horse people—their knowledge is not written down because they're not particularly literate. It's like the art of anything. How did the frontier people take care of these beasts? Horses were the way they moved from place to place. There were trains, ships, and horses. If you can control transportation, you control everything. But how did they keep these beasts healthy, sound, and alive? They had no antibiotics; they had no painkillers. So that's what I was reading for, their basic seminal knowledge handed down from generation to generation. What I noticed was that they were much better problem solvers than we are. Our solution is simply, "Buy another one." So I was looking for common ground and these little nuggets of things.

I look at those ruts in the road, and I think, "What they have endured!" I first saw the ruts near Baker, Oregon. Then again when I worked at the University of Wyoming. The fact that the ruts of the emigrants' wagon wheels endured for more than a hundred years struck me at the time. I have a photo of them from the Oregon Historical Archives. Somehow, the ruts became symbolic of their endurance. Of their perseverance and ability to push ahead.

Mr. Elija Welch, First Planting

Gray Back Flat

North of Powder River,
north of the Grand Ronde,
antelope trail my only footpath.
Not a tree, not even a rock
for shade, the stone-strewn
ash-colored ground grit-
fine, rocks and soap weed
the same shade, lichens
the only gaiety—that yellowing
green of unripe lemons
scattered across hills rising
up to a coppery sky.
Sun the color of the new
plow blade pressed
down, pushed forward,
breaking in oak handles
to the curve of hands.

Midday meal taken in the stream-
cool of a canyon bottom
while contemplating:
A hundred and sixty acres waiting
since before Moses to be
taught to bear wheat.

Returning, startled two
salt-hungry antelope,
tongues caressing
plow handles.

—*Jana Harris*

83

Sam Hamill
Port Townsend, Washington

We're headed for the first of two ferry rides that will take us from Seattle to Port Townsend, where I'm scheduled to meet with Sam Hamill, a masterful poet, translator, and the editor of the much revered—and poetry-only—Copper Canyon Press.

The ferry rides are spectacular. On the first one, a thirty-minute ride from the mainland to the southern tip of Whidbey Island, the sun rises behind us as we disappear into the frosty subfreezing fog that obscures the island from us. Once on Whidbey we drive into a little town that hugs the small two-lane. The sidewalks are dotted with kids headed to school, all of them bundled up in layers, not a serious winter coat anywhere.

The next ferry takes us off Whidbey Island, through a small strait, right to the attractively arrayed town of Port Townsend. Even from a distance, I can see white houses and buildings scattered over the hills. It's almost enough to make you miss noticing the towering range of the Olympic Mountains behind the town.

Once in Port Townsend we do some banking, check out some antiques, and then my wife drops me at the white clapboard building that serves as Copper Canyon's home.

Sam greets me, and we get down to business quickly. We pass a wall that contains a monumental stack of books published by his esteemed press over the past thirty years. I spot on the spines some of the names of poets I've already seen on the trip. He shows me where he personally hand sets and prints limited-edition broadsides of work from the press on two circa 1900 printing presses. He leads me into his office and settles in. I ask the first question and he answers without hesitation. He's sure of himself. It's a sort of confidence, I think, that comes when a writer knows what he's about and is ready to share it.

~ ~ ~ ~ ~ ~

How do you think place has impacted your work as a poet?

I think one's environment has an enormous effect on how one views the world. In my case I grew up in the deserts and mountains of Utah and Colorado, and then I lived for many years in California; but I migrated north until I came here thirty-one years ago. I cleared my own land here and built my own house by myself. And that has an enormous effect on how one lives. And the fact that I've been solitary and impoverished my whole life has an effect. So all of those things become terribly important. I'm sixty years old; I'm still bucking wood. I like to think of John Haines's lovely phrase, a "place of sense," rather than a sense of place. I've always liked the way he turned that particular phrase on its head.

What about elements of the natural world? This place is just astonishing, having the mountains and the sea on either side. Are there certain elements of the natural world that work on you more than others?
    Well, yes, but I would also point out that there is no unnatural world. There is nothing that is not nature. And when city people come here, they often say, "Oh, it's so wonderful to commune with nature," and I say, "So where do you live?" And they say, "Oh, I live in New York City." And I say, "What part of New York City is on Mars?" So it's really not a matter of being any closer to nature than anywhere else. It's simply a matter of being urban, suburban, rural, and in my case, subrural.

I've always thought of the Pacific Northwest as being one of the most clearly defined regions in the country. The Midwest can mean a number of different things to different writers—nobody, for instance, can exactly agree with which states make up the Midwest. But I never sensed that with this region. You've lived here for more than thirty years; are you a regionalist?
    I don't think of it with exactly that term. But I do think of myself as a westerner. But I don't think that the political, ecological, spiritual, moral questions of the West are profoundly different than they are east of the Mississippi, or for that matter, east of the Hudson. I brought Copper Canyon Press here specifically to become a northwestener. I came here with every intention of living my entire life here. And I still expect to do that. There are ramifications to those decisions, just as there are to decisions to pursue, for instance, a life with New York publishing. But does that affect in any serious way the poets that I publish? I don't think so. Ruth Stone, for example, is a New Englander. Tom McGrath was a midwesterner. Eleanor Wilner is from Philadelphia. Et cetera, et cetera. So the particularities of any body of poetry may be deeply influenced—and probably are deeply influenced—by the environment of the poet.

As an editor, have you noted that the work you see from younger poets is less rooted in a specific place or home?
    Given that the average American family moves every six years, it's not surprising to me that we don't have a body of poetry from younger poets with a deeply rooted sense of "I grew up on the farm in the Midwest." Children now migrate. And they have a migratory sensibility. There are

some advantages to that, and there are some drawbacks. But I think it has more to do with an ever-migrating population than anything having to do with poetry.

I direct the Port Townsend Writer's Conference. Twenty-five years ago I put on a little conference here called "The Power of Animals" with Gary Snyder, Barry Lopez, Paul Shepherd, and a corresponding conference on "Woman and Nature" with Susan Griffith, who had just published her remarkable book of that title. Those things came up over and over again, really in a sort of politically environmentalist sense. But one finds the poetry of place in Bill Stafford. I published a little book of his that was just poems written around the Northwest. Now Snyder, as I do, lives in a particular way, and he chose a particular path that has to do with becoming deeply rooted in a place. I took a similar route. But place means differently to each of us in different ways.

The Day I Did Winnie Cooper Wrong

The crunch was loud and thick. I looked at my wife and asked her if she had any ideas. I thought maybe a small deck chair we hadn't stowed properly. Maybe fifty tin cans.

We had just finished packing Winnie Cooper full after a lovely week on the Oregon coast. We had driven down from Washington and rented this house as a treat to ourselves for my wife's birthday. But now the schedule called to us, and the weather had started to turn. The rain, which had been spotty all morning, had now started to come down steadily. A light wind was coming off the ocean. But the view was clear. We had finished cleaning the house, had put the keys back in the lockbox, and we were headed out of the driveway when I heard the crunch.

When I got out, I saw the problem. I had driven the motor home into the roof overhang. A long board under the gutter had been torn off, about nine inches of it lying on the driveway.

The house didn't look too bad. I was grateful I didn't tear the metal gutters down. It would be an easy repair. A shitty break, but not the end of the world.

On the other hand, as I struggled to pull myself up Winnie's ladder, I kept thinking: "Please, God, I know I'm a sinner, a dirty-dog sinner. I know all about the gigantic catalog of mistakes I've made, the miserable gifts I bring to this sunny world. But this time—this one time—show me a little blinding mercy. Please don't let there be a tear in the fiberglass."

And, of course, there was. I could see through a foot-long gash right down inside the coach—I'm not making this up—to the Styrofoam insulation of the drop ceiling. Now the rain was coming down in sheets. The wind picked up and howled in my ears. I stood there on the ladder, twelve terrifying feet above earth, and wished with all of my strength for a lightning bolt.

My wife and I left a contrite note for the house owner and got rolling. The storm was swamping the entire coast for a hundred miles north and south. We just started driving on U.S. 101. My wife opened up the big RV guide, looking for a place in the area where we might find cover. She burned up the cell phone while I drove through the deluge. We finally located a place ninety miles north. It was Sunday afternoon. In this part of the state—sleepy little oceanside towns—most businesses are closed on Sundays. The streets roll up. The gas stations close at 6:00 p.m. The voice on the phone told us to come his way. Their service bays were closed till the next morning; but they had a big awning, and I could park there if I wanted.

The rain kept up, but now the wind was behind us. My wife kept checking the ceiling in the back, and the water kept coming in. She hadn't yet said a cross word. She knows me. She knew that I was beating myself up in exquisite ways, interesting ways, varied ways, ways that could not compare.

By the time it was dark, we had pulled Winnie out of the storm. We parked her and emptied out boxes of everything that was soaked. We put our clothes in garbage bags and then stood in the dark waiting for a cabdriver to come and deliver us to the nearest Holiday Inn. Once there, we arranged for another man to bring us some large pizzas. And then we slept.

Barbara Drake
Yamhill, Oregon

Barbara Drake lives on a vineyard amidst the rolling foothills of far western Oregon, surrounded by fields covered with hazelnut and walnut trees. Her land is crowded with sheep, chickens, one big rooster, and Guy, a large and happy border collie.

She and I walk through the farmhouse, surrounded by the smell of scones and hot coffee. She shows me the floors and ceilings that her husband Bill did himself. "They're soft wood," Barbara tells me. "The dog marks them up."

We sit in her sunroom as the Saturday morning light floods in.

We talk about her recent chapbook, Small Favors, *a gorgeous limited-edition offering full of earthy poetry, all of it rooted in place and the natural world. Barbara tells me about an old guy who showed up at the farm one day, a guy who had lived on this land almost eighty years ago. He remembered it as the place where he was happiest. They struck up some correspondence, and he sent her a photo of the place from the '20s that showed some of the same trees that are there today. Barbara likes living here a lot, and much of the reason for that is because she knows the history, feels the history of the place. She knows that the spirit of the place is something that existed before her, and she hopes it continues long after.*

~ ~ ~ ~ ~ ~

How did you end up in Oregon?

I grew up in Oregon. Though I was born in Kansas, we left when I was young. And I went to college out here, then lived in Michigan for sixteen years, then moved back. Even when I was in the Midwest, I often wrote about the West. And I drove out here in the summers. I bought a piece of land on the southern Oregon coast, so there'd be a place for the family. I just feel like I belong out here. Maybe it's an imprinting from my parents, who came from Kansas when they were very young. When my father met my mother, he promised her that when they married he'd take her to Oregon to live. So it's part of the family mythology that wherever you go, you return to the beautiful West.

In the time I've been traveling out here, talking to poets, I get the very real sense that the West is this really tangible thing, a place, an attitude, a way of living.

I think it's very physical. I love the landscape. Everywhere I look there are sights that please my eye. It's a physical, visual kind of thing, the way the land rolls, the trees, the mountains on the horizon. I feel like I'm at home so I feel comfortable. I also know about the past, the history of the place, so I have a connection in time to the area, which feels very familiar. I like being someplace where I know what it was like in 1945, 1953, 1962, and so on. I can write out of that with confidence about the beauty, and the history, and the people. It's as if being here, or looking at the world from the point of view of a westerner, even when I'm not actually here, I'm rooted in some way that puts me in touch with other dimensions of time and space as they are expressed or channeled through the touch point of place. I'm not being mystical. I just mean that my sense of being in the world and in the flow of history—and my understanding of that world and that history—is stronger because I know where home is in a very real way.

Are there particular elements of the natural world that show up more frequently in your poetry because you live where you do?

Landscape, events that happen here, the animals, and the weather of the place all get into my poetry, so I guess the answer is yes. I published a book of personal essays that have to do with the first ten years on this farm. I grew up on the Oregon coast, so I always felt a great attachment for the coast or the beach, and that's where I go to get away. But later on I also discovered the eastern side of the Cascades, and I've written some poems about that.

The variety in the state is just wonderful. I include landscape, birds, plants, local history, and so on, in my poetry. Because the landscape of the West is so rich and varied, I feel it's always opening up, not repetitious. The process of writing requires living with awareness in this world. Being mindful. Both familiarity and change can make that happen. But wherever I go, western Oregon is the place I come back to.

How did the move from a city to a rural farm and vineyard change your work?

In Portland we lived in a great house in a busy and interesting city neighborhood, and I loved that. I used to think that I could never live anywhere but Portland, but now that I'm out here I feel that the space and natural beauty around are more important, and if we want to go into the city, it's only an hour's drive. I think I used to write more about popular-culture subjects and urban subjects, about people and encounters in the city; and now I draw from the natural landscape. It's what I engage with all the time. It's there as a subject, and it's there as a sort of a quietness. I feel that there's peacefulness here. In my new chapbook of poems, there are poems about the physical place, the animals, and so on. But there are other ones that are about the spirits of the place. That's sort of hard to explain without sounding too metaphysical. But I definitely feel the current of all the lives and so on that have come through this place.

Of course, when I write out of the western viewpoint, I hope people will understand that I'm not just writing about my own little corner of the world. I'm trying to express the big, difficult stuff through a particular familiar place.

I'm always grateful to people who have done something good, who have left something beautiful or useful in the world. It can be something as common as old fruit trees. What if someone hadn't taken the trouble to plant those trees? People need to leave something good behind, rather than screwing up the world. I worry about that. I have three children of my own and five stepchildren, and together Bill and I have ten young grandchildren. I want the world to be good for them. I don't want anyone's children of the future to say, "If only our ancestors had quit making war, quit polluting, hadn't been so short-sighted." I want them to say, "Weren't they smart to have a left a good world for us."

Writing is part of that, too. You write your poems and enter into the ongoing dialogue, maybe leave something to speak for the place when you're gone.

from The Man from the Past Visits the Present

The man who comes up the road
is tall and thin and elderly, white-haired
with glasses, doesn't look anything like
the boy he says he was when he lived here
on our farm, eighty years ago.

Wanting to draw the missing figures
in my picture of this landscape,
I ask him about the house, the well, the trees.
He says he has never loved
any other place so well as this one.

He remembers Sunday picnics,
the community of Bohemian farmers
who came together on Sundays
to play their mandolins, eat from picnic baskets.
He remembers picking almonds from trees—
is it possible these spindly old trees
bringing forth eight or ten nuts each year
are those? In photos he shows me, I see
the familiar contour of our mountain,
much older than almond trees or any
growing thing on the place. And there
are the Bohemians, the family and friends,
men in straw hats and suits sitting on the hill
where the vineyard is now, once an orchard
of peaches, plums. Their musical
instruments are cocked across their laps.
The women wear dresses down to their ankles.

We have a lot in common, this man and I,
knowing how hard the ground is here, how dry
and ungiving except for Oregon white oaks,
the savannah grasses, the wild rose, poison oak
snowberries.

—Barbara Drake

93

Floyd Skloot
Amity, Oregon

Although the motor home is still being repaired, the trip must continue. I have one more poet to see in Oregon, the gifted and inspiring Floyd Skloot. Floyd and his wife live in an unexpected and round home on twenty acres, due east of Amity, a tiny burg with one gas station and one feed store.

I twist and turn up a hilly road through farm and ranchland (and vineyards), and turn down Skloot's driveway. Heavy stands of trees crowd in, providing a lovely green canopy as I travel the quarter mile to the house. I park and then stand and stare into a long, beautiful valley that sweeps away from me. I spot Floyd through one of the large windows, and I head inside.

We talk on the first floor of the house in a dark, small office with a window that opens into a heavily wooded area. Often during the conversation Floyd points outside at the view. He's not pointing to a scene in particular; he's simply referencing what is apparent: this place is beautiful. It's a peaceful place, dead quiet, and richly arrayed by nature.

In 1988, Skloot entered a terrifying and confusing new world after a virus caused permanent brain damage. He reclaimed the ability to read, speak, and write, and now lives with the damage, noting things on slips of paper that he knows his damaged brain might lose the next day. (The remarkable story of his illness is in the award-winning memoir, In the Shadow of Memory.*)*

During my visit, Skloot is charming, funny, insightful, and he energetically talks about his work. His illness limits the hours he can work effectively. So the work comes out more slowly. But it matches the pace of the life here. He motions out the window again.

~ ~ ~ ~ ~ ~

What role has place played in your poetry?

I think that place is at the heart of my project as a writer. Especially since I moved here. For me it's become a way of accommodating myself to the world that I'm in and of having a relationship with the world. This place permeates all of my work. And it's also forced me to look back on where I came from, a place on the absolute opposite end of this spectrum, not only the East Coast as opposed to the West, but one

94

of the densest, most urban places you can come from—Brooklyn, New York. I think there were more people in the apartment building where I grew up than there are in this town.

Growing up in Brooklyn, we didn't pay attention to birds, to flowers, to trees. A bird was a bird. A tree was a tree. I've read that in Yiddish all birds are called the same thing. There's no reason to specify which kind of bird. I grew up in that mindset. This has forced me to look very closely at the distinctions between these things that I had never paid attention to. To understand different species and different forms of life.

More perhaps in my prose, in my collection of essays about living with brain damage, I have explored the experience of deciding to live in the country and abandon the city. I thought I needed the city as a lifeline. I thought I needed to be near the doctor, near the bookstore, near the theater. Within walking distance of everything. I thought I had to be in the middle of the city where my friends could see me, where I'd be in the middle of life. And in fact, what I needed to manage my illness was to get away from all of that, where there was nothing to do, where there was nothing to distract. I wasn't fast paced and hectic and filled with things to do. So my prose particularly explores that experience of place, coming to recognize the potential of place as a healing entity.

Living where I do and the way I do, I have time. My health is such that my writing time is very limited. But in this place I can write when it feels right. There is no sense of time flying by. There is no hectic pace of commitments. There is little to impinge upon the things I need to do to stay in balance and maintain my health. I've had to learn how to adjust, take my time with my work, slow down with my work. Not rush to finish. Not rush to publish. Because I can't anymore; I'm not well enough. And trying to work that way only chokes off the creative work rather than enhancing it. So I've found it very compatible to be a writer in this place.

I live disconnected from the academic publishing world and academic life. At first I worried what that would do to my "career." As it turns out, it's been a blessing. I don't have to deal with those sorts of issues. I don't have to write under pressure. My work has finally reached a large audience with my memoir, despite the disadvantages of living far away from the center of activity. Which goes to show that it will find its way there. That you don't have to be in New York. It isn't as much about connections as I thought. It's about getting the work done.

A lot of work details events and places from your childhood in Brooklyn. You wrote these poems later, obviously. How did those places from your past turn into poems?

I think my experience growing up there was very intense and vivid, given the dynamics my family had, so the details always remained in place. The city and the family dynamics became good metaphors for me. To talk about the hardness and closedness and pressure that my parents created, being so hostile to each other. The sort of fury they created in the confined setting of an apartment building seemed to me to be an apt metaphor for the confined family and hostility that developed there, the explosions of violence that developed there that I wrote about in *Music Appreciation*. We moved from Brooklyn when I was ten, to Long Beach, a little barrier island off the south shore of Long Island. It was such a radical change of setting. I found that very dramatic. It became natural to write about that place, too, because the island was so different and so vivid. The storms and hurricanes that came with living on a barrier island became rich metaphors again. You can transplant the family, and maybe the setting is different—being closed into a little apartment or walking along the beach in the eye of the hurricane. They were all apt metaphors for what it was like to grow up in that family. So I was given, in a sense, places rich with meaning for the kind of experience I had.

Because of your medical problems and the permanent damage to your brain, do you ever think of your illness as a place, and with perspective do you think you can write about it as if it were a tangible, physical place?

It's a very chaotic place because of the damage to my brain caused by this virus. My experience is quite fragmented. My system of memory is fragmented. Abstract reasoning as well. To be inside my sick self is to be in a place which refuses to cohere and take shape. I find that to be both a place of great richness and also very scary. It helps to find organizational metaphors in the place where I live. To me, the match with the city was too close. There was no contrast between my chaotic, fragmented inner experience and the outer urban experience. There was nothing to help me get a form until I came to the country.

A Warming Trend

After three days of June rain
we kneel at our window
to watch hoary bats swoop
among the hemlock and fir.

In half-moon light, the right
music would be a fugue
for wind and erratic strings.

But all we hear is dripping eaves
and a gentle tap of moths
against the windowpanes.

We doused the lights,
but as long as our windows
hold the false moon
moths will flock to it.

Our shoulders barely touch
as a bat flies west to east.
Through my skin and bones
I can feel you breathe.

—Floyd Skloot

Suddenly in California

After Winnie Cooper returned to us, we made a hard push south through Oregon into California. We drove the Sacramento Valley, a long flat stretch full of pastureland and a variety of blank and similar midsize cities and towns. I'm sure that Merced and Fresno are more different than alike, but it would have to be proven to me. Highway 99 is hard like a washboard, more narrow than most interstates, and truckers raced alongside us, shaking our windows as they blurred by. Plates and glasses slammed in their cupboards. The TV rocked back and forth. The shower door slammed open and shut again and again.

After 100 miles of this, we were frazzled. At Fresno, we entered the San Joaquin Valley, and at a gas stop we pulled out the map and looked for the tiny gray roads that we hoped would take us off the interstate. We picked up Highway 180 to the east, up and toward the distant Sierra Nevada Mountains.

We started at 240 feet above sea level, but we went higher in a hurry. On the right were thousands of orange trees. They swept away from us into the rapidly deepening King's Canyon. On our left was scrub, some trees, rocky terrain. We passed a 1,000-foot marker, quickly followed by 2,000, 3,000, 4,000. Winnie was straining, and every mile or so we'd pull over into a scenic turnout to let cars go past. At 5,000 feet I could smell the engine running hot, so we pulled over for lunch.

It was absolutely dead quiet. Occasionally a car would go by. But we stared out into the canyon, the gigantic 11,000-foot peaks of the Sierra Nevada ahead of us. We had sandwiches, and we looked out the window and soaked in the quiet of the canyon. The sun was dropping below the foothills. Some big cows ambled along a fence line down in the canyon, maybe two thousand feet below us. It was clear that this was one of the things we'd been looking for, another miraculous view and another answer to the question we had asked before the trip started. Why are we going?

Afterwards, Winnie Cooper climbed the last five hundred feet or so and then started back down on the opposite wall of the canyon on Highway 245. When we rejoined 99, we were refreshed. We found a nice campground, backed the RV into the spot, and stared out at forty more motor homes just like it. We were in a town whose name I've already forgotten. That night I stared up at the ceiling and waited to fall asleep, but all I was thinking about was the canyon, that place, the trees, the sound of wind rushing somewhere.

Ralph Angel
South Pasadena, California

After weeks in tranquil mountains and forests, the arrival in Los Angeles is a little jarring. The whole "freeway nation" thing is not so hard to get used to. It's eleven lanes going every direction. Big deal. What's interesting about the ever-present freeways is the absolute necessity of knowing what they're called (number and name) when getting any kind of directions. Los Angelenos seem to delight in sending you on a pet path. It's impossible to get directions that don't involve you "hopping" on the 10 or the 5. Even to go to get milk, locals want to get you up on the Pomona Highway. They spend half their days looking at brake lights, and it brings them a bit of comfort to know that you will be stranded likewise.

This place is sold in so many ways that it's always been hard for me to see it as anything other than one of its many simulacrums from TV. I'm thinking "Chips," but maybe you're thinking "Melrose Place."

I'm always alarmed at how smoggy it is, how the haze greets you everywhere. There's a gauzy texture to it all. Most of what exists for tourists is hopeless, tacky; and even when I was a young man, I found it all depressing. Of course, it's also a place of great opportunity, a city of dreams for everyone from Mexican immigrants to runaways to actors, waiters, and guitar players. Some days the sun shines through the haze. You can get on an open-deck bus and ride right by Sly Stallone's house.

Like other tourist destinations, it's sometimes difficult to remember that it's a real place, too. And for someone who loves driving, it's a dream and a nightmare all at the same time. All those freeways, but all those cars.

No matter where you stand in L.A. or Orange County, you can see an on-ramp looming in the distance. And we hit and miss a lot of them today going across the city from Orange to South Pasadena to see Ralph Angel.

Ralph's got a two-story blue house from the '50s. He leads me down a slanted walkway behind his house that leads to a twenty-by-twenty-five office. One wall contains a large bookshelf. He's got two large desks, one with a computer, one with pencils and legal pads. During our conversation Ralph talks about the "trance," a period when he feels he is simply channeling information. "We're making our little things—poems, stories, art," Ralph says. "If you asked me my name, I wouldn't have an answer."

~ ~ ~ ~ ~ ~

What kind of role have the places of your life played in your poetry?

Let me use the word landscape instead of places, to begin with, because I think of all our places as the landscape of our lives, and that's huge. Especially as one gets older, and especially in our culture, with all our travel and moving around.

And yet I realize that I mostly carry this stuff inside, and everything's free game for me. I mean any given poem is always centered in a place, and it might be this city or that city. But it's really a composite of sounds and details and colors and light and any quality of any place I've ever been to or lived in that happened to be present at the time I was making the poem.

So place is huge for me. It is, in some ways, the intersection between what I'm making and anyone who comes in contact with it.

When you write about place, are you writing about a single landscape, one from your past, or are you writing about this place where you live now?

I think both are true. There's the place and landscape and the centering of the imagination in all of us, our internal reality. And there's also our physically moving through the material world. For me, time and location, place, landscape, characters, personas, they're all composites. In part, it's because it is my job not to censor myself, not to censor my own complex, internal reality. It's my job to hear essential language. I'm not interested in a more journalistic or information-based art, where the city I'm in, or my speaker's in, be an actual city. Because it is an actual city in my experience—it just happens to be made up of several cities.

So I am willing to move from the past to the present to the imagined future, from Tangiers to Billings to D.C. at any moment. And with weather and climate, atmosphere, light, all of it. There are parts of my reality that never go away. There are parts of my memory that never go away, and they are as real to me as the two of us sitting here right now. And I don't even know all the time if they make sense to me. It's immaterial to me.

What sort of impact does the natural world have on you?

It's not an easy question for me, because I am a helplessly urban person. But I did grow up in the Northwest, which helps, I suppose. And

I mention the Northwest, because even though I grew up in the center of inner-city Seattle, I was affected by the weather there. And I grew up in a house that overlooked Lake Washington and had a lovely view of Mt. Rainier. The vistas, the distance one could see at any given time, affected me and affects the way I look at the world today, whether I'm in a city or out in the natural world.

But to be perfectly frank, I'm afraid of the natural world, in the way that I'm afraid of death. I don't have a healthy relationship with death. I think it's fucked up and unfair and wrong, and it's stolen the best people in my life. So I have a great deal of respect for the natural world.

When I started making poems in my middle twenties, I remember reading an interview with Gary Snyder in which he said you have to be able to go outside and name every tree and every shrub and every mushroom. And that made sense to me. I've learned lessons from the natural world, and at the same time it's just a mystery.

How does an urban existence like yours affect your poetry?

I've always lived in cities, and I adore them. I feel most comfortable in them. One thing urban reality affords me is anonymity. I'm in awe of—and in my weaker moments, I envy—more regional artists and poets and writers who identify not only personally but through their work with a particular place or part of the world. In the abstract, it sounds luxurious and comforting. But I actually function best in anonymity. I can get quiet because I'm completely unknown in many respects. And in a tough town like L.A., nobody wants to know me anyhow. I can go to work, and I can be with family and friends in that kind of public, social way. I can go off and give readings around the country. But when I come back here, I can be quiet and solitary and get in touch with my soul.

Even being out there in uncultivated nature doesn't afford me that. Out there in the natural world I feel like I'm being observed by my impending doom. But here, gunshots mean nothing to me. I also like the fact that it's a twenty-four-hour-a-day reality, and if I've been in my trance and I want a martini at three thirty in the morning, I can have one delivered.

The city also sustains me with its diversity. I hear a number of different languages being spoken every day. And I encounter mannerisms that are foreign to me; and, even though I'm familiar with them, they remain foreign and, therefore, interesting. I love the fact that it's not about me. I'm just part of some bigger continuum, and that's the sense I feel when I'm in the city, especially in Los Angeles, which is such an international city. In my neighborhood here, there are seven, eight, ten ethnicities, and we all get along. It has shaped my orientation to language as well.

Do you feel an obligation of any kind to represent your places in your work?

I don't think I have a choice. I'm a westerner. But I grew up in a tight ethnic community, among people who were very happy to be in this country, and I was the first person in my family to go to college. I am who I am. I happen to prefer big cities. I happen to travel abroad a lot. I'm connected to my family history, and I'm connected to the West. And I don't think it ever really occurred to me to actively or consciously represent a place. I believe so strongly that the language that I hear and orchestrate is trying to do something that is both very simple and humble, and mostly impossible, and that is to enact the fact of my reality. And, in that way, making poems is an act of faith. And the poems just might intersect another person's reality or spin that person into his or her own internal reality. And, therefore, that person will know what I'm talking about and experience again what it is to be alive.

Carol Muske-Dukes
Los Angeles, California

A short distance from Rodeo Drive, we negotiate the gorgeous neighborhoods of Hancock Park on our way to see Carol Muske-Dukes. This neighborhood, filled with English Tudor mansions and built on wide avenues, is a quiet respite from our travels on the crowded and manic streets of Los Angeles.

Muske-Dukes lives in a stately home in this neighborhood just a little east of Hollywood. At the front door I hear barking, and I'm welcomed by Carol and her dogs, one who's just had an operation on his leg. While two of the dogs sniff me and then go back to their worlds, the injured pup joins us as we take our places in a beautiful high-ceilinged living room that is full with large sofas, paintings, a piano, gorgeous draped lamps, and a towering Christmas tree.

We talk a little about L.A. I'm intrigued by the folks who live here. Nobody thinks of it as a city. It's too sprawling for that. Carol tells me that it's really just a bunch of compact and busy towns built on desert and mountains, bounded by the sea on one side. There is a plant, native to South Africa, that grows all over L.A. called an "ice plant." "People used to say that the L.A. flower should be the ice plant—which is that stuff that grows near the freeways—because it's ubiquitous and about two inches deep."

But she loves it here and tells me that it's a good town for a writer, easy to isolate oneself from the fray. "You have to drive at least twenty minutes to get anywhere, so you're already in this enforced isolation of the car. So if you don't want to go somewhere, you can say it's too far to drive."

~ ~ ~ ~ ~ ~

Has place been important to you as a poet?

I'm not a big believer in place defining an aesthetic. The place where one comes from, and where one lives, and where one travels are all imaginary landscapes, especially for poets. I think we can be anywhere, and the imagination is portable. I was born in St. Paul, Minnesota, and I think that Minnesota has stayed with me. But again it's my own sense of Minnesota, not the state or the place. My mother came from that last generation of Americans who learned poems and speeches by heart. She was from North Dakota. She was from a family—my father, too—that had immigrated maybe one generation before. He was Norwegian, and she was Czechoslovakian. They spoke those languages on the farm. For them, growing up on the prairie, poetry was very important. Reciting the words that she learned in high school "elocution" class managed to keep my mother going when her mother died, when my mother was just sixteen. That sense of the Dakotas, Minnesota, and the prairie—even though I grew up in the city—has influenced my sense of space in poetry.

So my mother's imagination, her sense of poetry, her sense of place, the prairie, and thinking of snow as a landscape and that iron blue cold as a landscape is much more a part of how I approach poetry than I realized. Though I never really articulated it before. It's very strange to do so.

Is it Minnesota, then, that is your default landscape, the one place that has remained with you?

That's why I'm having trouble articulating that. I don't know how exactly. I've written poems about Minnesota; I've written poems about growing up in Minnesota, but I don't feel tied in terms of subject in any way to where I grew up.

But that's also true of my experience elsewhere. I learned to be a writer in New York. So New York is a part of that landscape. California certainly is now. Hollywood, even, since my late husband *(the actor David Dukes)* was so involved in that world.

I feel there's sort of a strange, shifting horizon that is the imagination itself. Keats's horizon. "The Vale of Soul-Making." You internalize that sense of place growing up, the space. But then that space, that imaginary geography alters as you travel, as you relocate, and as you are made different.

What about Los Angeles? Does this place have a role in your work?

There's this sort of unwritten sense of Los Angeles, this weird, centerless city, unlike New York or almost anywhere else. L.A. is a one-industry town, so everyone thinks of film. But then you have to think of what is Los Angeles apart from film, apart from Hollywood, and that's very hard to define. Because it is sprawling, and it really doesn't have a center. It isn't really a city, finally. Downtown is urban-like, but it's not like New York.

Steve Wasserman, editor of the *L.A. Times Book Review,* said that the streets in Los Angeles are like huge boulevards, made for giants. You know, there's something Franco-esque about it—though I don't mean it's a fascist place *(laughs).* Here, there's a sense of being giant, enormous. Maybe it's the Hollywood myth. The huge boulevards, the palm trees lining them, the huge sky, the white sky. It does have that alienating feel to it.

Do you think poets have any obligation to write about the places they live and work?

No, oh no. Not at all. I think obligation is a scary word connected to writing in any way. I think we're all trying to discover where we are in our writing. We're all trying to place ourselves, and we're all lost. And I'm not talking about place in the first sense you asked about. I'm talking about locating oneself in a landscape of the imagination. We're lost, and we're glad to be lost.

Twin Cities

I come from Twin Cities, where
the river between, surging, stands.

I believed once that what I called desire
flowed in that confluence between twins,

capitol and columned future. I come from
twin cities, Dark and Light. But the river was

dammed, managed for miles above the locks:
even at the source where the god's mouth opened

and what we call belief thundered down in
every synonym. Two mirrored cities:

their symmetry invented as my own present,
twinned to a past to which it is now forever

subordinate. Twinned to a future stunned
in its white eclipse. They killed the white

foxes, brought their pelts to market in the one
named for the Saint pierced by lightning.

The richer Sister prospered on the threshed tons
near the shared slaughterhouse. If the snow grew

steeped in blood, they raised a Court. But no one out-
thinks the two-in-one. The river was dammed, the moon

afloat, an animal face, in the crossed ambivalent tales
of my people and those of the suffering ancients.

Our gold domes on earth imitating the gold clouds
of the Chippewa, their vision-figures who doubled and

107

doubled but remained apart. Like this single mind,
forever unable to refuse its over-statement: blood on snow,

the gnawed bars of the trap, crack after crack in the
courthouse floor. And one irrefutable truth after another—

obliterated by the irrefutable dual: City and City and
river and river of this, my Ever-Dividing Reflection.

—Carol Muske-Dukes

David St. John
Venice, California

In a small sedan on David St. John's block in Venice, two lovers are actually smooching in the front seat. They're going at it like they're in an Adrian Lyne movie. There's no room to park, so I pull Winnie Cooper right up alongside them and get out. I'm sure they must sense we're right outside their window, but they don't even look up. I think about blowing the horn. My wife takes the wheel with the job of making sure we don't get towed. "U-turns," I say. "Just keep making u-turns."

St. John lives in a friendly and warm little house with a great porch. It's late in the day, so when we go inside, the living room is muted and dark. We sit at a thick wood table, and he gets us cups of tea. He tells me about his daughter who's on her way home from dance class. There's a recital coming up, and he seems as excited about it as she might be.

David knows nearly all the poets I've seen and so asks after them, their health, their happiness. It's a comfortable place to spend part of the evening.

~ ~ ~ ~ ~ ~

Have the places of your life had an impact on the poetry you write?

The place I was born, Fresno, in the San Joaquin Valley, clearly had a huge impact in those early, formative years. I'm one of a group of poets—Larry Levis, Roberta Spear, and Frank Bidart, to name only a few—who were all born in the San Joaquin Valley. I think that, in terms of "spirit of place," which we look to writers to embody, both Levis and Spear captured something about the Valley that's quite remarkable.

It's also important to remember the influence during those years of a poet like Gary Snyder and the early poems of Rip Rap. He had a tremendous influence on those of us just starting out. As much as the physical landscape in which I was growing up, the poets I encountered through reading gave me a way to see my own landscape through the ways they saw—and wrote of—their landscapes. I think this is an important thing we all learn, regardless of how different the landscapes are where we grow up. If we're writers, what we have to learn has to do with techniques and stylistic gestures that allow us to grant the natural world its own integrity.

You're pretty much a lifetime Californian. What other areas here have you mined?

Well, don't forget that I lived for almost twenty years in the Midwest and in Baltimore also. Still, quite obviously, from the very beginning in my work, the California coast was an extraordinarily powerful image and metaphor, especially the area from Big Sur to Mendocino. That long California coast became one of the twin compass points of the book, *The Shore.* The other was the Maryland shore. At that point I was living in Baltimore, so the sense of memory and retrieval and recollection of that other coast—the California coast—became a kind of necessary and living mirror for me.

Then I ended up—a kid from the San Joaquin Valley—having a kind of infatuation with European landscapes and the sensibilities they allowed. When I began to travel and live some in Europe, I really began to feel that Rome was a second home. Wherever my first home happened to be, Rome would always be a second home. Of course, I'm only one of about seven million people who feel that way.

One of the things I hope my work shows is that place in writing often exists at that intersection between the reality of place and one's imagination about that place, what one believes, hopes, or imagines about the various possibilities of oneself in that place, even if only as they can be held in memory.

When you're incorporating place, are you using place and/or natural world elements as context or foundation, or is it something even more subtle?

For me, it's often thinking of a place as it has shifted to the interior, by which I suppose I mean my own interior. Let me just say that a huge influence on me was Roethke's great poem, "Journey to the Interior." I'm seen to represent myself as having these French Symbolist sensibilities, but the truth is that poets like Jeffers and Roethke have always been profoundly influential to me. I just have found that place asserts itself according to the demands of the poem. So in *The Red Leaves of Night* or in the book *Prism,* place exists as a sequence of backdrops for some psychological urgency or some vignette or drama.

My new book, a book-length poem called *The Face,* has both unreal and specific locations. Sets or settings, I should call them, because it's very much a book that's configured like a movie. The poem is located in Southern California, where I live, which is both a real place and an unreal place, a place that is the product of many imaginations infusing the physical landscape with those material illusions we call movies. The conceit is that the speaker's life is the subject of a movie during the course of the book. There are other "locations" besides Southern California, of course. For example, there's a section that takes place in

Gainesville, Florida, and is meant to be quite literally there while I'm also thinking about a place in Hollywood, near to where my daughter was born. And then the next section of the book shifts to another "real" place—San Francisco—in order to twist a few strands of illusion, delusion, and "reality" together.

So the places give a backdrop, but why is using Gainesville or San Francisco important in the larger function of the poems?
    I think it helps to be placed in the world. As readers, we're always mapping where we are, both spiritually and psychologically. Even if it's an illusion, the knowledge of a fixed physical place gives us an experience of constancy, or even steadfastness. I think that one of the things that's disconcerting—and people who travel a great deal know this—is that if you do travel a lot, you have to bring your own sense of home with you. I think it's what we do psychologically all the time. We take a reckoning. Sailors used a sextant and the stars, and we're all trying to reckon where we are in our passage by many means, including poetry.
    Physical place, real places, real settings, real locations serve as a reminder that we won't fly off the face of the earth at any moment. And I think that's always our fear from the time when we are kids. It's why a sense of homecoming can be so urgent to someone, because it's a reminder of that first stability. We live in an increasingly fragmented and unstable world, so any way to fix ourselves on the map of our pasts and our world and our personal histories seems to me quite an extraordinary gift. I think that writers use that implicit consolation of place, which seems to me profound and constant, as a way to reassure the reader that they will be taken care of. Of course, once you make that reader secure, then you can pull that carpet of earth right out from under them. That's the exciting part.

Do you think poets have any obligation to write about—to capture— something of their place?
    I think the sense of duty connected to landscape is connected to a sense of duty about preserving memory, and it may be that places exist in order that memory itself has a home.

Dijon

The TGV sliced through the pulsing mustard fields

On its way from Paris to Nice
                Where he would meet her for coffee
At last after the months of calls & letters

& they'd walk along the promenade des Anglais

While she explained again all of those things
He could understand really no better walking alongside her

Than he could from his apartment off the *Rue de Bac*
That is all of those reasons he no longer stood

Within the frame of her future

No longer remained the body she preferred to all other bodies

& now the sun seemed to him to scour the sand & nakedness
Of the beaches there below them

With a blade as dull & yellow as his own final page of fear
                                 —*David St. John*

Sharon Bryan
San Diego, California

*We take a spectacular sunny drive between Los Angeles and San Diego.
We hug the coast the whole way, often stopping to gape at the ocean. At
one scenic viewpoint we rest on a faded white fence and watch gulls race
into the churning water for fish.*

*We get into San Diego, and my wife wheels us around; I use the
map. We find the spot, and I go up some stairs to Sharon Bryan's bright
apartment. It is at semester end, and a stack of graded essays rests on a
barstool, and a higher stack—waiting for grades—waits nearby.*

*While we're chatting, her cat (the beautifully hirsute and husky
Spencer) does an amazing trick. Spencer rises back on his haunches,
stretches his front paws up toward the ceiling. It's a sort of vertical
and supplicant offering to the God of cats. He pedals his front paws a
couple of times and then settles back down. After Spencer is done, he
turns around, gives me a once over and settles back into a more normal
horizontal pose on the carpet.*

*Sharon is a professional nomadic poet, able to move and stretch
and then settle again. She's been a visiting writer in a wide range
of disparate places—Ohio, Texas, Tennessee, New Hampshire, and
Washington. Born in Utah, educated in the Northeast, and a lover of the
Pacific Northwest—she calls Port Townsend, Washington, home—she's
a restless soul.*

*She has a love for anthropology and a keen desire to name and
understand our role in the bigger picture, the planet, the universe. That
love brings to her poetry equal parts science and spirituality.*

~ ~ ~ ~ ~ ~

What sort of role has place played in your own poetry?

I grew up as a minority—a little Methodist kid in Salt Lake City. I felt
as if I'd been kidnapped as a baby and dropped in this totally unlikely
place. I longed for the kind of intellectual life I associated with the East
Coast. And when I moved to Ithaca, New York, for graduate school, I was
thrilled. "Ah, people like me," I thought. It was wonderful.

But I'll always prefer the western landscape. I can't get the two
parts of myself together. When I was finishing my first book, *Salt Air,*
I saw that something was missing, and I was horrified when I realized
that I'd have to go back and write poems about the place I thought I'd

left behind. But that landscape, including my family, had the biggest impact, much bigger than anything that came after.

For whatever reasons, when I first saw the Northwest, I thought, "Yes." I think it's at least partly the water. I grew up in a landscape that made me thirsty. I thought the Wasatch Mountains were the most prominent feature, but I realize it was the absence of water that left the strongest impression. The dryness was an emptiness to me, and a loneliness. I went back and forth between my parents' and my grandparents' houses through a very bleak landscape. When I first read Frost's words, "I have it in me so much nearer home to scare myself with my own desert places," I knew exactly what he meant. You can die without water, and the person I wanted to be would have died if I'd stayed in Salt Lake.

You studied anthropology in school. Has your interest in that had any impact on your work?

I think the most important way I think of place comes from that background. What I'm really interested in is not "What's my place in Port Townsend or San Diego?" but "What's our place in the universe?" There's a poem in my new collection called "Charming Quarks." It seems ironic to me that vision is our dominant sense when we live in a universe that's mostly invisible "dark matter." What's wrong with this picture? Why don't we have enormous ears instead? We don't seem to match up very well with the universe we live in. The title poem in this book—"Stardust"—began with a trip to the Rose Space and Science Center in Manhattan. They try to give a sense of scale, in time and in space. There's a spiral staircase that begins at the top with images of what the Big Bang might have looked like. Then each step you take down is 145 million years. Along the way there are accounts of the first stars, first constellations, first planets. At the very bottom there's an actual human hair that represents the time of human life on earth.

"Stardust" is a meditative poem. Obviously our lives were not the point of evolution. I never thought they were, but the museum exhibit really reaffirmed that. The universe is not about us. But at the same time, our lives are so enormously important to us. How do you reconcile those two things? There's a point in the poem where I get angry. We're the ones who give it all meaning, and I want to shout up the staircase, to the stars, back to the beginning of time, "We're coming. Life is coming. We'll make something of you—but there is no *you*."

Death Valley

This project started in part because I believe that *where* we live and work has a tremendous effect on *how* we live and work. I grew up in small towns all across Canada, but in my adulthood I have lived in cities all across the U.S.—Phoenix, Dallas, D.C., Miami, and others. I romanticized this trip out of all proportion for several months before starting it, but I continue to be amazed at how gorgeous and varied the big country is.

A short break in the interview schedule allows us some time, and we decide to take a couple of days in the remote and beautiful Death Valley National Park. We arrive at Stovepipe Wells at midday, the temperature a polite and friendly 65 degrees. Stovepipe Wells is a little outpost in the middle of the big valley. There is space for about fifty RVs in the national park area—no electricity or water. And there are fourteen spots with power and water right alongside the desolate and barely traveled Highway 190.

At night the place is dead silent. About every hour or so a car might headlight through, headed either to Los Angeles or Nevada. We sit out under the stars and a three-quarter moon and just soak in the quiet. The desert gives up its heat easily out here at night, and the lows are in the mid-thirties.

In the mornings we sit outside again in our coats and watch the sun poke up over the Funeral Mountains and light the desert floor all over again. We don't talk about it. We just let it bathe us, warm us. Sometimes my wife will get up and wander away, through part of the desert. A quarter mile away, and I can still actually hear her shoes scuff the desert floor. I watch some kind of hardy spider work out from beneath a rock and then head out on his own path.

Out there, I think we both feel it. The cares and worries of our old life, the working life, the city life, have disappeared. This is not a vacation. It was a breaking of one life and the opening of a new one.

Donald Revell & Claudia Keelan
Las Vegas, Nevada

Donald Revell and I stand under a brilliant blue sky laced with Las Vegas's ever-present jet contrails. We're in the backyard of the house that Revell shares with his wife, the poet Claudia Keelan, and their son, Ben. We're south and west of Vegas near a tiny settlement called Blue Diamond.

Like most people who live in Vegas, Revell lives nowhere near The Strip, the gaudy and garish main drag littered with gigantic casinos. Vegas is a city like most cities. You've got your downtown, your suburbs. There's industry (here it's roulette, showgirls, and magicians). And it's populated by a wide variety of folks: friendly, happy, creepy, noisy, kind, et cetera. People from all over the world come here for vacations, but the real citizens shop, drive, work, just like it was a regular place.

Keelan runs the MFA program here in Vegas, but Revell commutes once a week to Salt Lake City to be a part of the excellent program at the University of Utah.

When Keelan joins us, we sit in patio chairs near their newly installed lap pool. Revell points out the spare desert landscaping. Everything out here was planted by him and Keelan, including a lovely acacia, and—surprisingly—seven full-size Christmas trees. While we're talking, I can see their son Ben peering at me through the blinds of a back window. I suspect he'd rather be inside than listening to the old folks outside.

Keelan is originally from California, and Revell comes from the Bronx. But they both are at home in the desert. Their work, too, is heavily influenced by the empty spaces of their adopted home, especially in Keelan's Utopic *and Revell's* My Mojave.

~ ~ ~ ~ ~ ~

What sort of role has place played in your life?

DR: I must be naive or just lucky. I've found every place I've lived to be—essentially—pastoral. I didn't know the South Bronx was a slum until years after I'd left it. I grew up in a three-room apartment. My sister and I had the bedroom; my parents slept on the sofa bed in the living room. It was sort of like "The Honeymooners." That was our apartment. The laundry went out the kitchen window. But I have nothing but good memories. I remember what might have been the only tree. I remember a little bit of grass, and I remember nice people. I know it was a very dark, urban landscape, but I just don't remember it that way.

My whole life has had that continuity of pastoral, green decency. I was so lucky because my parents were very kind. I think everyone was aware that the physical circumstances of my childhood were difficult. In terms of material things, in terms of access to certain kinds of pleasures, we didn't have those. But if you've never had them, you don't miss  them. And as they did become available, they were wonderful. A class trip to the Metropolitan Museum of Art. A class trip to a farm in upstate New York. Sort of like a Thomas Traherne moment *(laughs)*. Wonders!

As the understanding of my circumstances grew, my circumstances became easier, gentler. Only in retrospect can I say I grew up in a terrible slum, because I have no memory of a slum. Going back there now as an adult makes me sad. I'd never live in New York again. My mother still does, and she'd never live anywhere else. I've lost the knack. I must have had whatever mindset is necessary, but I couldn't go back there. And I've never written a word of poetry there.

As I've gotten older, I've had to work harder and go further to maintain my innocence, my pastoral naiveté. You have to be crafty to be naive.

You guys really have a nice spot here, and it looks like a great place to live. Are you conscious of the fact that you're building a place to live, but also a place for your son to grow up?

CK: What you see now is the finishing of seven years. Mostly we planted everything by ourselves. Every year we've gotten a Christmas tree—in fact we're going to get one tomorrow. *(She starts to point at them.)* There's that one, and look at this one over here. This one's huge. That's not even the oldest; it's only three years old. I think it's in the septic field *(laughs)*. There are more over there.

So we planted most of these trees by ourselves, which was very hard, because this is all caliche. And we didn't have enough money to landscape it until this last summer. For a long time it was very daunting to be here. It's hot six months of the year, really hot. The kind of way people feel in Alaska, where they get housebound. You get the same kind of thing here. The children can't play outside. For me it was really hard to imagine a landscape. For one thing, I grew up in California in a really lush landscape and lived in Boston, lived in the South. And when I came here, I was terrified. It was really my concept of a kind of a hell.

And then I started to open myself up to the place. And now I notice any color there is. When I go anyplace else now, I'm just in awe of color. Here, the sky is dominant. And I love that. And it's empty. And that emptiness has become an important part to me. So much of American poetry is about the eye, and it seems to me that here I've developed my ear a lot more, listening. Listening to solitude. Listening to what happens in the desert, which is interesting.

Donald, in your most recent collection, My Mojave, *place exists but is not always named or obvious. How do you think you use place?*

DR: Place uses me. Because more and more over the years I've come to trust in what's given at the moment of composition rather than what's intended. I've been rereading George Herbert's *The Temple* these past mornings and noticing, as I didn't notice when I was a student, how much he surrenders himself to his eyesight. I loved that in Traherne but didn't remember it in Herbert. And in poets of the twentieth century, like (Ezra) Pound and Ronald Johnson, I've really treasured that sense of "I will open my eyes and be given the poem." As Herbert says, "If I but lift mine eyes, my suit is made."

The place will compose itself via me. Writing becomes more and more an act of trust and less an act of craft. So place isn't just important, it's almost everything. The poem will be what it is because of where I'm writing it. Luckily for me, where I am is where I am. For the most part, and in *My Mojave* entirely, the place wrote the poem. In terms of "I lifted my eyes," as Herbert says, and there it was; there was the poem. And the poem continues as long as my attention continues. I'm always telling my students, "The longer you look, the more you will see." A Yogi Berra sort of thing, but it has some bump to it. If your eyes stay open, your eyes will be filled. When first you move to the desert, you almost recoil. How can we do this? How can we live here? And then slowly, if you pay attention, the desert teaches you how to live here. It teaches you what to look for; it teaches you to see how beautiful it is, how subtle it is, how full it is. It translates into a way of thinking about poems. A poem is not empty. Even if there are twenty words in it, it's still full. And if there are twenty-one words, the poem is still just full.

Claudia, how do you use this landscape in your own work?

CK: There's a lot of space in my poetry, especially in *Utopic*. That book was really informed by absence, and by waiting, and the solitude.

For a long time there were only two houses here. There was no wall. I sat at the table and just looked out the window. Or sat out here and wrote and was informed by my breath and by the relative lack of vision, but also of rhythms, internal rhythms and natural rhythms of living in a place for seven years. So that space, that emptiness. And the wind is everywhere in my poems because the wind is dominant. Ben's first word was "wind." "Wind wind." And he was really trying to figure out what it is. Because it howls. And when that wall wasn't there . . . *(makes whooshing wind sound)*.

My father died two years ago here, in our house; and we just sort of decided that we, too, were going to die, and we were going to finish our house and live in it.

There's also the sound of construction around here all the time and the sound of airplanes. It's very funny because it's a desert that's being invaded. But there's always the sense of the invasion. When you first move here you think, "So what, it's just a bunch of scrub grass." But then you start to notice the one-barrel cactus out there that blooms. The purple sage that comes up at certain times. And really know the flowers. And start to feel this sense of propriety.

Donald, you and Claudia and Ben live here, but you commute regularly to Utah. Salt Lake City and Las Vegas seem like an odd combination? Do you see similarities in them?

DR: Both cities, both cultures are improvised in a vacuum. Both cities are tributes to the improvisational nature of American spirituality. Is that a real religion, or did you make that up? Is that a real city, or did you make that up? It's like that Robert Creeley line: "Is that a real poem, or did you write it yourself?" It has that kind of weightlessness and goofiness that is, nevertheless, compelling. Believing in something believable doesn't impress me. But believing in something you know is about an hour and a half old requires a leap of faith. Both of these cities were built by faith alone. There should not be a city here, in Las Vegas. And there shouldn't be a city in Salt Lake. I get the feeling they made a wrong turn. They really should have been going further north, because the Cache Valley is so green and beautiful. It's the combination of faith and goofiness that connects the places. I find myself fooled and awed by it. I don't use that word goofy dismissively. I use it with a tremendous respect and desire to be able to emulate it. In the days right after September 11, I felt that we were living in the last innocent places in America. That somehow Salt Lake City and Las Vegas hadn't changed. They weren't rooted. They could simply float above events. I'm sure the city fathers of both cities would be troubled by that.

Both cities are founded on the idea that "Well, we're not going to be here long." In Las Vegas, you're going to make a lot of money and go somewhere else. In Salt Lake City, you're going to heaven. These are way stations.

CK: They're both promised lands in a sense. One is a religious Zion, and the other is a capitalist Zion. And they float around those promises very well. And on the other hand, Las Vegas is a place where people come to be unreal. And it's very interesting to be a person conducting a life where people come to forget their lives. And in a certain sense there's a sorrow in the life of a city that is used in such a way.

You see it in the old casinos and the old casino workers. The fact that their lives are the background for America's playground. That's poignant. It's also a very utopian place for a large part of the population who wouldn't be able to own a house or get a job that paid good benefits and let them put their kids to school without the casinos. Housemaids own houses with pools here.

There's the poignancy of the unreality of the city. Because Las Vegas is a simulacrum of all other places.

A Parish in the Bronx

The moving filaments of traffic shadow
the people and jagged, stationary cars
in a church parking lot below the highway.
Anyone leaving the late mass has a choice,
a lucky one. He can look up as far
as the highway and believe in so many lights
moving fast. Or he can look up farther
to the spire razored in floodlights,
taller than the traffic or the near buildings,
and picture himself that high, that visible.

Some choices are too easy to make
only because nothing hangs in the balance.
Coming out of the darkness of a church
into a dark neighborhood smeared beneath pylons,
nobody has anything to lose
between the heavens of the fast cars
and of the spire razored where everyone can see.
I felt so lucky when I stood there.
I felt like the last organ note of a hymn
huge inside of the nothing that comes afterwards.

There is no room between eternity
and the loneliness inside a car
and the loneliness of the floodlights cutting
a tall scaffold into the night sky.
I came out of mass and made a choice
lucky to believe the choice mattered.
The fast cars sped out of the city to dances
and marriages. The sharp spire
laddered upwards into the easy fame
of the last note of a hymn held forever.

I am no dancer. And marriage
never gets to the end of anything.
I chose the perspectiveless, tall nonsense
of God's noise aloft over the jagged parish,
thinking everything else was a dream
too lonely for words. It was, but just as lonely
is praying that all wives return, all dogs live.
Eternity takes up all the room in the world.
You can't drive fast enough. You can't picture yourself
so high that the dead see you and come home.

—*Donald Revell*

Alberto Rios
Chandler, Arizona

Alberto Rios and the family dog Kino welcome me to their home in Chandler. We're just south of Phoenix, where Rios teaches at Arizona State, my alma mater. I went to school here in the late '70s and early '80s, met my wife here, and drove fast and wild on the desert highways in and around Phoenix when I was indestructible. It's my first visit in almost twenty years. Oddly, I hardly ever think about this as my college hometown. I just wasn't much of a student. I didn't think much about class, went as seldom as I could, and really just visited campus when I had to. (Not that I'd recommend that for any of the kids . . . stay in school, stay off the pipe!)

Rios and I read at the same function more than twenty years ago, although neither of us remembers too much about it. We sit in the front room, and we talk about what it's like for me to be back in Arizona after all this time.

He tells me about his first poetry, scribbled in the back of his school notebooks. As he recalls it, the only thing the back of the notebook was used for was spitballs and stuff you could write but couldn't show anyone else. He remembers that he was writing for himself then, not for school, not for assignment, not for a grade. It was an important but solitary part of his progress, and he wonders what a more organized introduction to poetry might have done to him.

As an important and influential poet, he clearly has had numerous opportunities to go elsewhere, nearer the hubs of publishing and academia; but he's chosen—both consciously and subconsciously, I'd imagine—to stay here, within an easy afternoon drive of his hometown. The Southwest is his place, a place to live and work, but more importantly the place that is inside him and his poetry.

~ ~ ~ ~ ~ ~

What has been the impact of place on your poetry?

I think it's been profound. It's everything. I grew up in Nogales on the border, which is a line, and knowing that if you crossed that line, something else, something different was going to happen. Different laws. Different people. Different language. Different ideas.

Even as a child you recognized something about that liminality, about that in-between place. And I've since thought it was a lot like

125

going to sleep and beginning to dream. You cross over into something. And even though I spoke the language and knew what Mexico meant—I was living on the Arizona side—I still recognized that something was changed. And when I say "changed," I don't just mean in a surface way, not just the decorative nature of what the streets looked like. Everything that you could count on here was simply turned around there, the way you turn a diamond around. It's an equal shine, an equal glint, but it's not the same glint. And it's never ceased to amaze me. Even today, I think I write from that. It's what gives me a sense of freedom in that I never have to be happy with saying one thing about something.

I think that also comes from growing up with multiple languages and multiple cultures. For every single thing, one name, one word doesn't work. And that has helped me as a writer. So when I think of place, I don't just think of a physical land; it's a sensibility of groundedness. When I write, I don't write about this house, and I don't write about the Chandler I'm living in now. And it's not that I write out of childhood necessarily, but I think I write about that time which childhood marked. When I say Nogales, I don't mean Nogales today. It's a very different place, and I have a hard time recognizing it myself. And when I say Nogales, I mean both sides, and the paradigm of the two Nogaleses.

What sort of role do you think landscape or place is best used for in poetry?

To me, it's to raise something of my humanness. It goes back to that diamond turning I was talking about before. Poetry is a lot of fun because you get to do it quickly, where you just start with something like a nature image that I've just encountered. I just turn it over and let it take me where it wants to go. So metaphor and simile and the wild adventure that they offer take over. If I'm patient enough, that thing will eventually come around and tell me a story or a poem. It's an examination. Each time it's a discovery, and if I can convey that suddenly new moment—it's the age-old notion of "make it new"—I let language and experience take part in that moment. As writers we're all too eager to answer questions neatly, but that having been said, there are no rules. Everything I've just said I'm just as likely to break the next time I'm into a poem. That's a hard thing to explain to the world, because everyone wants to buy a book or go to a class and learn how to do it. But the fact of it is you learn how it's been done, not how to do it. That part is up to you.

What is it about Arizona? What is it that makes it such a big part of your poetry, and what is it that keeps you here? And do you think poets have some sort of responsibility to their places?

I am a native and have lived here all my life. Even though I've visited many other places, Arizona is so central to my whole life that I probably don't know the answer to that. I probably don't have the perspective to answer that with real clarity.

When I went to high school, it was an astounding time. It was before we were doing all these education initiatives. It was before we were worrying about dropout rates. There were about a hundred of us who graduated high school, but there were a thousand in the freshman class. It was hard, because in Nogales there were things like the produce industry where you could make a lot of money real fast in six months, but that amount of money was all you were going to make. It seemed like a lot. There was also the beginning of drug trading and a lot of other things. And that dropout rate was astounding.

Nogales High School in that sense was more of a vocational school. It wasn't a college prep kind of school. And if it was, it was a dismal failure. It meant that I wasn't particularly prepared for college, and in balance, after a long life, that's been a positive thing for me personally. I certainly wouldn't recommend it. But it meant that college was an adventure. College was no big looming thing. For me, it was just thirteenth grade, because I didn't know how else to experience it. And I went through; I survived it.

There were only a few who made it through. The others have all gone away, because they're commodities. People who made it who had that background, particular abilities in language and all that sort of stuff, were commodities, and they've all gone away. And I've had every opportunity to leave as well.

The hardest choice—and I've tried not to make it a confrontational choice with myself—has been to stay. Because I could have done all sorts of things, in all sorts of places, had a very different kind of success, I think, had I been willing to go where the action is. I think staying here has been an act of responsibility. People often ask me if I'm happy here, and that's completely the wrong question. And in fact it's one I try not to even ask myself. Because I might be happy in Paris! But is this the place I can probably make a difference and where I need to be? I think so.

Richard Shelton
Tucson, Arizona

When Richard and his wife Lois built their house in the foothills of the Tucson Mountains in 1961, they were one of only three residents in the vast and unscrubbed Sonoran desert some ten miles west of Tucson. They and their young son relished the remote location, but scorpions and one spectacularly dog-hungry Gila monster made the land a little more hostile than a similar area nearer the city.

But Shelton wouldn't trade the experience or the location. While it's true that the neighbors have arrived over the past thirty years, the spot is still breathtaking. Unlike the desert areas right around Phoenix, which I've just left, Tucson's desert is packed with cacti, hundreds of thorny "platypus" or pancake cacti jammed in every square city block of space. And up on the foothills where Shelton lives, the inhospitable nature of the place is still apparent. Sure, there are concrete roads that wind in and around the adobe-colored homes; but a foot off the main road and you're on gravel and rock, and the desert is everywhere.

As always, I'm interested in a poet's place, and it's obvious this place has beauty. Shelton talks about the transformational nature of the desert, a place that in summer can still be scorching in the middle of a moon-filled night.

~ ~ ~ ~ ~ ~

How do you think the places of your life have influenced the work you've done as a poet?

I think they've influenced the work I've done profoundly. I have always lived in the desert or on the edge of the desert. I was raised in Boise, Idaho, which is on the edge of an incredible desert, the Snake River Plain Desert. Then I went to west Texas to school, in the Chihuahua Desert. And then I came here; the Army sent me to Fort Huachuca, and I was so fascinated with the landscape that I decided to stay when I got out of the Army. I took the closest job. In a sense, I've always lived in or very near a desert. When I get into the deep woods, I become claustrophobic. I notice that in the city—tall buildings—I get a little claustrophobic. I enjoy going to New York, but after a week I'm quite ready to leave; the excitement is over. I think it's conditioning from earliest childhood that the desert landscape suits me.

Big vistas; big distance; I have to see the spaces. From this house you can see completely across the valley to the mountains. I don't think that's an accident. Space is what I've always needed.

Because this landscape has been so much a part of your life, do you think that there's anything in the desert that has had an influence on the process of your writing? What kind of habits do you have?

I'm very slow. Undisciplined. Terribly undisciplined. I'll write in spurts. I did write for many years only at night, because that was the only time I had. I was teaching full time and wanted to spend time with my family during the day. So after they went to bed, I'd write, and I'd write all night. This was the first house here, and for all those years all I had to do was walk out that door and I was in the desert. I could go out, hike around for a couple of hours, and then come back and write. I didn't necessarily write about what I saw in those couple of hours, but I do remember going out and staring at the moon—and I have a lot of moon poems.

So that certainly shows up in the work. You get the nocturnal desert again and again and again, because I would wander around in the desert at night. I have no fear of the desert. A lot of people are afraid of the desert, and I don't understand that. It's much safer than just about anywhere else you can be. It's certainly much safer than downtown Tucson. I don't know if it's had much to do with process, except that my process is very relaxed, open, and sort of disheveled, the way the desert is.

I'm seeing all of the regions of the U.S. this year, and every region has something singular about it that makes it unique. What is it about the Southwest for you?

The quality of the air and the quality of the light. It's more nearly like the Mediterranean than anywhere else in this country. And there's a similar quality of light and air in southern Italy, Greece, and so on. I don't know of anywhere else in the country with this light and air, and, of course, it's because of the light that so many painters come here.

And that intense, dry heat. It's an astonishing thing. I remember the first summer I spent here. I'd spent nearly all of my summers in Idaho, so it wasn't so hot. The first summer I spent here, I can remember going outside at midnight or one in the morning and it was still 100 degrees. And that does something very strange to you. It disorients you, and you do things you wouldn't normally do—fortunately not too many of them are illegal *(laughs)*. It excites you, stimulates you, and I think that may be one of the reasons why so much of my poetry was written at night in the summer. It's a combination of the air and the dry heat at a time of day when your body is not accustomed to it. Your body expects things to cool off, and it doesn't here, not all the time.

So you don't see the desert, with all of its critters, rocks, and cacti as a hostile place?

No. I think the desert is about the most benign environment I can think of. There's space. Because of the lack of water the plants are spaced. Yes, a lot of them are pretty dangerous—prickly. A lot of cacti, but you soon get over that. But things are spaced so you can walk right through the desert. It's not like a thick forest with a lot of undergrowth, something impenetrable. It's open.

And the moonlit nights. Because of the color of the earth—it's very pale—it's very light. In the fall semester, I normally take a group of students to a wash, way out in Saguaro West, and we read poetry by moonlight. We don't need a flashlight. It's bright enough that you can read by moonlight. Those washes are like desert beaches, white sand and gorgeous.

Over the past forty years, Tucson has gotten closer and closer. How do you feel as the city encroaches on your desert?

Many of my poems have to do with the destruction of this desert, even this part of the desert, the Tucson Mountains. We do have the Saguaro West monument and Tucson Mountain Park, which has saved a great deal—so you can see what it was like. I did buy land further out to try to escape from the crowd, but my wife didn't want to do that. She wanted to be closer to town, so we stayed here and just added on to this home. But I would have preferred to be further away.

I think what I have done in my poetry is interpreted the desert, the Sonoran desert, through the lens of my own despair at its destruction. I think I have done more to write about what's out there *(pointing to the foothills behind us)* than almost anybody, but that doesn't mean you're getting a photograph, a painting. You're getting an attitude.

Local Knowledge

For Michael Hogan

on December nights
when the rain we needed months ago
is still far off and the wind
gropes through the desert
in search of any tree to hold it

those who live here all year round
listen to the irresistible
voice of loneliness
and want only to be left alone

local knowledge is to live in a place
and know the place
however barren

some kinds of damage
provide their own defense
and we who stay in the ruins
are secure against enemies and friends

if you should see one of us
in the distance as your caravan passes
and if he is ragged and gesturing
do not be mistaken

he is not gesturing for rescue
he is shouting *go away*

—*Richard Shelton*

Jane Miller
Tucson, Arizona

Like her colleague Richard Shelton, Jane Miller lives across the valley from the gorgeous Santa Catalina Mountains, which ring the eastern landscape outside Tucson, Arizona. It's been nearly twenty years since my wife and I left Arizona, so before I knock on Miller's front door, I stand there and soak in some of the endless and bathing sunlight. It's cool today, in the seventies, but I know what it's like here. In a few weeks it'll be 110 in the shade, and by then we'll be many miles down the road.

Miller greets me at the door in the midst of this little daydream and invites me in. We look around her stunning and large adobe home and then sit in her great room: Mexican tile, twelve-foot windows, a piano that Jane is learning to play.

She tells me a little bit about hiking the trails in and around this hillside house. I ask about the local wildlife (spiders, snakes, and such), and she admits that she's skittish about the snakes and sees a variety of these desert creatures regularly enough. She tells me about a recent party they had here where visitors from elsewhere came across a scorpion out on the back patio; and I spend the next several minutes watching around my feet for something speedy and small.

~ ~ ~ ~ ~ ~

Do you think place has played a role in what you write?

Yes. I've moved around a lot, from Provincetown Bay to Tomales Bay and all points in between; and topography, weather, the bustle of the marketplace, the presence of a border here between southern Arizona and Mexico—all these manifestations feed my imagination. Reality and the imagination, it seems to me, have an inexplicably successful marriage.

I like to walk as much as I can. The first thing I do is set out every morning. It's a meditation. Not that I then set about describing impressions; I'm not naturalistic in the way I write. I like to leap and make associations and unusual, even unrealistic, connections. I prefer the expressionism that results, and which, for me, makes a heightened reality. For example, on a very hot day here in the desert, when I'm out walking, all the dirt and cacti and gravel are a moonscape. Cacti don't really blow in the wind. There's a feeling of stopped time that has advised me about exploding, expanding a moment in poetry and prose. I'm sure this is quite different from the action of, say, a flat Floridian landscape. So, form—diction, syntax—is a kind of dreamscape of the terrain. And then, of course, subjects rise up as matter-of-factly, and as forcefully, as islands appear to someone sailing a ship. Who could live in this place and not be aware, for example, of Mexicans trying to cross into this country every day, many without enough water, and against all odds?

Are there specific places that may have had an even more direct effect on your process?

When I'm happy and have been able to make a place home, I feel free to write. I don't write very well when I'm miserable, and the feel of a place, with its friendly or unfriendly trees, coyotes with nerves on edge—it can all get rather anthropomorphic—definitely affects my internal weather.

I remember the wonderful trails of Humboldt County (California) with spongy soil. I felt buoyant, really, and that no doubt got projected onto the page. And the place was glowing in mist. Thinking of those days, I am certain that the landscape and the spirit of the place had a huge effect on the thinking I do.

Experiencing a wavy landscape—heat waves, ocean waves—creates a certain harmonic peace for me, which may have led to my long, clausal sentence structure. And, of course, it's no surprise that the desert, with its exposed lumpy ocean floor, offers a wonderful metaphor, wonderful encouragement, for writing. You know the old story of the nomad on a quest for an oasis? Is what is out there a mirage? What's reality?

When you were painting, did you find that elements of that endeavor had companions in your work as a poet?

Absolutely. It served as ballast to my tendency to perceive of the world as super-amped. That is, things could be as simple as the blue table, the red hat, the green chair. The world gets complicated soon enough by language. My poetry gets complicated very quickly. I think in associative ways and expressionistic ways, so before I know it, I'm off and running. This reminds me of that—reminds me of that. But having to portray the world in color was a kind of relief. A way to keep a place simple. Spare. But I gave up painting because, in fact, the world does need to be represented in its layers, in its thickness, and I wasn't able to

achieve that in oil. Still, I'm grateful for what, in many ways, was an idyllic time.

You've been in Arizona since the late 1980s. Is it a tough place to live, given the rocky and somewhat inhospitable landscape?

Certainly there are a lot of snakes, and I'm very cautious about them. I had a recent encounter with one while I was recycling my trash, and it was a formidable experience. My blood drained out and ran into my shoes!

And the landscape is formidable because of what you can and can't touch. If you're used to lying down in the grass or feeling the sweet leaves of the almond tree—forget about it. It's not a very welcoming landscape.

Do you feel any responsibility or obligation to capture anything about this place where you live?

I feel a heavy responsibility. I don't know if "capture" is the right word though. I'm not an environmentalist or a scientist; there's a lot I don't understand. But I spent some years researching the efforts to create the bomb out in New Mexico, when I was writing a book that worked that theme a bit. Driving around the remote Southwest can no longer be a naive experience of strange beauty—it turns out that the ground underneath is ticking. Toxins have been leaking into the earth for sixty-odd years. I became obsessed with nuclear waste material and its effect on the landscape here, not to mention the human population. So I spent some time getting involved in politics in that way. I was outspoken without being terribly knowledgeable. And then I realized that it wasn't really my job; I wasn't trained. However, I was thinking about what evil is, and the question has stayed in my work at the metaphoric level. Poets have vivid imaginations and can imagine the very worst of what must be going on.

I would describe myself as a writer who is forced into the real world every day. And I think we absolutely have an obligation not only to describe what we see but also to rail against any further deception. It's just not enough to say, "Things are a mess." We have to prevent them from getting worse. That's a challenge. And I don't have a blueprint for how to do that. But, as a teacher, I feel that I have to participate in a conversation about the responsibilities of the poet to the world. It's not about the sounds of the words we use, even as they echo sounds in nature. It's not about recreating pictures "of a lost world." That's only the beginning.

#15, from *A Palace of Pearls*

What is it about Americans
we bully the first people we meet
whole villages of Pima Indians
moved into saguaro forests every June
with long picking sticks they poke the green fruit they scoop out the
    pulp
and toss the star-shaped rind down to inspire rain
the innards ripen to iodine-red centers and tiny black seeds
they're made into syrup and jam and pressed into cakes for later
should they need to be shared with manbeasts like us
our prophecy has been written by Shakespeare
"you'll be rotten ere you be half ripe"
the long picking sticks are made by tying their ribs together
WHEN THE SOFT FLESH FALLS OFF THE FALLEN GIANTS

—*Jane Miller*

New Year

The days have become weeks, and the weeks have counted off the months. It seems that yesterday we lived in suburban madness, commuting hours a day to satisfying but exhausting careers.

Then the trip. And it's as if the old world, the old ways never existed.

It is 4:45 a.m. as I write this. New Year's Day. We have crossed over from one year to the next. When the sun went down last night, we cooked dinner, popped a bottle of champagne we've been carrying around for months, and then—under only the light of the half moon—we scoured the sky with our binoculars. Stars upon stars. Countless dots of light, light hurtling at us—like the light of the North Star—sent this direction hundreds of thousands of years ago. And then, like old people all over, no matter the home or location, we turned in early, long before the big ball dropped in NYC or anywhere else. At midnight we were asleep as one year clicked into the other.

I woke up very early, and I began to think about the journey and what it means. Towns, places, and the highways that connect them. Always lurking is "What's next?"

This trip is full of things that are named and unnamed. I'm writing a book, trying to figure out if I want to keep teaching. My wife is deciding what's next for her, a business, back to her career, something else we don't even know.

Loose ends. The money is disappearing. It's not an endless supply, I can tell you. I have the small white bank receipts to prove to you that the time is dwindling. But we wouldn't go back now. We're something like halfway. Half the poets. Half the miles. Half the country. We wouldn't turn back for anything. It's a road that we chose and one we're going to hurtle down until we finish the journey. When the interviews are over in a few months, I suspect the sadness will be real and overwhelming. The real world will intrude like never before. But there's time still. Time still to continue the dream.

Just now, the light is appearing in the east, over a hill whose name I do not know. My wife sleeps. I leave Winnie Cooper for a bit. The desert is always cold in the morning, but I stand out there for a while anyway. The only sound—I mean the *only* sound—is the rush of blood in my temples, the sound of my breath. The sound of a new world coming on.

William Wenthe
Lubbock, Texas

To get to Lubbock, we have to go north and east out of Arizona and through New Mexico. We charge headlong into the panhandle of Texas, my favorite part of my favorite state. We're ahead of schedule, so we spend the day north in Amarillo. We eat gigantic slabs of beef, walk under a swirling, changeable sky, then take a ride out of Amarillo to Cadillac Ranch.

Long one of the best and most wondrous nutty roadside attractions, Cadillac Ranch sits benignly but queerly alongside the interstate between Amarillo and points west. Ten vintage Cadillacs are lined up, their front ends lodged in the earth, the back half of each car rising up at about eleven o'clock. They are heavily laden with psychedelic, swirling colors and graffiti: "Jeremiah," "Kelly," "Jared W. age 8 was here for the first time 2004."

When we get down to Lubbock, we find something just as odd: Bill Wenthe—a kid from Jersey—happily stuck halfway into the ground of this hardscrabble windy city. Although Lubbock was a sort of geographical shock for him, he's adapted beautifully. He tells me about a visit from one of his New York pals a few years ago. As they drove a highway north of the city, Wenthe was reveling in the texture and variety of grasses, the birds on fenceposts, the railroad track, the various structures along the road, the sky, and what the sky was telling him. His pal said, "Boy, there's nothing out here."

It was then that Wenthe knew he'd crossed a threshold. The geographic shock was over. The landscape had taught Wenthe what to see and how to see it, and suddenly Lubbock was home.

~ ~ ~ ~ ~ ~

After a childhood in New Jersey and before coming to Texas, you lived for a long time in rural Virginia. Was that a culture shock of some kind?

It was a very welcome move, but not so much a difference of culture as of geography. I was living in Manhattan, in the East Village, before I went to Virginia; and I'd go backpacking in the Blue Ridge Mountains. On one of these trips I stopped at the University of Virginia in that quiet period between graduation and before summer school, when the campus is really quiet. Walking in these gardens that Jefferson had designed, one could get this kind of eighteenth-century feel, and I remember thinking that this would be a nice to place to come and study. Virginia

138

was the first place I ever lived where I really felt like I understood the place in terms of natural and human history.

When I moved to Virginia, I found a landscape that was just stunningly beautiful. Rolling hills, woods, and farms, mostly pleasure farms, that often looked very picturesque, like English farms. And nearby, there were national forests and wilderness.

For three years in that time I lived in a structure that, to call it a cottage would be to ennoble it. To call it a shack might be to disparage it a bit too much. It was an old barracks structure from World War II that someone had towed out into the woods. I heated it with wood that I cut from fallen trees. I lived on 500 acres of woods that had been in my landlord's family since colonial times—it was granted to them by the King of England.

There was a slave cemetery on this land, hidden and overgrown in the woods. Just adjacent to the land was a ruined antebellum mansion. There was an antebellum house that was still lived in by a very old woman that was featured in the poem "Enniscorthy, Virginia," in my first book. There was also a walled, well-kept cemetery that held ancestors of my landlord and other families. One of the things you'd notice were the gravestones of men who were born in the 1840s and who died in 1863 or 1864, presumably in the Civil War.

So there were all these layers that I could see of American history. And layers of society: the rural people who lived there who didn't have a lot of money, the families of old money who'd owned the land for a long time, and then the new incoming money.

At the same time I had a very intimate sense of the immediate woodland surroundings. I had a sense of time that was measured by the cycles of insects, wildflowers, birds, and the growth on the trees around me.

What was it like for you when you came to Lubbock?

Having lived the first thirty-five years of my life on the East Coast, I was nervous about moving so far away. In fact, I swear, when people would ask me where I want to teach, I'd say, "Anywhere but Texas." It was a joke, and all I meant was that I didn't want to move to a flat, dry place. So, of course, I ended up getting a job in one of the driest, and certainly the flattest, places in the state.

My first reaction was, again, a kind of geographic shock. I wouldn't call it culture shock. Because in many ways this is a very accommodating town, a very friendly town. A very interesting town with its own kind of creativity and diversity. The overall climate, culturally and politically, tends to be conservative—and I'm not—but no more so than Virginia or much of New Jersey.

What continually amazes me about Lubbock is the birds here. This neighborhood I'm in kind of looks like the suburb where I grew up in

New Jersey. Of course, there's no major metropolis, but the impression is suburban. And yet, there are so many kinds of birds that I can see from my backyard or in the park down the street. Dozens of varieties of raptors, waterfowl, wading birds—bizarre things, like pelicans even. And that doesn't even include the songbirds.

As a bit of an adopted Texan, do you feel any responsibility or interest in capturing something of Texas?
    I'm finishing my twelfth year here. My sense of responsibility comes, first of all, in realizing that I'm not a Texan. Texas is a place that many people are deeply attached to, whose ancestors are buried here, and whose lives were shaped here. I know I can't simply move here and call myself a Texan.
    I look with some envy at that strong identification with a place, which is something I don't quite have. I can observe that identity, but I can't write from inside that identity. I want to present the place where I live in its complexity. There's a poem in my second book called "White Settlement," which takes its title from a local historical marker that notes—without actually mentioning the cruelty, the massacre—the defeat of Indian tribes in this area. The marker's inscription ends with the phrase, "thereby opening western Texas to white settlement." The speaker of this poem, like me, is a newcomer trying to make sense of where he lives. He considers the violence behind the euphemistic word "settlement" and the layers of human occupation, from earliest hunter-gatherers from twelve thousand years ago to the later Plains Indians, to the Cavalry and the white settlers, and the contemporary overlaying of asphalt, which seems to wipe out, like a kind of amnesia, these layers of human occupation. That's a poem where I really try to grapple with the history, a history that is only mine in the last twelve years.

When you use place in a poem, what are you trying to accomplish?
    The way I usually work to create a sense of place, or to ground a poem, is that I talk about places in relative ways, types of places. I might speak of our street or backyard, or I'll talk about a park. Or I might talk about a trout stream. But then I'll try to present that place in such a way that you can see it in time, in a particular and dramatic way. I'll try to make the poetic experience of that place specific, whether it's a direct physical experience of a place or a memory of a place. I want to describe it in such a way that it's being experienced at that time, and not just as some file photo I'm pulling out. I think I'm always trying to arrive at a sense of place, with emphasis on the sense—to discover where you are and how it is that you're there at this particular moment. Ultimately it's about intensifying the experience of being alive and human, which is what all poetry, or all poetry that I could care about, tries to do.

Alien

They can be found, we've been told,
west of Roswell; some who claim
to have seen them, even
caught them. The idea of them
teased us until we made contact
with a rancher on whose land
they've been reported, and we set out
to investigate ourselves. Route 380
led through downtown Roswell,
where the silly and the earnest
keep each other honest—*Alien
Souvenirs* on one side of the street,
UFO Research Center on the other.

Later, ranch roads gave out
in rock, ocotillo, straggling
juniper, a land strange to think
would be hospitable to what lives,
naturally, so far away.
We made our preparations—
polarized glasses, special boots
and vests, the graphite rods—
then hiked to the creek
where we worked apart, probing
every rock, undercut, and downed
log, every fluid seam
where current slips past
stiller water.

When Loren gave a shout, I ran—
and when I had reached him,
he held it for me to see.
There it was, undeniable; still
this proof was not exactly
what I would call knowledge;
it only confirmed
a sense of something other.
And yet this being
at the edge of our being
is all we had come for.

We caught several more: greenish
above, waxing to yellow underneath,
scarlet gills and gelled, lidless
eyes—though I cannot really
describe them, or even see them
clearly for the coat of clear
slime that made them shimmer,
and shift, reflecting back at me.

It was night when we returned
to the truck. A sky trout-
spotted with stars; the lateral
line of our galaxy shining—
that stream still moving, as
the astronomers tell us, always away.

—*William Wenthe*

Naomi Shihab Nye
San Antonio, Texas

Nye lives in a beautiful 100-year-old house in the fabled King William district in downtown San Antonio. The neighborhood—which boomed originally in the middle of the nineteenth century—is an eclectic collection of two-story houses painted in festive and funky colors. Right across the street is an empty park, and I stand there and look across at it for a while before going in.

We go through the house to a back room that looks out over the backyard and garden. Nye gets me iced tea and a tray of nuts and candy. She shows me some pages from a new anthology she's put together, one that pairs poems and paintings from Texas writers and artists. It's large, colorful, and rich inside with many folks that Nye has known after a quarter century in the state.

As we sit and nibble, she tells me about a five-day trip through Louisiana that she took with her husband and son in the waning days of 1999. They took turns being in charge of all the events of a single day. The trip they called a "meander." On one day they all went and sat in a field, sketching. On another, they knocked on a small-town mayor's door to ask some questions. "We sat with the mayor; he ended up giving our son the key to the city."

She tells me about the last day of that trip, indeed the last day of 1999. They were driving toward Homa, Louisiana, where they would stay that night. A train was crossing the track in front of them after sundown. It pulled a number of odd-looking flatbed trailers, and they couldn't tell at first what was being carried on them. "We realized that these were tombstones on the train," she said. "It hit me that we had left the century in which we were born, and we were entering the century in which we will die."

~ ~ ~ ~ ~ ~

What sort of role do you think place plays in your own work?

I think place is really the gravity for poetry. Poetry exists in terms of how it springs out of the earth that you're in, the earth of your memory, and the gravity it gives you, the compass, how it holds us together and keeps us linked to what we need. I read poems out loud every day to wake our son up—been doing that for years.

There's a sense of deeper connection and belonging when we hear poems read aloud, because they give us the sense we're back on the true earth, not restless and not preoccupied or lost in empty language. Engagement with a poem is greatly helped by hearing it and saying it.

So, the places of my own life become that earth. But I feel at home very easily in places. I don't have the sort of dislocation feeling that many people have who travel a lot. I feel at home in about two hours when I get somewhere. And I like that nomadic switcheroo in the psyche. But I also like being on my own humble earth, in our little hundred-year-old cottage near the San Antonio River and the way the light comes in.

I think about place obsessively, maybe because part of my own family was made refugees by the state of Israel in 1948. I carry their sense of exile. Many of my cousins, who live in Texas now, and my dad, of course, really bear a profound ache of exile as Palestinian refugees. I think my awareness of displacement and diaspora has marked a certain way that I think about place. We're very lucky if we have a little piece of ground, house, or an apartment that we can feel secure about. This is a great American luxury; we might wish it were a universal human right. I have known so many in my life who have always been in flux and who have had so many things taken away from them that I don't have the delusions that many Americans have. "This is mine and I'm keeping it!" I'm haunted by what a luxury this "simple basic right" would be for so many people in our world.

Last year we were renovating two rooms in this ancient house and living in a hotel for thirty-four days down the street, because we had no water at home. During that time I was reading the news as Texas suffered terrible flooding and houses were washed downstream. I was also reading about Palestinians having their houses crushed by bulldozers, a popular Israeli hobby. So at the same time as we worked on two little rooms, our labors seemed so pathetic, like an embellishment. Why am I working so hard picking out tile when I should just be grateful to have a roof?

Poetry helps us acknowledge and notice our own places with more care.

What does San Antonio smell like? Jasmine adrift. Honeysuckle, mountain laurel. When we have houseguests, they say, "My God! Your birds are so loud!" Or, "Oh, those trains at 2:00 a.m. How do you sleep?" After all these years they have become our lullabies.

In poetry we have detailed, interested, reverent engagement with our surroundings.

Do you feel any kind of obligation to write about the places of your life?

Definitely, but I don't know if obligation is the right word. Someone asked me recently if I felt "recruited" to speak up for Palestinians, and I said, "I don't know if I've been recruited. Maybe I'm recruiting myself." There's a sorrowful cause, so many people in a bad situation, and the turmoil and sorrow remain unresolved, so I feel that it's a part of my calling to speak up about it—although we all must speak about many things. Iraq, now. So, so many places.

I've heard Robert Bly talk about how we continue to return to the trees of our childhood, the land of our childhood, our first spot on the earth, all of our lives. That's true, but I think other later places can overtake that place in our metaphorical realm and our deep-heart thinking and seeing. I know I think more about San Antonio as a physical place, or even Jerusalem because it's a struggling place, more than St. Louis *(where she was born)*, which will always have a childhood-wistful air for me.

We're always looking at place, always thinking about it and wanting to convey something of what it is. I love when I can read a poem by Mary Oliver, say, and feel completely wrapped up in Cape Cod. A poem will transport us to another whole sensibility of air and earth.

Arabs have a phrase, which I've always loved, that my father used a lot when I was young. We have a duty to go outside and smell the air. Some evenings, we'd all be in the living room, and he'd say, "Let's go outside and smell the air." Other kids used to say, "What's in the air? Is something burning?" But it just meant being part of the evening, feeling the light, seeing the sunset and sky, smelling the earth. And it is very, very important. It's still the one thing I do when I first get to any town—take a walk and smell it.

I do think we live in a particularly disembodied time, and I'm concerned about kids growing up—and I have one—who don't have a strong allegiance to what makes a place distinct, the soulful elements that we should try to protect.

About two months ago my husband and son were out of town. I had been working all day, and I was going out with some friends, and there was about an hour in between all that. I went and sat on our front porch step with a perfect view of the sunset, the buildings, and trees. One of my neighbors passed by and said, "Are you all right?" And I said, "What do you mean?" And she said, "Well, the way you're sitting there like that, I thought maybe you were locked out." And I thought that's so weird. What is a porch, if not for sitting on? But then I thought, when was the last time I just sat there, with a little glass of rum and lime, staring at the sky? It's my job.

Sitting on one's porch step is a lost art. I think that poetry calls to us—by its very nature, by the kind of consciousness it requires or invites—not to believe in the word "busy," not to apply it to ourselves. Poetry calls to us to *(banging on table)* sit on the step.

Pause

The boy needed
to stop by the road.
What pleasure to let
the engine quit droning
inside the long heat,
to feel where they were.
Sometimes
she was struck by this
as if a plank had slapped
the back of her head.

They were thirsty
as grasses
leaning sideways
in the ditch,
Big Bluestem
and Little Barley,
Texas Cupgrass,
Hairy Crabgrass,
Green Sprangletop.
She could stop at a store
selling only grass names
and be happy.

They would pause
and the pause
seep into them,
fence post,
twisted wire,
brick chimney
without its house,
pollen taking flight
toward the cities.

Something would gather
back into place.
Take the word "home"
for example,
often considered
to have an address.
How it could sweep across you
miles beyond the last
neat packages of ice
and nothing be wider
than its pulse.
Out here,
everywhere,
the boy looking away from her
across the fields.

—Naomi Shihab Nye

Peter Cooley
Jefferson, Louisiana

Peter Cooley's house has a purple door. It's a rich and powerful hue, and we see it from well down the street as we negotiate the narrow passage. We're in Jefferson, just minutes west of New Orleans proper. Winnie Cooper is north of the city in Slidell, Louisiana, and we've taken a rental car to spend a night and a day in New Orleans, a city with brilliant but narrow city streets.

When the purple door opens, I'm welcomed in by Peter and his wife— and the delicious smell of a chicken cooking.

Peter and I sit in the living room, and I arrange the gear. As always, my small digital camera sits on a tripod off to the side, where it will work on its own, shooting images once every ten seconds or so. I get out my indestructible minicassette recorder and place it somewhere vaguely pointed at Peter. (At this point, all of my gear is dented in some way, as I've dropped everything from a variety of heights getting into and out of poets' homes and offices.)

The purple door that led us here comes up during the interview because Peter wants to talk about the rare quality of light that exists in New Orleans. He's always had a debt to light in his work, but he really became aware of it during the research and writing of his celebrated volume, The Van Gogh Notebook. *This part of Louisiana has just the right climate and humidity to give colors their due. The reds have a rich redness, the purples really pop. I wouldn't believe it if it weren't for the door that I look at more than once during my visit.*

Cooley's work is not a natural or obvious fit for a book about "place," but I've long since learned to look past the obvious things. Peter's landscape is internal, questing. The speaker in many of his works is caught inside a frame of his own design, looking out, peering out, wondering if indeed there is a way out. It's heady stuff—and rich in place in ways that don't require the occasional name of a town or street or roadside bar.

~ ~ ~ ~ ~ ~

What kind of role have the places of your life played in your poetry?

I'm very interested in place as a reflection of the inner self. But you can't have the inner place without the outer. The outer has to be expressed through the inner; that's how poetry works. We can't understand each other without images. So we have to imagize the internality, and place is—finally—extension of the imaging.

So this place—because I've lived here for twenty-eight years—has a lot to do with me now, but not in any obvious ways. There's a poet I won't name who has written a lot of poems with street names from the Quarter. I can't stand that kind of thing. I hate this "Now I'm on Frenchman Street. Now I'm on Decatur Street" kind of poetry. That's just local color, and local color is the most transient form of literature.

But I didn't set out to be in a certain place at all. I'm a southerner by adoption, and that old-line southerner thing is very important to many people. You have to be from here, and your granddaddy has to be from here, too.

Jefferson seems like a quirky little multi-use sort of place. What is it like to live on this nice residential street with an industrial area looming?

We've lived out here in this little no-man's-land since 1978. We moved here simply because we could afford to live here. But it has become a part of my poetry. This is a very quiet residential area. Originally, a lot of very old people lived here, but now young people have moved in as the old people died out. But it's right off Jefferson Highway, and we have some of the New Orleans weirdos wandering up and down the highway, and they have figured in my poems as the "lost" of New Orleans. And I think we have a larger proportion of lost people here for a number of reasons. It's easy to be lost here. You can live on the street. There's the whole party culture. The laissez-faire culture takes in a lot of different people, and anyone might be included.

Do you think poets have any obligation to write about these places where we live and work?

It's going to happen anyway. Do poets have any obligation to use images? It's going to happen anyway. Do poets have any obligation to be musical? It's all just inevitable. I determined I wouldn't write about New Orleans, but I ended up doing it anyway. I've always had this field of opposition in myself; if I said I wouldn't do something, I'd end up doing it.

I think the reason I have this antagonism about writing about this place is because it's a tourist town. When we think of New Orleans, the first thing we think of is tourists and a lot of very trite images. They're commercial, and I'm not interested in using commercial images, the images of Mardi Gras.

I'm much more interested in the place inside and in the place outside and the place I make, which is a mediation between those two realities. And the place I make is myself—the person I'm carrying around—and the poem. They're both made-up entities.

Your work is quite spiritual, lyrical. Are there natural world elements in your work that do double duty?

The light. The light is trying to keep the inner light lit, the spiritual light. And I can only keep the spiritual light lit by a relationship with a God who is inside myself and outside myself. This light in reality keeps that light lit. And the light in New Orleans is very important to me. I think it's a very special light. I wrote these poems about Van Gogh. When I was studying him in the late 1980s, I discovered that the light in a lot of his paintings had to do with the humidity in the south of France. In densely humid places, the hues of colors are more intense—red is redder, blue is bluer, and so on. And then I discovered that there was a great similarity between that climate and a New Orleans climate. The French poets saw those percepts of external reality as being part of the spiritual condition, as Rimbaud did. Red is a spiritual red. I can't say it equals "blah blah blah," but it's all part of a spiritual landscape that I'm trying to create in my poems. So it's inner and outer, and the light is the connection.

There's a really claustrophobic sense in some of your poems. At times for me I feel like I'm closed in with the speaker, trapped inside that moment. What are you doing with that?

I don't have any sense of open space. Most of my poems deal with room, and one of the typical situations in my poems is a speaker being in a room and being confined there. Now that's a room of his own soul. How can he mediate the distance between his room and the outside world? As I said earlier, the light is the mediating source between those two things, and the light is a spirit in itself. The light carries him out and carries the world in so he can get out. I think my work is constantly bringing the world in. In my final poem the wall between inner and outer would come down, and the room would be all light.

Miller Williams
Fayetteville, Arkansas

From New Orleans we head toward Arkansas. We get to poke along through countless little towns in Louisiana and Mississippi as we take a leisurely path north. We've got two goals: (1) to visit with the venerable and much beloved poet Miller Williams, absolutely the first poet I thought of when I was planning this trip, and (2) to see our house and the disastrous array of furniture and boxes that fill it.

Were we to begin work on the American poetry version of Mount Rushmore, I'd like to volunteer to start work on the chunk that would become Miller's face. It's a miraculous face, one that is wise and welcoming, genteel and grizzled, open, inquisitive, and always alive.

Miller's home—a virtual treasure trove, museum, and love letter to his family, his countless friends, and his work—makes a splendid place to meet. We repair to an airy porch off the side of the house, where the sound of a burbling fountain eases into the infrequent gaps of our conversation.

We talk about Miller's southern past, a biography of travel, civil-rights protests, music, family, and love that pour out in his lifetime of work. He recalls for me some of the stories behind his poems, turning pages in a collection, running his finger along lines, sometimes—surprisingly— reading with a sure and soothing rhythm.

We spend some time in his study, where the photos of his friends and family peer down on him as he works his way through yellow legal pads of new work. (He fills these pads, sometimes an entire one to create a single piece.) While we get acquainted, he sits in his writing chair and points out U.S. presidents, musicians, poets, and pals on the walls. He points out his family: the ones ahead of him, the ones behind. It's a small room, but comfortable, and it buzzes with the lives that his work has touched.

~ ~ ~ ~ ~ ~

When I first raised the question to you about place in your poetry, what places did you think of right away?

I thought of not a very well-defined or local place. I thought of the South. I think of myself as a southerner before I think of myself as an American. It's a matter of personality and character and lifestyle, and it has nothing to do with conservatism or racism. My father was a Methodist preacher, who was a socialist, union organizer, active integrationist, and feminist. And first of all, a southerner.

And he felt, as I feel, that a southerner has a slower lifestyle, which is valuable to us, certainly to me, and a sense of irony that is not always found in the rest of the nation.

I worked in New York in the 1950s, and I began to feel that I was surrounded by bricks, where I had grown up surrounded by stones. I simply like the texture of the South. And especially in the South, I want to live in the hills. I published an essay titled "Hill Folks and Flatlanders." There's a real difference in the way the world is seen by people, like my wife, who grew up in a delta, and myself, who grew up in the hills. I'm not only a southerner, but I am a hill man.

I asked my wife, "What is the place in my poetry?" and she said "It just smells southern all the way through. Do you realize how many southern towns you have in your poetry?" She realized it, and I didn't. These yellow tabs *(showing me a copy of his collected work—*Some Jazz a While*—with more than a score of yellow slips sticking out of the pages)* all indicate poems that happened in the South.

Some of the poets I've talked to identify themselves quite strongly as regional poets, poets from an area or a state. You've already identified yourself as a southern poet. Do you think that's big enough; does that cover enough territory?

I think that the subjects of my poems answer that in the affirmative. Because I have written about everything from creation to the possibility that dogs might have souls, to the meaning of evolution. I don't think there is any subject that is not available to me just because I like the tonality of the South. You can deal with any subject with any tone. I was called by one critic the Hank Williams of American poetry. And what it meant was that I use ordinary language that is accessible to squirrel hunters and taxi drivers. And that's important to me. But it doesn't limit the subject; it simply limits the approach to it.

My poetry is as colored by my scientific background as it is by the fact that I'm a southerner. I can think of a new poem that bears that out. In "An Answer to a Young Woman Who Said That She Never Had Any Luck," I went back in the poem and showed this young woman how in following her genetic train back, that every time a sperm met an egg, that there had been a hole left for her. Generation after generation. So that somebody who is nobody but her could be born when she was born, just at that moment when that sperm got that egg. Now if that's not luck, there is no luck. But without my scientific background I couldn't have explained that to her in the poem.

There's a poem of yours called "Rock" that seems to me to be especially vivid, certainly one that couldn't have been written without your keen attention to the place that's described in the poem.

The poem is about what we do with our lives, the pursuit of our lives, the goals of our lives, and finally, they are simply something to keep our attention. It was here in this front yard where we did it. The rock is metaphorical, of course. We all have rocks in our lives that we have to move. But finally, the rock is simply an obsession, as Sisyphus had an obsession. We are not going to be here forever, and you have to understand that here, unlike forever, it's six o'clock. Forget it, man, cool it. Leave your obsession alone. Your career is not the most important thing on earth. But finally, it's just a rock you're trying to move. In the poem I say, "Every two hours, I've earned a beer." It's a metaphor for what we dedicate our lives to. Finally, just go in the house, and let your wife give you a mug of beer.

RV Life 2

After one night in our own bed—surrounded by splendid stacks of boxes—we got back on the road, headed east through Arkansas, south of Memphis, and down toward Mississippi. We spent the night at a mammoth RV park that was emptying out after a two-day swap meet that had been held on the grounds. We steered Winnie Cooper into our spot and set up. We waved at some neighbors who were next door in patio chairs, sitting in the gentle glow of a bug zapper. Outside the tiny trailer were two parents and three school-age kids. Dad was spooning out a casserole of some kind while Mom fed a newborn. The kids squabbled, and Dad had some sharp words.

Some RV parks are like resorts. They have swimming pools, jaunty workers who buzz around in white golf carts; and the grounds are immaculate, cleaned by unseen hands in the overnight hours. You can pay more than fifty dollars a night, and you park alongside rigs that sometimes cost up to a half million dollars. Other parks are full of broken-down trailers and motor homes, some thirty years old, many clearly not going anywhere ever again.

Most parks, like this one, are in between. Rent is cheap in these places, sometimes as low as ten dollars a night or a hundred fifty dollars a month. When people's options narrow, RV parks and campgrounds—always with bathrooms, showers, and coin laundries—become homes. Folks struggling to put food on the table for their kids share spaces next to rich retirees, who might be towing a stainless steel barbecue the cost and size of a small car.

State or national parks offer the fewest amenities—but the best views. You're lucky if you can get a water line; it's very rare to have power. High-end campgrounds allow you to plug in not just water and electric, but sewer lines, cable TV, and telephone service.

The typical RV park is more "RV" and less "park" than we first thought. Some larger parks have five hundred to a thousand spaces. There may be trees dotted through these places, but for the most part they're parking lots with water and electric stands popping up every few feet. The showers, bathrooms, and laundries are usually in good shape, clean, located well. But it's not very verdant.

Once we're parked, though, we're home. There's a soft fabric cover that we connect to snaps that separates the cab of our rig from the back; and once that's in place, we don't even think about Winnie Cooper as a moving vehicle. We cook. We fire the computer up and tell folks where we are. We take a stroll through the park. We peer in at folks playing bingo in a small hall. We might take a shower, do some laundry, and then catch "Sex and the City" reruns before going to sleep.

When we got up this morning, I opened the blinds to the family next door. They were eating cereal out of plastic bowls, and the oldest two kids were putting on shoes and socks. Dad was buttoning up a blue work shirt that had "Chet" stitched above the pocket. On the furthest reaches of the park I could see a small yellow school bus weaving through the disappearing rows of RVs. It kept rolling until our neighbors flagged it down. The bus driver talked to the Dad for a bit while the two oldest kids filled a plastic bread bag with unwrapped sandwiches, an orange, and a banana.

Beth Ann Fennelly
Oxford, Mississippi

Beth Ann Fennelly has just finished a fifteen-page poem about kudzu, the climbing and unstoppable vine that covers millions of acres in Mississippi, Alabama, Tennessee, etc. Kudzu is a southern touchstone; and when my wife and I lived here in the mid-1980s, it seemed an exotic and frightening natural world element, too spooky and mysterious to ever fully understand. We left Mississippi after only about eighteen months, so its reappearance as we drove into the state last night set us thinking about the South, a place, a way of life, a varied and multifaceted landscape vastly more intriguing than the easy and lazy stereotypes that abound.

But Fennelly is from the North—suburban Illinois, specifically. So I wondered how she came to be here in Mississippi, and—more importantly—how she got so in touch with the evil vine.

We park alongside her home's huge corner lot, and Beth Ann greets me and lets me into her delightful and airy home just minutes after putting her daughter down for a nap. I sit opposite her, my back to an entire wall of book-filled shelves, white cupboards with glass doors.

She met her husband, the fiction writer Tom Franklin, in Arkansas, the furthest north Franklin had ever traveled (he's from Alabama) and the furthest south for her. After some years in Illinois, they've settled in Oxford, a hip and wonderful Mississippi town, home to the venerable college where Fennelly teaches, Ole Miss.

Fennelly tells me a little about kudzu, an Asian vine that grows best in the climate of the southeastern U.S., where it is free of its homeland's variety of pests and bugs. In the summer, the vine can grow a foot a day; and it does, obscuring fences, trees, power poles, sides of houses, etc. Most folks see it as a nuisance, but for Fennelly, it represents one of the things she loves about the South, its places, and people. The kudzu is mysterious. It covers up some things that would normally be too in the open, too easily seen. Like her favorite elements of Mississippi, the kudzu conceals some of what's underneath, leaving rich stories for writers to unearth. She believes that in her own work she's doing the same thing.

~ ~ ~ ~ ~ ~

How has place had an impact on your work?

For a long time I thought I was interested in place in my writing, but what I was interested in was places where I was not. I'd go to Krakow and write a poem about the salt mines or go to Japan and write a poem about the tea ceremony, but I never engaged with my native landscape of the Midwest; home was the negative. Then I went to the University of Arkansas for my MFA; and I fell in love with the South, the landscape, the mountains so old they're only hills, the lushness, the decay, the seething semitropical humidity, and giant blossoms and giant bugs. Although this landscape felt exotic, it also felt like home. I'm not sure why this is; my life prior to that point was mostly spent in a suburb of Chicago. It might have something to do with the fact that so many Scotch-Irish settled that part of the South. And many of the things I like about Irish heritage I also love about the South—the importance of storytelling, music, family, and celebrations. So I started writing about the landscape that I was in for the first time.

After I finished my MFA, I went back to the Midwest for three years, one at the University of Wisconsin, where I had a fellowship, and two years teaching at Knox College in Galesburg, Illinois. That's a prairie town, and I thought I would continue to write about the landscape around me, but I didn't. I remember making an effort to study the landscape and make myself love it. But I failed. People said it takes a while to see the beauty of the prairie, but I never did. Maybe it's too subtle for me.

We came down here to Mississippi, and I fell in love with landscape all over again. I just think it's something about the South that calls to me.

It may be that I'm so interested in writing about the landscape now because I really feel like I've finally found my long-term home. Other places where I lived, I knew it was just for a year or two. I wasn't going to get to know the neighbors or the neighborhood or the woods behind my neighborhood. But I think we'll stay in Oxford until they make us leave. We bought a home, and it feels so good not to be renters anymore—not to have checks with low numbers, not to have the phone number for U-Haul scrawled on the fridge. When I walk to the university past the graveyard and see Faulkner's grave, I imagine my own plot there some day. Graveyards never seemed comforting before.

And the final reason that the roots we've put down seem strong is that we're raising a family. The pace of life in the South is slower and more old-fashioned, and that's why it seems a good place to bring up Claire. I'm very conscious, however, of the downside of that. The South still feels twenty years behind the rest of the country in terms of human-rights issues. I've found more sexism and racism here. So my love of the place becomes problematized and challenged.

You've already noted that you come from a much different physical landscape. How different are the natural world elements of, say, Illinois and Mississippi?

Everything in the prairies was flat and straight, even the prairie-style architecture, which is really beautiful and features wide doorways and large fireplaces and big horizons, free of rococo scrolls and finicky flourishes. And I think that contributes to the character of the people there, who are very open, forthright, honest, practical, and down to earth, unironic, and pleasant. But I confess, I've always loved flourish, sequins, and boas, always loved the theatre and costumes; and that's what the landscape provides here. There's more room for mystery and convolutions. Skeletons in the closet. Even the way things are always draped with vines. There's a great sign outside of town that says, "Trespass," because the kudzu has covered the "No" and the "ing." And to me that just seems a metaphor because the landscape provides its own masquerade and doublespeak; it covers and reveals. There's a sense of play in the landscape.

Over the years, have you noted anything about the kind of physical or mental space or place you are in when you're writing?

When I was a real beginner, I would sometimes read in an interview where a writer would say things like "I can only write with a sea view" or "I can only write with a number two pencil on a yellow legal pad." I remember thinking that those writers sounded glamorous and had some secret knowledge; "If only I had a sea view and number two pencils . . . ." But now when I hear people say things like that, I think, "Oh, they have a trust fund and a maid." With teaching full time and traveling a good bit and raising a toddler, I can't allow my preferences to harden into necessities. I'd write with my Revlon Fire and Ice lipstick if I had to.

That being said, I've noticed I've moved progressively to quieter and quieter places. And that makes sense with the process of getting older—becoming an old married woman *(laughs)*—and having a baby. But I do think it's allowed me to find a kind of silence in myself that I've needed to nurture in my poetry. Maybe you can't write loud poetry unless you have a silence in yourself as a gauge.

from The Kudzu Chronicles

The Japanese who brought the kudzu
didn't bring its natural enemies,
those hungry beasties sharpening their knives,
and that's why kudzu grows best
so far from the land of its birth.

As do I, belated cutting, here
without my blights, without my pests,
without the houses or the headstones of my kin,
here, a blank slate, in this adopted cemetery,
which feels a bit like progress, a bit like cowardice.

When I die here,
for I sense this, I'll die in Mississippi,
state with the sing-songiest name
I remember learning to spell at six,

my singular stone will stand alone
among the Falkners and the Faulkners, the Mizes and the Avents,
the Neilsons and the Howorths, these clans which spill down hills,
angled and directional as schools of fish.

I'll be a letter of a foreign font,
what the typesetter used to call *a bastard.*

And even when my husband and daughter
are dragged down beside me,
their shared name won't seem to claim my own,
not to any horseman passing by.

Well, I wouldn't change that, I suppose.
It's just another compromise where no one fully wins.

Listen, kin and stranger,
when I go to the field and lie down,
let the kudzu blanket me, for I always loved the heat,
let its hands rub out my name, for I always loved affection
from the locals.

                                        —*Beth Ann Fennelly*

Natasha Trethewey
Decatur, Georgia

No city offers a more stunning transition from its ring of highways and interstates to its inner hub of suburban plots. Coming into Atlanta is like driving on the Ugly Highway to Ugly Town. The gray slabs extend to four and five lanes in every direction. Cloverleaf after cloverleaf—almost all of them under construction—web together endlessly. The pines that line the road obscure everything else that might resemble a place where one would want to spend some time; and the cars just hurtle onward, onward, deadeye stare, smoldering tires, eighteen-wheelers pinning you in one lane or the other.

But once you leave that behind—and in our case, skirt the southern bypass and then slip into Avondale Estates—large sweeping yards and one-story ranch houses line each road. Businesses cluster at intersections; but as soon as you leave them behind, you are back in another pleasant neighborhood. They all have churches with towering steeples, small parks with grinning kids. Houses are brick, surrounded by bushes and trees.

We find Decatur, another beautiful suburb. Natasha Trethewey has told us there's a church parking lot near her, and we find it easily. I stroll across the street to a two-story, weathered-brick building. It's from the '30s, was a boarding house for years, and is now a set of small but cozy condos. I poke my foot in the black dirt along a walkway and straighten some pink and yellow pansies that look like they're fixing to go across the road. When they're back in place, I go to the front door.

Natasha buzzes me up, and I meet her and her husband. We stand in their glittering kitchen—not just spectacularly clean, but ringed with stainless steel appliances—and then Natasha and I go and sit on two overstuffed couches in the living room.

She was born in Mississippi and now makes her home next door in Georgia. While she's spent time elsewhere, she's back home in a sense here in suburban Atlanta. She feels totally at ease in this pretty New South suburb.

~ ~ ~ ~ ~ ~

Do you think the places of your life had an impact on the poet you're becoming?

I do. I think that it's true for so many people who come out of Mississippi. If you're born into a place like that with that landscape and that history, because it's so troubled, it fuels you, trying to grapple with that beautiful and troubled history.

The landscape where I'm from—Gulfport, Biloxi, Ocean Springs—has the longest man-made beach in the world—twenty-six miles. It used to be a mangrove swamp, so they bulldozed that and dumped sand there to make it more like a beach resort you'd see in Florida. And that seems so metaphorical for me, because there's so much buried history—people's lives who have been left out of the public record and people whose lives have been erased. And if you look at the landscape, it suggests that. There's so much of the natural and man-made landscape of my home that reveals and conceals at the same time. For example, they've gotten rid of the swamp, put all this sand there, and then put all these sickly looking palm trees, trying to make it look like a different kind of beach. They point to and suggest something else that is beneath the surface. They point to a kind of evidence or a way to dig below and see below the layer of sand that's been dumped there.

You spent a great deal of your life in the South; has there ever been the thought in your head that you might not remain here?

I went to the Northeast for graduate school, and I lived in Massachusetts for six years. I often thought that I could have stayed. I didn't expect to come back to the South. When I did come back every year to see my grandmother, I came with a weird chip on my shoulder. After having been in the Northeast for a while, you begin to internalize ideas that Northerners have about the South; and I came down here with the same ones. *(Laughs.)* Not that there's nothing to complain about.

I think about the monuments. How the narrative that they have tried to impose upon the landscape is of the Confederacy. You see it in the town squares and public buildings that are named for Confederate heroes. The monuments, the graveyards, the flag still flying. That's the narrative that's been inscribed upon the landscape, and I think it takes a different kind of narrative to reveal what has been covered over. Narratives of Native Americans, for whom many of these states are named, the rivers. It's a weird contrast of the naming of those things and, say, the naming of roads. Jeff Davis Highway.

In your second book, Bellocq's Ophelia, *you write about the life of a New Orleans prostitute from the turn of the twentieth century. Obviously you had to do a fair amount of research, not just into Bellocq's photographs, but also into the time period.*

I did a lot of research. Gulfport is only about an hour from New Orleans. My father did his PhD at Tulane, so as a child I spent a lot of time in New Orleans. I had a certain image of it in my head and a certain idea of what things were like there. The climate, the way the air smells there. It has a scent that's different from anywhere else.

One thing I did was actually go and spend a month there, because I wanted to be reminded of all of that and to be reminded of that little thundershower that happens at the same time every day. And then it's gone, and it's sweltering. The photographs were my main documents, but I read actual published letters of a real prostitute who lived in Philadelphia—but at the same time—renamed "Mamie" for the collection. I read lots of histories of New Orleans, histories of prostitution, theories of prostitution. Histories and theories of photography.

I also read the kind of thing you might find in almanacs, stuff about the mosquitoes in a certain year. Stuff about sewage, the cisterns, stuff about rats in New Orleans. And the cockroaches!

Are there elements of the natural world that have a role in your work as a poet?

My landscape was always the natural world sliced or divided or undercut by a highway. The first place that I called home, and the place I return to the most, is my grandmother's home. Her house is in an area of North Gulfport that for a very long time was very rural. Highway 49 runs through it, but it was just a tiny little highway that blues singers would sing about. There were still lots of people who had farm animals around. I remember pigs underneath the house and chickens from someone's yard. Cows in the yard. And that changed rapidly when they built the new Highway 49. The old highway was on one side of her house, a few blocks away, but they built the new one right next to her house. Some men came and asked her—this must have been in the early '70s—if they could put up a billboard, and one of the big poles was going to be right in her yard. I think they paid her a hundred dollars a year for that.

That's what it was like for me. There was this rural world with fig trees, pecan trees, and persimmon trees, turtles. But there were eighteen-wheelers zooming through at the same time.

South

Homo Sapiens is the only species to suffer psychological exile.
—E. O. Wilson

I returned to a stand of pines,
                bone-thin phalanx

flanking the roadside, tangle
                of understory—a dialectic of dark

and light—and magnolias blossoming
                like afterthought: each flower

a surrender, white flags draped
                among the branches. I returned

to land's end, the swath of coast
                clear cut and buried in sand:

mangrove, live oak, gulfweed
                razed and replaced by thin palms—

palmettos—symbols of victory
                or defiance, over and over

marking this vanquished land. I returned
                to a field of cotton, hallowed ground—

as slave legend goes—each boll
                holding the ghosts of generations:

those who measured their days
                by the heft of sacks and lengths

of rows, whose sweat flecked the cotton plants
                still sewn into our clothes.

I returned to a country battlefield
        where colored troops fought and died—

Port Hudson where their bodies swelled
        and blackened beneath the sun—unburied

until earth's green sheet pulled over them,
        unmarked by any headstones.

Where the roads, buildings and monuments
        are named to honor the Confederacy,

where that old flag still hangs, I return
        to Mississippi, state that made a crime

of me—mulatto, half-breed—native
        in my native land, this place they'll bury me.
                          —Natasha Trethewey

Denise Duhamel
Hollywood, Florida

Denise Duhamel lives on the ocean under blue skies year-round. She lives in Hollywood, Florida, a place full of retirees and vacationers. But she's young, hip, working, and getting all of the benefits most of us dullards have to wait for until we're sixty-five. So it'd be easy to hate her if she weren't so wonderful—as wonderful as her work.

A Rhode Island native, she's logged her time in Boston and New York, so sunny climes are a gentle and wonderful reward for all of that. She tells me about some of her favorite writing spots—a local coffee shop, the wide and windblown boardwalk just north of her apartment, the beach itself, just steps away from her building.

Like some of the other writers I've met, Denise revels in the anonymity of a large, bustling city. She can escape in public places and take in the characters and stories available only to someone who's a great listener. She writes in notebooks while on the town, then comes home to her office to turn the scratchings into full-blooded poems.

In person, she's a dynamo, eager to talk about the powerful effect this newish place has on her work, her health, and her happiness. She's animated and lovely, and we sit in a large living room, where light pours in on us.

~ ~ ~ ~ ~ ~

How have the places of your life influenced the poetry that you write?

I grew up in Woonsocket, Rhode Island, a dying mill town of about forty thousand people, most of whom are French-Canadian. My first two hundred poems or so and a novel all took place there. I was then mostly concerned with "How do you get out of a small town?" There were no bookstores and only one movie theater. Very working class. Mostly barrooms and churches. And, even as a teenager, I just wanted to go to a Broadway show or something.

It was my childhood home, so all of those issues were there. I'm sure that I wrote in my journal from the age of ten to eighteen: "Get out, get yourself out!" *(Laughs.)* Also I censored myself back then because I thought, "Oh my God, what if someone finds this?" And I felt as though I was the only one who wanted out. "You don't want to live here? You snob. Who do you think you are?" There was so much shame growing up French-Canadian. And when you grow up a working-class kid, you want to be better, but not that much better. So it's comfortable; stay where you are.

But when I was six years old, my parents took us from Rhode Island to New York. And they said that at six I said, "Mom, why can't we live here? Why do we live in Woonsocket?" I just loved it.

So that's how your love affair with New York started. How have the cities of your life influenced you?

In my twenties I lived in Boston and New York. I wrote about New York while I lived there. Walking down the street from your apartment to the subway, getting to your job, might be ten poems. There's so much stimulus. There's something about the rhythms of walking, the rhythm of poetry. Sound overload. You hear ten sounds all at once. New York was my favorite place to write. You hear all these different languages. You eat a lot of different kinds of food. You see everyone from homeless people to gazillionaires. It's almost impossible not to write there. I wrote on the subways and buses and commuter trains; I was always writing. There was something about the vibrancy of New York. I could grow there as an artist.

And now I live in Miami, which is a car culture, and I'm not a very good driver because for a decade and a half I lived in urban areas. You can't drive and write at the same time, though the drivers in Miami are so erratic, I wouldn't be surprised if that's what some are doing. But I am still able to walk a lot because we live right on the ocean. And a few blocks up is a boardwalk, a big pedestrian walkway. And many times I take my notebook there and watch the people.

I've visited writers who definitely fall into one of two camps, city or country. You come from a small town but have lived your adult life in cities. What sort of perspective do you have on that axis?

City poets have to deal with more. Rural areas are usually about one or two cultures at the very most. So if you want to know how people speak in a small town in Arkansas, you can hang out there and get that in your blood. I can still get the Rhode Island diction down in two minutes, because I was steeped in it for eighteen years. I can do the French-Canadian accent.

But if you're in a city, it's polyphonic by nature. What you're hearing every day is this wide variety of voices. No matter where you live, if you want to do anything or get anything, you have to leave your neighborhood and go experience all these other different neighborhoods.

In a small town everything is right there for you. Of course, I hated that when I was a kid. But now I romanticize it. "Ahh, they help each other. Everyone knows each other." That is the positive side of small-town or country life. If you're in trouble, someone's going to help you. If you're living in a big city, you could be dead in your apartment for five days and nobody would know.

But if you're in a small town and you're the oddball, it's not so easy. My small town didn't embrace its oddballs. I think the South might have a different tradition with that. And in big cities, there are so many oddballs it's easy to feel at home.

Valentines, Hollywood Beach

That night we took a walk and saw a young couple eating dinner on a deck of one of the lifeguard huts. I imagined the boy ordering his girl's favorite takeout, picking it up at Giorgio's, and putting it, along with the wine, into a cooler; the girl shopping for plastic cups that didn't look too tacky, the right tablecloth, candleholders and candles. I imagined them lugging the card table and folding chairs into, and then out of, the trunk, and even if it meant two trips from the car to the hut, and the loads were heavy, and they had to run back a third time because one of them forgot the matches, look at them now, I thought—pillars of romance, the poster couple for how to do it right.

My husband squeezed my hand, forgiving our failure of imagination, vowing we would have a lifeguard hut, candlelit meal next year. He wore his vintage golf shirt even though he's never golfed. We climbed through the sand to the boardwalk where the oldies from Green Briar Condo waltzed on the cement around the pool, Frank Sinatra pumped in through the sound system, hotdogs and hamburgers flipped on the grill and served by man with a spatula and chef's hat. I saw a ghost couple hovering on lounge chairs. A few days ago, at a yard sale at the same condo, I bought my husband his Valentine's gift, a never-been-worn pullover shirt with a tiny golfer's silhouette sewn on the pocket.

The daughter, my age, was there to clean out the apartment, her mother dying only a few months later than her father, after being married fifty years. She'd spread her mother's dozens of Grasshopper sneakers on a ping-pong table in Green Briar's rec room. "I guess she bought all these through mail order," the daughter said proudly. She didn't know her mother could manage mail order by herself. According to the receipts, her mother had purchased them after her husband's death, her husband whose favorite movie was *Caddyshack*. I stared at the pastel shoes, the checkered ones, the stripes, the four identical pair of white, then turned over a pair to inspect their new pink rubbery soles. "I don't know where she thought she was going without my father," the daughter said. Such tiny feet, size five, or I would have bought them all.

—Denise Duhamel

Campbell McGrath
Miami Beach, Florida

Campbell and I are standing in front of his gorgeous garden home plugged serenely in a bucolic neighborhood in Miami Beach. He shows me two trees in his front yard, both planted and grown by him over the past ten years. One is a Royal Palm that is as big around as two bulldogs and must approach forty feet. It started as a stalk, not even waist high. The other palm is a little shorter, but thicker, and grown from a coconut that Campbell stuck in the ground ten years ago.

We go in Campbell's bright yellow home—under an arch, scooting past his sons' skateboards—and sit in the front room, the outside air wafting in through two elephant-eye-high gated windows that are open to the street.

Campbell's a Chicago transplant, but he's fully at home in Florida now after a decade. He's happy to call himself an urban poet, and his work has long explored the commercial landscape of America, the strip malls and convenience stores that are undeniable cultural and physical landmarks.

We talk about south Florida, a region that Campbell says is distinctly Latin, not like the American South at all. He's interested in it and his bilingual students who come to him with a dense mélange of cultures. Campbell tells me that a history of Florida's culture is something he went in search of when he first moved here, but he found it missing. It's as if the place developed and grew without a record being made of its spurts.

~ ~ ~ ~ ~ ~

How has place influenced your poetry?

That's a pretty good question for me because I write directly about place as a subject. And I have tended to move around a lot. So I've written a whole book about Chicago, and I've written a whole book about Florida. And places of all sorts are central to individual poems, from Brazil to North Dakota to Tunisia to Vanuatu.

Place is not something I strive to write about—it just manifests itself naturally. Richard Hugo was a poet whose work really influenced me when I was just learning about poetry, and his notion of the "triggering town" really resonated. It's not just landscape or geography that interests me but the sociological or sociopolitical aspects of place as well. The human and the natural worlds. Often I use place as a way of writing about larger cultural issues, as a way to consider America in particular.

At many levels, Chicago and Florida are so different. But they are two sides of the same coin; in Chicago you hide away from the weather for six months in the winter, and down here you hide away in the summer. The kinds of people who live here, the kinds of organizational patterns of the city, their histories, myths—and the natural world—everything is different. But that's kind of the point. To recognize what the diversity of America is really like, you need to hold both Miami and Chicago in your mind, along with North Dakota, New Mexico, and Maine. And you would need to understand each of those places, which obviously I do not. But I have tried to understand certain places. I write poems about place, about the physical world, because I'm trying to document it, so that I can understand it.

Specifically, what are your thoughts on Florida?

Living in south Florida is like living on a different planet, just in terms of the physicality alone—the light, the moisture, the colors of the flowers and sky. I feel like a different person here. So writing about Florida was also an internal act, at first: a response to the world around me. But *Florida Poems* did become, at some levels, a book written for an audience. When you start to research Florida, you learn how little has been written about it. It's so new, and little that matters has happened here; and few people have really bothered to think about it much. And historically the various regimes have systematically erased the record of the previous regimes: the Spanish erased the Indians, the English the Spanish, the Americans the English, and the current-day Americans are busily erasing the presence of the last generation. So writing about Florida also became an act of creating a cultural record of a mysterious and undocumented place. It was written to Floridians, at some level. And when I read those poems around Florida, I get a very strong response and recognition; and when I read them other places, I often get—"Hmm, what's that all about?"

In some sense, I was trying to locate or create a creation myth for Florida. The Fountain of Youth is that myth, that great image—and the fact that it's illusory is all the better. But what I decided, I guess, is that it isn't fictive, it's actual. First of all, the physical "fountains" exist—they are these fantastic springs that Florida is famous for up in the central and northern part of the state. Just last week I was up at Blue Spring, near Orlando, swimming with my kids in the gorgeous spring, when a manatee came up the spring run, and we got to swim with it. And then at another level, youth itself is the fountain of youth. Florida's very youthfulness, its human potential, is a cultural fountain of youth. Florida is still becoming whatever it is going to be—it's a kind of gawky adolescent, but not yet fully grown. And Florida is going to have to decide "Are we going to pave it all over" or what?

You're on record as being a big fan of the 7-Eleven as a sort of cultural icon of huge importance. Are you still captivated by it?

This is the only place I've ever lived where there aren't that many 7-Elevens! The chain isn't big down here. Seven-Elevens were part of a younger, urban identity for me. Everywhere I lived—Washington, Chicago, Los Angeles—you conducted much of your life at the 7-Eleven. That's where you got things. If you needed to get a beer. If you needed to get money. If you needed to get a Slurpee. That's where it was.

To understand American culture, you have to focus on its commercial aspects. The country is an empire of commerce. It's nice to see the historians validating this notion again right now. In a way, Wal-Mart has replaced the 7-Eleven, as it has replaced and displaced so much. 7-Eleven has turned out to be too small for contemporary tastes. You can only get a certain amount of stuff there and how much further is it to Wal-Mart, where you can get Slurpees and snow tires and groceries and whatever. These kinds of corporate changes indicate deeper cultural changes, obviously, and so they attract my interest. Wal-Mart is "landscape," that's what I'd say.

Terrance Hayes
Columbia, South Carolina

Our appointment to meet with Terrance Hayes in Pittsburgh, where he lives with his wife (the poet Yona Harvey) and their two kids, is more than a month away. But I get an email from him telling me he'll be at a book fair in his hometown of Columbia, South Carolina, about the time we'll be headed through there. We decide to make new arrangements and capitalize on geographic fate. All of this planning goes on while we're on a brief break down in Key West, Florida. We reluctantly pull out a day or two early, leaving behind the little electric cars the tourists rent to zip from bar to bar and saying good riddance to the always-present packs of aggressive roosters that have inundated that town.

When Terrance arrives in Columbia, he calls to tell me that he's brought his nine-month-old son on the trip—to allow the grandparents some time to dote and fuss. He figures we should find some place to meet other than his house, which will be busy and noisy. I think of the relatively cramped quarters of Winnie Cooper and tell him we'll be at the first Holiday Inn I run across. The next day we splurge on a king-size suite and park Winnie Cooper by some dumpster behind the hotel.

In addition to the displacement of being out of the motor home, it's the first time a poet is coming to me on this trip. Usually we're circling some foreign neighborhood, running over curbs, and consulting a map of our own evil design, arriving with a giant bag of recorders and cameras, bowling over any children or animals who may be too confused or slow to clear a way.

There's a sense that we've abandoned the journey, but the promise of a "free continental breakfast" convinces me we're doing the right thing. My wife takes a cab to a nearby mall, and I set up my cameras and recorders and wait. When Terrance arrives, we talk about his being back home for a visit, his reading coming up, and the trip I'm on. We sit at the chintzy hotel room table and talk about poetry, Pittsburgh, sports, his painting, et cetera.

A word Terrance uses early on is "compartments." He is able to keep the parts of his life and work separate from one another, sort of like—he says—the greens and the potatoes on a plate of food. He's a teacher and a writer, a poet and a painter. He acknowledges that these things have something to do with one another but doesn't always see vital or obvious connections.

~ ~ ~ ~ ~ ~

I haven't seen many poets in their hometowns. Most of them I find in adopted hometowns or even in places where they're just visiting for a year or so. What is it like for you—on this trip and others—to be home in Columbia?

I've lived out of this state now almost as long as I lived in it, so with these latest visits—more and more time seems to pass between them—it's always a matter of getting used to the place again. I don't know if I ever thought of it as a permanent home though. My dad was in the military, and we moved around quite a bit. So returning, even my parent's home is a strange, vaguely familiar place. I stumble a lot in the house. I stumble coming down the stairs. "Was that stair there?" I get lost even driving to old hangouts.

These few years removed, is South Carolina still in you; does it seep into your poetry?

Interestingly, in the last year or so I've been writing more about South Carolina as a physical place. It's a curious thing.

I've been asked, on more than one occasion, "Where did you grow up?" And when I say, "Down one hill there was a cow pasture and up the other hill was a horse ranch," folks look surprised since those kinds of things are nowhere in my work. I never paid attention to any of it. I'd see people riding horses right through my backyard. There was a lake not far off. But what I remember are people. Friends. Girlfriends. We played in the woods and all that, but it never had any real impact on me that I could mark. Most of my poetry is about people, characters, and figures. In that way my poems are like my paintings. I think I'm interested in the body, the personality—in memory as a kind of place. I've been thinking more about it recently though. I've tried to write specifically about South Carolina. One method I'm using now is beginning with the landscape and letting that shape the poem. There was this abandoned house where people would go to make out *(laughs),* and so I thought about that house, the tree limbs reaching through the windows, the splintered shabby porch, the sunlight coming through the roof. There was no path to get to it. Typically, such a poem would have started with something about goofing off there with my friends.

You've been in Pittsburgh now for a while. Is there something about cities and their energy that works for or against you when you write?

What I most value about living in a city is my access to so many different communities; the chances to float between them. In Pittsburgh I'm able to go into almost any circle—and even when I was there as a grad student, that was the case. I had a circle of friends in the university. But I had a circle of other writing friends, and a circle of musician friends, a circle of basketball friends, a circle of knucklehead friends. In South Carolina I have my family and the friends I've known since childhood. I don't meet many new people when I visit; and I think my work, the poems and the paintings, are limited by this. Or have seemed so in the past. I'd like to think that would change if I spent more than a week or two here.

Threshold

No steps remained, but we did not leap
from the knee-high grass of that house
abandoned in the woods to the porch

with the planks that were as loose and warped
as those of a small boat beached long ago
by someone who rowed one last time

from a lake in a kind of reverse drowning,
the kind that calls one permanently to land
when some one has been lost, the water opening

indifferently and closing in the same manner
until even the oar strokes were traceless,
the boat left to become more and more

vaguely like the ribs of something that lived once,
that had purpose, but now could not hold a body,
could cradle nothing except the occasional rain

and wind as we cradle our breaths—
the warped, narrow wood of the porch
reached past us, me and the daughter of a man

who had been like me, who had been young
when this house was new and warmed by people
we would not ever know except by way of a black sock

someone had used to wipe away shit or semen
and left in the corner before going out again
to the porch and yard to sink

into the will of what ever else makes up the woods.
Seeing the sock then told me some of the possible history
of the world around us: that others had come here,

probably the girl's older brother had been hiding here
while their father knocked at almost every door
in our neighborhood looking for him one night,

and maybe the cool somber-jawed drop outs
had been here, and other couples
who could not afford hotels,

others had left crushed and uncrushed cans
and clouded bottles and stick porn and mottoes
and aliases on the walls, they'd left their smell too

and the roof seemed to want to guard it
though when the windows were smashed,
the doors kicked open, some of their scents

had been swept into the woods where it met the two of us
approaching with nothing but our caution
and green irrevocable hunger, and we could see it

would not hold us, the old porch,
so we did not leap from the knee high grass
to get in, we stepped as lightly as others had crossing

planks that splintered and cried out
as if to the old house and maybe to the deep, deep woods
and to the path others had not intended to leave.

—Terrance Hayes

Alan Shapiro
Chapel Hill, North Carolina

We are in Chapel Hill between winter "events." Snow lies alongside roadways and mounds up six feet high in parking lots. Tomorrow freezing rain is expected, but today is nothing but blue skies and temperatures in the forties. It's hard to believe that four days ago we were sweltering in Key West.

We roll into a picturesque neighborhood just north of the University of North Carolina. Bare trees tower above us as we meander down a thin neighborhood road. We find the driveway to Shapiro's house and don't even think about turning down it. I load up the equipment and head off on foot while my wife begins the process of looking for a place to turn around.

I knock on the door, but nobody comes for a minute. I hear music coming from the backyard and make my way toward it. I pass some stunning seven-foot-tall metal sculptures, salvaged metal welded into figures reaching up.

In the shed I see Callie Warner, Shapiro's wife. She emerges from a smoking piece of metal that she and her assistant are working on. She takes off her work glove and shakes my hand, offers to lead me back to the main house to see Alan.

We go in; and after we all chat a bit about the trip, Alan and I take a tour around the house. He shows me several of Callie's pieces—furniture, a breathtaking dining-room table made of metal, some paintings. He tells me something about each piece, and he's as proud of the work as if it were his own.

But, of course, he's an artist too, a tremendous poet and essayist, whose work unstintingly peers into human relationships to uncover the elements worthy of praise or investigation. His collection of essays, The Last Happy Occasion, *shows Shapiro at the height of those particular powers.*

We go into his study and sit facing each other, the backyard framed by a large window that Shapiro admits usually closing tight with heavy drapes when he writes. We talk about the psychological landscapes that make up the work, the interiors where his characters play tense and beautiful scenes.

~ ~ ~ ~ ~ ~

You're a northerner who's lived in North Carolina for almost twenty years. What kind of relationship do you have with the South?
I was dragged kicking and screaming. My aversion to the South was based entirely on ignorance and provinciality. I didn't know anything about it except the clichés I got through the media. I didn't think it would be a place very hospitable to a Jew. One thing that I was afraid of, and it's true, is there are no sidewalks. Nobody walks. There's no public transportation. It's bedroom communities, and you have to live in your car; and I hate that. I grew up in a city where it was an inconvenience to own a car. And I liked getting on a trolley, getting on a bus, and going anywhere you wanted.

But when my marriage fell apart, there was no way that I could leave since my ex-wife and I had joint custody of our two children. My son is with me and Callie full time, and my daughter goes half time with us and my ex-wife. It's unthinkable that I would move.

What do you tell others about the South?
One is that the cliché about southern hospitality is true. People are extremely hospitable and generous. Of course, we live in a cosmopolitan pocket of North Carolina here in the Triangle *(Raleigh, Durham, and Chapel Hill).* But North Carolina also is the state that sent Jesse Helms to the Senate time and time again, and there's a strong conservative redneck element to the area. But it's not all there is. Most of the people who live here now come from elsewhere.

But the other thing I find truly attractive here is the relationship between the races. In fact, it's the exact opposite of what I imagined before I came down here. I imagined, when I lived in Chicago—as if that was a city of racial harmony, not to mention Boston, I mean where whites and blacks are often at each other's throats—that the South was still the South of the antebellum era. Of utterly oppressed black people and utterly racist white people. And that is simply not the case. There's the racism you'd have anywhere, but there's much more intimacy between the races here. Whites and blacks live together and interact in ways that simply don't happen in the north.

I had a friend I played basketball with in high school, a black kid named David Williams, who still lives in Boston. He had moved to Boston from South Carolina as a freshman, and that's how we met. A few years after I moved down here, I went back to Boston to give a poetry reading, and David and I got together and we were talking about the differences between north and south. He said that in the North the white man will let you rise but won't let you get close and that in the South he'll let you get close but not let you rise. There is more intimacy here, and I value that greatly.

There were tremendous surprises that I had in store in living here. And, of course, now I'm married to a southern woman, so I married the South.

What about your work habits and the time you spend in this office at the job? What's your relationship like with this room?

Working is the one place I go to feel at home. It's the one place that hasn't changed. My home has changed, my work has changed, but the joy of working hasn't changed. (John) Keats says, "In times of difficulty, our objects of desire become a refuge as well as a passion." Writing, working, reading, sitting at the desk has become as much a refuge as a passion.

When my brother died in 1999, his death coincided with the disintegration of my marriage. I had always assumed that I was going to be somebody's brother, and suddenly I was nobody's brother. I had always assumed I was going to be my ex-wife's husband, and now I was nobody's husband. I always assumed I would be somebody's son, and my parents' health was so precarious at the time that I felt that soon I would be nobody's son. So I wondered, "What am I still?" What sources of continuity did I have? I still had my children; I was still a father. I was still a basketball player, so I played a lot of basketball. And I was still a writer. I could write. I could go to my desk and write, and I could find the kind of joy and solace that I could find nowhere else.

But the muse is a very jealous mistress. When we're not writing, most of wish we were. The problems I've had with girlfriends and wives have never been infidelity or restlessness. It's always been, "All you want to do is work. You never want to be with me." And in a way, it's true. Because the experience of writing is so profoundly satisfying.

So all of that is awful and frustrating. And so why do we do it? Because it feels so damn good to do it. So good to be in that place, that hallucinatory Zen state of mind that we get into when we're working. Writing is a way of being happy, a way of being at home.

Bower

Our bedroom in a small
house in an old
forest where trees
lean down over
trees around
this opening
that they enclose—

neither apart
from the world, nor
altogether
in it, of it,
where what comes
to us comes through
what holds it back,

scrimshaw of leaves
on leaves, the farthest
stirred by breezes
we can hear
but don't yet feel
through the open

window where
the drawn curtain
too is stirred
and lifted like
a breeze-shaped
vagrant boundary
set to make

what's coming in
to us come more keenly,
not to keep it out.
Shadow of leaves
commingling
with the single
shadow of our bodies

stirred and lifted
on the lifting
scrim between what's
near and far,
inside and out,
all held now
and slowly moving

toward the sudden rush
of downpour and
love cry becoming
bird call sifting
in the plush dripping
of the downpour's
aftermath.

—*Alan Shapiro*

Nikki Giovanni
Blacksburg, Virginia

Nikki is wearing a medal when I meet her at her office on the campus of Virginia Tech. Her poetry has won almost uncountable awards, plaudits, and honors, but this is an actual medal. It's from the National Academy of Recording Arts and Sciences, and Nikki received it earlier this week at the annual Grammy Awards dinner in Los Angeles. Her spectacular spoken word release of The Nikki Giovanni Poetry Collection *lost; but the nomination, the medal, and the good seats she had (near Carole King) made the trip a great success.*

She's wearing the medal because her students wanted to see it. Just before our chat starts, she even gets a call from a student who wants to know about the medal. Did she wear it to class? Did the other students like it? Was Nikki on TV? Nikki answers the questions, reminds the student to turn her paper in, and has to admit that she never got her mug on the TV. And it's too bad, because it's a great mug—open and vital.

On the walls of her office she displays posters of Tupac Shakur, Bob Marley, and Prince, and her long love of music fills her work in the same way. I can see the campus out her window behind her. The blinds are wide open, and the sun on this seasonable winter afternoon pours in, lighting up Nikki from behind, giving her spectacular white-platinum hair a real glow.

~ ~ ~ ~ ~ ~

How has place affected your work as a poet?

Well, actually it's been the same place. It's all Appalachia, because Cincinnati sits at the top of Appalachia. I was born in Knoxville, Tennessee, and I've only moved four hours due east into Blacksburg. Essentially it's been the same place.

As an adult I lived in New York for eleven years, which I totally enjoyed. And if my father hadn't fallen ill, I'd probably have stayed. New York is a fabulous place for writers because so much is available to you. And so much of what any writer does is this recall thing, and memories don't really change. You don't even have to go back. Of course, I go back to Knoxville and Cincinnati, one of the great hidden cities of America. Great restaurants, great ballgames. In a sense, I've never really left Cincinnati or Knoxville, and I've been here in Blacksburg for sixteen years.

My sense of place, in other words, has not been violated. Ernest Gaines, who has been a friend and a nice man, spent a lot of time in California. But Ernest talks about leaving Louisiana "in time." He says, "If I had left Louisiana later, I'd have been beaten down. If I'd left Louisiana earlier, I wouldn't have remembered." And I was always enchanted by him looking at his childhood that way. I think that my relationship with Knoxville, Cincinnati, and—now—Virginia has been essentially on time. I have reached a point that I can utilize the knowledge that I have.

You're certainly in demand as a visitor, and I know you travel a lot. What's hard about taking yourself out on the road so much?

Holiday Inn's a fine hotel. I'm not knocking it. Because Holiday Inns are just like McDonald's. Whenever you buy McDonald's on earth, you're going to get the same thing: two all-beef patties, special sauce, and you know the rest. But you wake up in the Holiday Inn in Johannesburg or in Buffalo, New York, or Portland, Oregon. It doesn't matter. It's always the same. You never know where you are.

I had a friend tell me, "I always sleep in my watch." We're all old road warriors, so we're always sharing tips. And I asked, "Why?" And he said, "At least I'll always know what time it is." Because there's nothing worse than waking up and not knowing.

But I thought, "I need to get out of staying in Holiday Inns." If you can stay in a Hyatt, or a Ritz, or a Four Seasons, they're all different; and you'll wake up in a room that is not what it was the other night. I've just come back from Los Angeles. I had dinner in the hotel and signed the bill to room 312, which I'm going to remember now because that was the room I had the night before in Hartford, Connecticut. My room in Los Angeles was actually 507, but it didn't dawn on me until I went to the third floor to get into my room and the key wouldn't work *(laughs)*.

There's a poem in one of your recent books about space travel. That's a place I haven't been to on this trip. What interests you about it?

I'm a futurist. I'm so in love with space and the possibilities that it offers. I'm a University Distinguished Professor. And I sit in a meeting with the man who discovered the crystal that proves there was water on Mars. It's so thrilling. He wears his khakis, and he's, "Yeah, I'm just a scientist." But, of course, there's water on Mars. What do you think the icecaps are about? We just can't get it back to the surface because the surface is a little bit colder than what we know it to be.

But we're going to Mars because they're our neighbors, and it's possible. And even if we found nothing there, we know that there's life on Mars because we'll be on Mars. Some people say, "Well, we can't survive." Well, I don't know if we can survive *here*. I know that we have to get over things like oil, because we can't keep killing people because you want to drive a Humvee getting two miles to the gallon. What kind of sense is that? There are people hungry on earth, but our response is, "Well, I want an eighty-thousand-dollar Humvee."

If they send people to Mars soon, do you think a poet should go?

Oh, God. A black poet. I'm going to be specific. A little old lady. That would be lovely. Toni Morrison always says that a black woman is both a ship and a safe harbor. And I always loved that description because if anybody could go into the heavens and light on a star and be well received, it'd be a black woman. And definitely I would carry a beer, because my mom drinks beer, and I would never go that far without one. I'd pop a beer *("shpeeeee"—making noise of beer opening)*. "Hey, anybody here? Come here, sugar, what's your name?" Because that's what my grandmother would do. And everybody feels the comfort of a black woman. So I think we need a black woman in space, an older one.

Charles Wright
Charlottesville, Virginia

Wright has been a titanic figure in American letters for forty years, and his most recent work continues to amaze. I appear at his three-story home in Charlottesville on absolutely the crummiest weather day of the trip. It's 30 degrees, and it's been raining for nine hours. Trees and power lines are ice coated. The main streets are clear and wet, but the small road in front of Wright's house is like a skating rink.

I'm in a rented car. It'd be impossible to steer Winnie Cooper through this.

I slide into the circular driveway in front of the gorgeous and imposing gray house, and Wright waits for me on the porch. He's a little surprised I'm sans hat, umbrella, galoshes, and such. We go inside the dark and warm first floor, and he leads me up two flights of stairs to his study.

We emerge into the spacious attic, really more like an entire floor of the house, shaped like a cross with four annexes to the outside world. Wright's lived in the house for twenty years. It was the previous owner— an artist—who fixed up this great floor.

I spot a large table in the center of the room and begin getting equipment out. The furniture up here is lovely and heavy, and I'm afraid to sit in any of it as I'm soaked from the weather. I notice a little beaten-down chair next to a small table in one of the nooks and ask Wright if I can use it. He nods. It will be in the middle of the interview below that I realize—when Wright points to the table where he writes all of his poems in longhand—that this is his chair, the one he sits in when he works.

~ ~ ~ ~ ~ ~

How has place affected your work as a poet?

The places of my life, the geographical places, have started, sustained, and—ultimately—will end my poems. I write out of landscape; I write out of what I see, not out of what I make up. Although what I make up comes out of what I see. Every poem I start comes out of something that I'm looking at or have seen or thought about seeing. Even the places that are behind the places that I've been—in other words, the more nontactile landscapes that I tend to write about—come out of the landscapes that I look at.

I started writing in Italy when I was in the Army, because I was taken by what I was seeing; it was so different from what I was used

190

to seeing in Appalachia—east Tennessee and western North Carolina where I grew up. Then for several years I wrote out of that experience; and then suddenly one day I realized that I had a past and a childhood, and it all came sort of flowing into me, through me, and out of me, I guess. My madeleine is a pine cone. It brought back the landscapes of my childhood.

And wherever I've gone, I've written out of those landscapes. For years when I lived in California, I wrote about east Tennessee and western North Carolina, my remembered landscapes. As soon as I moved back here to Virginia twenty years ago, I never wrote another poem about them, those places of my childhood. Until recently, when I realized it was those remembered landscapes, still, and I was doing it at firsthand instead of secondhand. You always want all of your landscapes, your poems, and your imagination to seem firsthand, even though most of it—and most of us—use secondhand experiences to write out of.

Virginia was basically the old landscape, a laundered and crisped-up version. Much brighter and luminous than it was. I had a very nice childhood. We lived—for a child—in very interesting places. Probably not for my poor mother because they were out in the woods, on TVA *(Tennessee Valley Authority)* dams, Oak Ridge, Tennessee *(the site of the Oak Ridge National Laboratory, established in 1943 as a part of the secret Manhattan Project),* during the war. All of these places that were fascinating for a kid.

I wrote about that, and then—as the years went by—it began to stand in for what was beyond that landscape, an imaginary landscape, a more spiritual venue.

Do you think your poetry is a way in which you try to make sense of where you are in the world?

Ultimately, yes. That's what I came to understand it to be. In the immediacy of it all, it was something so different. Ever since college—really since puberty on—I had had this desire to write. But I didn't know how in the hell to do it. And back in Davidson College in the '50s they didn't have any courses, so I didn't know anything about it. But I had this great yearning; and it spilled over into something tangible there in Italy, and I began writing letters home to my mother about it. And I started reading some poems, and I began to think, "Maybe I could do it this way."

So I found the lyric poem. I was reading the selected poems of Ezra Pound, and I found a poem about the place where I was, Lake Garda, Sermione Peninsula. Then I got the fever. And once you get the fever, it never goes away. So, as they say in the narratives *(laughs),* one thing led to another; and there I was, thinking about it all the time.

Do you think poets have an obligation to write about their surroundings, the places of their lives?

I don't know. Since that's all I really know about, that's what I write about. Mark Strand, for example, who's a good friend of mine and a wonderful poet—a great poet of our generation—grew up in Nova Scotia and other places. But Mark mostly writes out of his head. Recently he's written some poems about his childhood, but I don't think that he feels obligated to write out of where he was. Another friend, Charles Simic, certainly does. He writes about Yugoslavia a lot. I don't think it's my bounden duty to do so, but it's what I keep turning back to; and it's the one thing that seems to spring me beyond it.

Are there certain elements of the natural world that have an impact on your writing process?

The natural world is my process. It just is. When I moved here from California, I started writing poems set in my backyard. I never wrote poems set in my backyard any other time in my life. I didn't have a backyard most of the time in California. In Italy, my backyard was the Italian landscape in a larger sense. As for Appalachia, it was the whole spread and flood and overflow of memory. Now Montana—the valley where we have a place in the summer—has become my new backyard. But I'm writing the same poem I did when I started writing forty-five years ago in Italy. I find the same kind of poem. Of course, some might say, "He's writing the same damn poem; I wish he'd stop." *(Laughs.)* But I can't stop.

High Country Spring

It's not so much the description, it's what you describe,
Green pox on the aspen limbs,
Lilac bud-bursts set to go off,
                              suppuration of late May.

The world is a tiny object, a drop of pine sap,
Amber of robin's beak, like that,
                              backlit by sunlight,
Pulling the glow deep inside.

                              —*Charles Wright*

Choosing

About a third of the poets I meet ask, "Why me?" It's a fair question, but I don't think I've ever given a completely satisfactory answer.

The work of some poets just screams out "place" to me. Poets like Miller Williams, for example. It's always been impossible for me to read his work without feeling the South in every line. So I sought out many poets like this when I was first putting the list together. I wasn't trying to stack the deck in favor of the conceits of my book, but I did want to talk to some folks who would think that the question "Has place influenced your work?" was a satisfying and enjoyable place to start a conversation.

Sometimes it was just geography. In the beginning I had a huge road atlas in front of me. I knew we'd be traveling thousands of miles through countless towns, and since we were passing through so many areas, why not talk to someone? I will confess that there are some poets I've met this year whom I hadn't read before this trip, and lucky geography has led me to them. One of these poets is David Romtvedt. Our route was taking us to his part of Wyoming, and I happened across his name. I read some poems online, loved them, and I'm very grateful I took the time to contact him and visit his picturesque little town.

Since I went to college in the late' 70s and early '80s, many of the writers I studied are now part of the established and older generation of poets. Because I wanted a good cross section, I knew I'd need to find younger poets as well. It's easy to pick someone who's been in the game awhile and has fifteen collections. It's a little harder to find someone more or less just starting out. But as the overall list was being created, I began to work on adding younger poets. It was in this way that I discovered Beth Ann Fennelly and others like her.

Some poets I wanted to meet with disqualified themselves by noting that place just wasn't a concern for them. They didn't see how they'd fit into the book's conversation. Some poets have bowed out because they were too busy finishing books, doing research, teaching, dealing with new children, etc. Sometimes it just was simple bad timing—poets on sabbatical, poets out of town during the week I was going through their area. When a number of poets from one area couldn't meet with me, it left a few blank spots on our map—the Bay area of California for one, upper New England for another. And then, of course, time itself worked against us. There were finite amounts of time and cash for the trip, and those occasionally stopped us from traveling further and staying longer to catch up with folks.

Finally, I can say that the process of choosing poets for the book has been a fascinating challenge. It's a rigorous thing I'm asking. Not just "Let me ask you some questions," but "Let me into your home and your poetry and allow me some time to root around in there."

I correspond with the writers ahead of time, get directions, ask some preliminary questions, and sometimes ask the poet to look at his or her own work with an eye for things that might be useful in our conversation. When I arrive, I have a large bag of equipment that I spill out on the couch—three cameras, two tape recorders, notepads and books in quantity. Not only do we sit for the formal interview, but oftentimes poets show me around the house or the neighborhood. I often take the writer outside to a nice spot and shoot a dozen or so photos.

And then in the aftermath we exchange as many as a dozen emails as I work toward an accurate and interesting transcript of our chat. It's been—as the poets will tell you—a protracted investment of time and energy. I know I started the project somewhat naively, but in the midst of it, it seems like the only fair way to go about this job is the way it has worked out. The poet and I wrestle with the ideas and the words until we've accurately captured the special things that place brings to the poet's work.

Additionally, because of the tireless schedule we're on, I often arrive at a poet's home after driving 200 miles. There may be another 200 miles to go later that same day. My wife is in the motor home circling the narrow streets of the poet's neighborhood while we talk. I occasionally forget what town we're in—or what state. I have asked poets questions about poems they didn't write and towns they never lived in—a result of my ever-increasing piles of research that clutter Winnie Cooper and my own brain.

But throughout, the poets are happy to have been chosen, and I feel lucky that in some way they've chosen me.

Rita Dove
Charlottesville, Virginia

Rita Dove lives in a spectacular and quiet neighborhood outside Charlottesville. In the directions to her house are these words: field, meadow, ivy, pond, lane, hills, and rolling. I stand outside the house and look down at this little body of water behind her house. It's partially covered with ice, but the sun is beaming down on it, shining up mad shards, erratic ribbons of light.

Rita and her husband, the writer Fred Viebahn, greet me, and we try to remember the details of the first time we met two decades ago when I was a panicked undergraduate psychology major seeking a transfer into the English department. Rita was new at Arizona State, and she drew the short straw and got me as a charge.

After we all catch up a bit, Fred goes off to his study, and Rita and I sit in the living room on large white couches. There's a piano in the corner. An acoustic guitar leans against the wall behind an occasional chair. Rita looks exactly like she did twenty-two years ago. She smiles at some of the memories I recall at the beginning of our chat. I'm trying to give her a sense of how important that first visit was, without making too much of a fool of myself. My life changed that day. I gave away one path—one that I thought would please my parents—and took charge of doing something for myself. I chased a dream that was my own, a dream (reading and writing?) without obvious and sensible rewards. And the past two decades were possible only because Rita helped me fill in some forms.

Rita is a brilliant poet, one of extraordinary grace. Her books are rich, textured, funny, beautiful, honest, fearless, enlightening, and—always—sharply wrought. Her poems swirl into life and then explode into clarity with one final line or stanza. Sometimes they end with just the right word.

She is one of the most admired and honored poets of her generation, a Pulitzer Prize winner, a Poet Laureate. She has collected awards and achievements of a remarkable range. But one thing she tells me today obscures all the rest: she and Fred are ballroom dancers.

She talks about a wild notion that drove them and their neighbors into some lessons. She and Fred were the only ones who stuck it out, and now they dance in the style of the "American Smooth," a somewhat loose interpretation of the arcane and rigid rules of classical ballroom dancing. The foxtrot. The waltz. Samba. They have outfits. I've seen photos. Fred in a tuxedo, his flowing gold mane blurred in motion, Rita in a spangly purple number, caught mid-spin.

~~~~~~

How have the places of your life influenced your work?

It's a big question, because it changes according to where I move. I think I've detected a pattern. It takes me a long time to write about the place that I'm in. It took me a while to figure that out, because I like to keep all these processes buried, until they finally say, "Look at me."

I'm profoundly influenced by place. One of the primary reasons for moving to Virginia was that it was so beautiful; the whole area spoke to me. *Thomas and Beulah* was influenced by Akron, Ohio, though it took me many years to recognize my hometown as a place that was possible for poetry, because Akron, Ohio—and I don't mean to put it down—is not a pretty place. It's a busy place, an industrial place, but it didn't seem to have poetry in it.

I was living out of a suitcase somewhere in Europe when I reread Rilke's *Letters to a Young Poet;* in one of those letters he says—I'm paraphrasing madly—if you can't pull forth the riches of a place, don't blame the place, blame yourself, because it is you who are not rich enough to pull them. And it hit me like a lightning bolt, and I thought, "I have Akron. I've got to do Akron."

I think Virginia's influence is finally coming out in my next book. What fascinated me about this place initially, when I came to look it over, was how many American myths seemed to converge here. It was Thomas Jefferson—dear, conflicted Thomas Jefferson—who built the University of Virginia, who built Monticello, and at the same time had slaves, fathered slaves, the whole shebang. The Declaration of Independence! All of that stuff is here.

Though I loved Arizona, one of the things that began to get to me was that everyone was new there. There was history with the Indians, but the plate I was working off of was clean, tabula rasa. In Arizona I did not even experience that much racism, covert or otherwise. Everyone came from somewhere else, so everyone was friendly; you could just sail through life. Not that I'm a masochist, but I used to stand there, look at the eternally blue sky, and think, "This is la-la land!" Now, I don't experience much racism in Virginia either—because racism has a lot to do with class, and when you become an intellectual, you're in a whole other category. But here I see the consequences

of racism; I see the history, the past, and the guilt. What wonderful material for a writer.

There's a fairly recent poem of yours with these lines: "Who am I kidding? Here I am." I get the feeling that you're really content here. Is this the place for you?

As soon as I say that, I'll probably move! But, yes, I'd say so. This is where I feel good. That doesn't mean I won't go off, like you have, for a year or so to travel around. But this is where I'm going to come home to. I can't explain it; from the first moment I walked into this house, it felt right. Charlottesville, too. It's a wonderful place to be, a wonderful place to write in. There's enough distraction to irritate me, and I love my students. But I also love this specific spot on the earth.

Our house burned down in 1997, and we rebuilt it right on the same spot. After it burned down, the memory of the fire and going through the ashes also became part of this place. And it feels fine. It feels good. The fire was not about loss, though we did lose things. I was lucky in that most of the writing I was working on was in my cabin out back. My study in the house was water damaged, and all I lost was a couple of notebooks.

The fire was about recovery. It was about discovering things again. I'm not going to say it was a picnic, but there were more moments of joy than there were of despair. What I remember is standing outside for the first couple of hours. Lightning had struck the roof, and the attic was burning. I remember standing there watching the flames. As the rooms ignited one by one, I discovered there was a heck of a lot I could live without. I would say, "Okay, I can live without that." But wonderful things were saved from the start. Like our photo albums happened to be on this floor, and the firemen covered them with tarps to save them from the water damage. They saved everything on this floor, including the piano, by lugging everything outside before they had to break holes in the ceiling to let the water through.

Once you've saved the photo albums, you can pretty much say, "Okay, now I'm fine."

I'd be remiss if I didn't ask about your own RV experiences. What does moving around do to your reading and writing?

This past summer we took a motor home to Alaska. Our daughter was with us for a while; there was a lot of territory—thousands of miles—to cover, and we were just driving along. I had just come out of a very busy semester, where I hadn't had time to read anything I didn't have to read. So I'd taken all these books with me. My idea was to read in the evening, but you never read at night in a motor home; you're always busy cooking and cleaning. So here we are, driving through these incredible landscapes with my husband and daughter in the two front seats; he's driving and she's navigating. And I'm sitting at the table in back while the world rolls by—the incredible Canadian Rockies—and I'm reading. Oh, I'm looking, too; I have vivid memories of this landscape, even though I didn't stare at it nonstop. I was just in a trance. So I'm reading, and occasionally I look up. They'd call out, "Look at that, Rita," and I'd look up and say, "Oh my God, it's amazing"; and then we'd talk for a while, and I'd go back to my book. I never left the trance, really. It was one of the best reading experiences I've ever had.

The House on Bishop Street

No front yard to speak of,
just a porch cantilevered on faith
where she arranged the canary's cage.
The house stayed dark all year
though there was instant light and water.
(No more gas jets hissing,

their flicker glinting off
Anna Rettich's midwife spectacles
as she whispered *think a baby*
and the babies came.) Spring
brought a whiff of cherries, the kind
you boiled for hours in sugar and cloves

from the yard of the Jewish family next door.
Yumanski refused to speak so
she never bought his vegetables
at the Canal Street Market. Gertrude,
his youngest and blondest,
slipped by mornings for bacon and grits.
There were summer floods and mildew

humming through fringe, there was
a picture of a ship she passed
on her way to the porch, strangers calling
from the street *Ma'am, your bird
shore can sing!* If she leaned out she could glimpse
the faintest of mauve—no more than an idea—
growing just behind the last houses.

—*Rita Dove*

Henry Taylor
Bethesda, Maryland

I went to Washington, D.C., in the early '80s to work in the MFA program at American University. Once there, I was turned on to An Afternoon of Pocket Billiards, *a recent collection of poems by the program's director, Henry Taylor. It—and indeed all of his work—was deft and exacting, funny, and finely fashioned. What set Henry apart though was his teaching. In the classroom he was gifted and gentle and, as I came to realize over the years, a man of immense humanity and talent.*

Although we've been in touch sporadically, it has been twenty years since I've seen him, and he is the same—smiling, bearded, and comfortable in his own skin. He lives with his wife Mooshe on a spectacular and spacious wooded lot just north and west of D.C. It's a forest in there, and the city seems miles away. We sit on soft couches in a room with floor-to-ceiling windows and catch up a bit about the trip. He tells me about his new book. We remind each other about my time in D.C. two decades ago.

Henry and Mooshe are champion RVers, so we talk a bit about that. They are leaving later this week for a week's excursion in their lovely gold Class A. After we chat, we talk about what's next for me—once an advisor, always an advisor. I'm embarrassed to admit we still don't know. Maybe we're not ready to stop yet. Maybe we're still going to keep moving. But where? Why? What will be waiting?

~ ~ ~ ~ ~ ~

Do you think the places of a poet's life influence the work he or she does?

Sure. There's no way they can avoid doing that, it seems to me. Where you are in your deepest memories, the things that you go back to when you're dreaming, those are the places that you were. In some cases they are the places you've found along the way. I don't see how surroundings can be anything but influential.

You have individual temperaments that are—let us say for the sake of simplicity—inclined to a very spare kind of free verse or a very lush kind of formal verse. Some readers will want to point to the spare free verse and say, "Well, he's from eastern Montana; it's no wonder he writes like that." But someone else will note that Robert Creeley's not from eastern Montana, and he writes like that. J. V. Cunningham, one of my favorite formalist poets—who hardly ever wrote a poem more than eight lines—claims that being out there around Billings, Montana, kept him from talking too much.

But it's very complicated. The influence of place on every person is very profound. What it ends up meaning to your poetry is a matter of temperament. It matters a lot to me, and at the moment it matters more than it ever did. I'm finishing a book now that is really focused on a very tiny place, Loudoun County, Virginia, where I grew up. That's a very conscious return to a place I remember. But there, even, if you went there and looked at it, you'd see some of the same things. If I go there, I see many things that aren't there anymore. Or I see things the way I saw them when I was eight years old. The feeling around that place is comprehensible to a person visiting it, but not the same to somebody else.

How are you using place specifically in this new book?

Over the years I've written a good many poems that are set in the countryside around where I grew up and where I later spent some years living as an adult. So I'm not sure I could point to specific ways in which these poems are very different from those, at least in terms of their native lands. There are some technical explorations that feel new to me. Some of the poems are longer than usual for me and lean far over toward prose in some places. But I'm interested in mixing these impulses—the lyric and the narrative—in the whole book and even in single poems. The book is called *Crooked Run,* after a stream in the middle of western Loudoun County that, with its small tributaries, drains an area of maybe twenty-five square miles. It occurred to me a few years ago that every home I have had in Loudoun County has been somewhere along a branch of Crooked Run. I started walking up and down the banks of it, both in actuality and mentally, picking up this and that, throwing a good deal back, and writing these poems, some of retrospection, others of present observation.

Do you think poets have any obligation to capture the places of their lives?

No. I may myself feel some sense of obligation to the place I'm working with. But I think if poets have any responsibilities, they are the same as any other citizens have. As artists, I would like to think, we have responsibility to be faithful to our craft and our vision.

Your responsibility to a place is you don't want to betray it. Consider Faulkner, who did this amazing combination of seeing an actual place and inventing another place using the same ingredients. He drew maps of Yoknapatawpha County, and they are entirely plausible. People have gone to that part of Mississippi, taken pictures, and come back saying, "This is Yoknapatawpha County."

I don't feel quite that kind of obligation.

But do you relish the opportunity to do it?

Oh, I do. I have a great time with it. If there's a Southern element to it, it's a certain kind of storytelling, which is more typical of the South than some other regions. Storytelling is not regional as a phenomenon. But storytelling devices and mannerisms can have regional flavors. Trying to put into a poem some of the same weird moves that are available to a skilled southern storyteller is one of the things that is preoccupying me now—although it always has to some extent.

What value does place play in your own poetry?

Even in the case of the shorter poems, there's always a narrative element. I don't often write a poem that doesn't have a story line. Once you have a story line, you're likely to have a setting. You're not obliged to, I suppose—it doesn't absolutely follow—but it tends to follow that you'll have a setting, a kind of grounding. If I settle down to write a poem and I realize it's taking place on a very familiar piece of landscape, I have the same feeling that maybe a happy teacher has walking in to the same old classroom. It won't be just like yesterday, because it never is. There are an infinite variety of things that can take place in a small space. But there's a familiarity to the practitioner that—in a kind of paradoxical way—makes other technical risks easier to undertake. We risk failure. And without a good many failures, I don't think I can have successes that would be very meaningful. That is, in trying to do what I haven't done before, I will run into things I can't do after all. But some of them I can, and there's where the rubber meets the road.

Harvest

Every year in late July I come back to where I was raised,
      to mosey and browse through old farm buildings,
      over fields that seem never to change,

rummaging through a life I can no longer lead
      and still cannot leave behind, looking for relics
      which might spring back to that life at my touch.

Today, among thistles and ragweed, I stumble on
      a discarded combine—the old kind we pulled
      with a tractor to cut and thresh barley and wheat.

Now it lies listing into the side of this hill
      like a stone or an uprooted stump, harboring snakes
      and wasps, rusting slowly down into the briars.

Still, I climb to the seat, wondering whether it will
      hold me, fumbling for pedals and levers
      I used to know by heart. Above my head,

the grain-pipe forks down to the bag-clamps,
      and a wad of tie-strings, gone weedy and rotten,
      still hangs by my right hand. As I touch these things,

this machine I once knew by many unprintable names
      moves out through barley in late July, and the stalks
      fall to the knife as the paddle-reel sweeps them in.

On wide canvas belts, cut grain rides into the dark
      insides of the combine, where frantic shakers and screens
      break the grain loose from the stalks and the chaff;

almost invisible, small spines from the grain-heads
      pour out through holes in the metal, billowing
      into a cloud that moves with us over the hills,

engulfing me, the machine, the tractor and driver,
      as we work in a spiral to the center of the field,
      rolling back through the years in a dust cloud.

The spines stick to my skin, work into my pores,
      my bloodstream, and finally blaze into my head
      like a miniature cactus of hatred for all grain,

for flour and cereal and bread, for mildewed surplus
      swelling in midwestern silos. Never again,
      I thought once, as I rode out the cloud until sundown,

never again. I climb down and walk out through the thistles,
      still breathing fifteen-year-old barley. The years
      in the cloud drift back to me. Metal rusts into the hill.

Barley-dust pricks at my brain, and I am home.
                                —Henry Taylor

Dave Smith
Baltimore, Maryland

I ran the undergraduate writing program at Johns Hopkins University for three years, so today is a bit of a homecoming. We drive through the dirty inner city, each street a long row of townhouses—some thriving with greenery, cats, and patio chairs, and some nothing but rotted wood, broken windows, and empty beer bottles—past the bustling commercial pleasures of the Inner Harbor, and then up toward the university. We pause briefly south of the school at the greatest diner in creation, the New Wyman, where I can see Mike and Pete handling the lunch rush, and then head over to campus for a quick look around.

Time is short, as it often is on the journey, so too soon we are forced to leave campus behind and follow another map.

Dave Smith arrived at Hopkins during my last year there and now has been in Baltimore for only about eighteen months. We find his beautiful and imposing stone house, and Smith welcomes me at the front door. He's very much a man at home and comfortable. We move through the first floor to a back room surrounded by windows that open into the backyard. A cat scurries across. I meet Smith's wife, and they settle some plans for later while I get my gear out. Smith coedited the Southern Review *for a dozen years and is as well known for that as he is for his vast production of poetry.*

We sit at a wood table, facing each other. Smith has on jeans; a purple shirt pops out of a nice blue sweater.

I mention where I'm headed in the coming weeks. He hears one name and asks me to take along a special message. His eyes light up a bit. It's a fond memory or an inside joke, I think. I promise to pass along the greeting.

~ ~ ~ ~ ~ ~

How have the places of your life influenced the poetry that you write?

In some respects the places I've lived have been irrelevant. After I have lived long enough in a particular place, because I'm temperamentally receptive to the local environment, the culture of a place does tend to seep in on me. But in a way it's largely very superficial.

My historical and self-identity was always rooted in tidewater Virginia, which is my native area. My wife has maintained that it was less literal Virginia than an imagined place. Having lived in Louisiana for

206

twelve years, I now live quite near Virginia, and it feels to me no closer emotionally or spiritually than Utah or any of the other places. I now feel homeless. In a way there was a part of me that always thought I was going back to the landscapes—the emotional landscapes—of Virginia. I suppose in a way I never left them, because they always undergird the things I write about. But after many moves, one loses that feeling of belonging to a place.

Yet landscapes are resonant to me. I think this proceeds from a historical sensibility. I am responsive to the history of a place, and I mean even particular local history. I'm an inveterate reader of newspapers. If I fly into an airport, I'll buy the local newspaper. I don't know a thing about the town, but I'll read about what's going on in the local clubs and so on. I don't know why that's the case. I don't know what feeds into the things I like to write about. But it has always been the case. Perhaps because local, specific stories with actual people in them matter to me. And to that extent, I think I could be called a poet of place.

Are there elements of the natural world that have impact on you? Does the world itself start poems for you?

Some poets, as I'm sure you know, are triggered into their verbal response by sound or by abstractions, possibly even by ideas. But I believe that over the long evolution of poetry in the last one hundred fifty to two hundred years, there has been an increasingly naturalistic attention to the real and implacable surfaces of the world. The idea that the world somehow speaks, and everything in it somehow speaks, is real to me. So it follows that my task was to learn how to listen and to learn how to observe as accurately and present as accurately as I could. Toward the middle part of my writing life, I began to feel that this wasn't enough. That one had to listen beyond the realistic surface to discover something else, something larger, more resonant that was already there in the phenomenal surfaces.

For example, Theodore Roethke is well known for writing about his greenhouse memories and the specific flowers and using them as metaphors. But he's not using them as metaphors at first. He's simply writing about what he remembers and what he has cared about in some very personal way. Still, Roethke understood that this would only be of value if it could permit him to see something else. To use the thing as a kind of lens, or an oral device. The German phrase, *dinglichkeit*—or "thingness" of the world—was always strong to me; it has become not just a strong sense, but a kind of door.

I will only succeed if I can make that door your door as well, as a reader. And when I don't, then all I've done is a kind of verbal photograph.

There are elementals—elemental images—which were initially interesting to me, which were in the middle interesting to me, and which remain interesting to me. For example, any body of water, but particularly an ocean or salt water. But any body of water is a trigger for me, is immediately interesting. And almost anything to do with its marginals.

A number of poets I've met with tell me they are regionalists, suggesting that there is a certain area, a certain region, where their work comes from and where they as artists are most comfortable, not just living, but examining, writing, and working.

I think any good poet is first of all a regionalist. We tend, at least in the public media, to speak of a regionalist as somehow a lesser creature, but it wasn't true of Faulkner. It wasn't true of Conrad. It isn't true of most writers. I simply believe writers—to the degree that they are good writers—are, first of all, regionalists. I mean that the region in which their psyche is located becomes the matter they most intently draw upon and try to ultimately generalize to the level of values, to meaning.

My feeling, and I say this without too much fear of upsetting anybody, is that right now the best writing poet in the world is Seamus Heaney. Heaney is as much a poet of place as has ever existed on this planet. But I don't think you could take it any further and say he's only a poet of place. If place equals regionalism, then I fully subscribe to it. But I don't view poems rooted in place as limitations, but opportunities. All any poet wants is the opportunity to have opportunities to make the world's voices come alive in his saying.

Gaines Mill Battlefield

Just off Cold Harbor Road we entered the woods
for squirrels, solitude nearly two hundred years
deep, oaks, hickories, the American
chestnut gone that once would have soared.

All the cold morning light does is leave
us standing, hands number, mute as crows
where wind off the bloody millpond
still brings the howl of a dog, a cow's low.

At noon we give up, shoulder guns, and step
over mounded leaves like trespassers.
On the way out we find the grandfatherly
pine toppled by no storm we remember.

Tall as a house, its root-mass blackly waves.
A clear stream trickles over red layers of leaves.

—*Dave Smith*

Nicole Cooley
Glen Ridge, New Jersey

The journey continues north, and the difference is enormous as we leave the verdant Mid-Atlantic of Virginia and Maryland, skirt the nation's capital, pass through schizophrenic Baltimore—Southern charm and Northern hustle—and emerge into the wall-to-wall townships of New Jersey that lie in the shadows of New York City.

We are here in Glen Ridge to see Nicole Cooley, a young poet who welcomes me into her home on a very cold Sunday morning. Nicole is the daughter of Peter Cooley, whom I visited in New Orleans earlier on the trip. She wants to show me her study first, a light and airy room at the top of a steep flight of stairs. It has purple walls and two desks. An easel is set up to the side of Nicole's computer. This is where her oldest daughter Meridian sometimes scribbles and draws while Nicole writes. On the large pad are two drawings of Glinda the Good Witch. While I set up my gear Nicole recalls how when she was a little girl she'd go with her dad to readings, crayoning away in the back row. She remembers playing with his pens and pencils while he wrote. When she tells me about this, I see the light of recognition in her eye as she sees the easel and realizes that Meridian is getting the same start she did. Nicole grew up with a poet in the house, and now so will Meridian.

~ ~ ~ ~ ~ ~

How have the places of your life affected the poetry you write?
I think part of it is I've lived so many places—starting with Iowa, Wisconsin, New Orleans, Providence, Atlanta, a small town in Pennsylvania for two years, New York City, and then here—that I paradoxically became more interested in the idea of place. I think it's why I wanted to write my second book, *The Afflicted Girls,* about the Salem Witch trials, because it's all about place, all about people being constrained by place, which is not what I've been.

But there's something about moving all the time that got me interested. My time in small-town Pennsylvania really made me think about what it's like to live in a close-knit community, and then immediately we moved to Queens, which is the polar opposite. Suddenly we were living in this superurban environment, where you don't know your neighbors at all and where there are millions of people on the street. Constantly being jolted out of my sense of place made me think about it.

210

What was the transition like between rural and city life for you?

When I lived in small-town Pennsylvania, what I did for fun was stroll through flea markets. They're so full of old stuff: samplers, tea dishes, clothes. I spent all this time going up and down the aisles thinking about home and place and all the things that had belonged to people, going through old boxes of photographs. Looking at the things people had touched and owned and loved, the signatures on the ancient postcards. It's what I did to start writing. I'd go to the Roller Mills flea market, wander around, and come home. It made me wonder what was home for me and what home had been for these people.

Then being jolted into this urban environment was totally different. We lived in this old Italian neighborhood. There were no flea markets, and it was a totally different way of thinking about home. In New York, home is out on the street. Your apartment is your sanctuary, but home is all around you.

I spoke with your dad, Peter Cooley, a couple of months ago. What was the impact of having a poet for a father?

My father used to help me write little poems when I was a kid. He would encourage me to write these poems, and he'd type them out for me. He'd transcribe them when I would say them, before I could even write. And then my parents would put them in a little book, so it felt as if I'd written a book. I was four. They were silly little poems, but I still have them.

From my father I got that you have to be able to write anywhere. You can't have the perfect garret, the perfect silence. When my family would go to Sarasota, Florida, my dad and I would go to this dilapidated shopping mall, sit in this crummy food court, and drink coffee. We'd sit together and give each other assignments. Usually words. We'd open up whatever books we had and pick three random words. We'd have timed writing where we'd sit in silence and have to create something. At the end we'd read it out loud to each other if we liked it, or we'd just junk it. The hubbub of the mall would be going on behind us, and it would become something. Some of the stuff in my first book came out of that, and I know it's the case for my father, too.

The mall has since closed, so we need to find a new place. It's a good lesson that you have to be able to write anywhere. You don't have to wait for the perfect moment or inspiration. You just do it.

You've got a great room here at the top of this house. It's all cut up, being an attic room, but it's very bright. It feels like a real retreat. How does it play a role in your work habits?

This is the first time I've had a sanctuary. The first time I saw this room—it was a baby's room—I thought, "You couldn't make a more perfect room for me." The room was purple; that's my favorite color. It was the most perfect room I could imagine. I didn't do anything to it. They took out the baby's crib, and I moved in.

Before that, I had always worked in the room with my husband or in a kind of closet. I had the dining room. I didn't have the space. That was good, though, in a way, not to have the space, because I was always forced to work in spite of situations.

I'd find places in New York City, Iowa City, or Atlanta—coffee shops, park benches, whatever. It kind of forced me out of myself. There was always noise in the background. Things to do, hard to shut out the outside world. But now, with two small children, this place is really a relief. But it was good to have to adjust to the outside world, because how often does a writer have that sacrosanct place?

Unfinished Sketch: Green Sandbox Winter Sky

At the fence two small bodies the cat has split apart

In the middle of the yard my daughter fills her dress pockets with sand
as if she can weight herself to the earth

I want to believe in language fastening the moment to the present

On the grass I watch her knowing I'll never equal
shelter to anyone again

She sifts dead grass through her fingers under the sky
white as paper on which nothing is written

Here is a scene in which I can't plot myself as the heroine

There is only this small girl who knows nothing of the hazards
of joined bodies or separation's safety

—Nicole Cooley

David Lehman
New York, New York

It's 28 degrees in lower Manhattan, and we're eating gigantic chicken wraps inside a car we've rented to—get this—drive into Manhattan. We got the wraps at a funky convenience store, where I mostly am amazed to see cigarettes selling for nine dollars. Where are we, on the moon?

We're here an hour and a half early because I foolishly insist on driving everywhere, even Greenwich Village. I love cars. I love pushing the tin back and forth. And besides, this whole trip has hinged on a manic devotion to living on the highways and roads of America. So instead of taking everyone's advice about the A train, F train, whatever, the 6, the 4, etc., I've circled the soda-straw-narrow streets near Washington Square Park for forty minutes before finding a perfect parking spot. My wife used to travel by train to New York regularly, but when I started dialing Enterprise Rent-A-Car from our campground in Jersey, she just shrugged.

I'm here to see David Lehman, the man who—I'm willing to bet—reads more poetry than anyone else in the country. For more than a decade he's been the series editor (the only series editor) of Best American Poetry, *a sprawling and crucial collection of the year's best work (chosen in concert with a guest editor).*

Lehman also is widely known for an experiment he started in the late '90s of writing and finishing a poem every day. This experiment yielded two phenomenal and well-received collections, The Daily Mirror *and* The Evening Sun.

A lifetime New Yorker, Lehman sometimes splits the city for his house in Ithaca. But he spends the majority of his time right here, in a tiny book-and manuscript-filled apartment. While we chat, Lehman shows me a dozen scraps of paper with ideas and lines for new poems, some on the back of envelopes, some on the back of a memo, even some in a small orange notebook he carries in his back pocket.

His work can be sharp and snappy, tight lines, no punctuation, vital, moving. But other poems stretch out, become floating narratives. Lots of women and men and the troubles therein. Always quietly, subtly funny. Crack-across-the-knuckle realizations abound.

214

~ ~ ~ ~ ~ ~

What is your relationship with New York like?
I'm a New Yorker. I'm from New York; I was born here. I grew up here. Went to high school here. So I have all the loyal feelings of a native son. And then I chose to live here as an adult, so I guess I'm a very passionate New Yorker.

Like everyone else who lives in New York, I have complicated feelings about the city and about being here. One thing is indisputable: it's a tremendous generator of inspiration. It's the capital of inspiration. There are dozens of things going on at any given moment that are worthy of your attention, so you get used to having a very high level of stimulus. It's the capital of so many things that one feels close to being at the center, whether it's finance or advertising. Wall Street. Fashion. Media. You feel at a place where reality is at its most intense. That's an exciting feeling.

Is there anything particular about the pace or the energy here that translates into the forms of your work?
A lot of the poems I wrote in the period when I was writing a poem a day as an experiment were influenced by the pace of living in New York City. In those poems, there's often an absence of punctuation; lines are short. Some of the poems are fairly short and have a kind of breathless urgency, either in the lines or in the arrangement of lines. In those books I think that I got more of New York City into the poetry, not only as a subject—which it often is—but in the very texture and form of the lines.

Do you think poets have any obligation to write about their places?
You're talking to somebody who doesn't think poets have obligations in the sense of being the "conscience of the race" or the political advisers to the President. I think poetry has to do with freedom and not with duty, as a general rule. So I wouldn't legislate and say that poets "must do" this or that. I think that in my own case, my poems are infused with New York City, and that sort of tallies with my own feeling that New York City is my own default reality.

While you know that every place in the world is real, and equally real, where are you

when you close your eyes and are existing in a purely metaphysical plane? For everyone it's a different answer. Perhaps it's where you were born. Perhaps it's where you grew up. Perhaps it's where you live now. But whatever it is, it's a place of your inner sense of reality. And I know that New York City is that default landscape for me.

One of my books is called *Valentine Place,* which is the actual street address in Ithaca, New York, where I own a house and spend a lot of time. It's as though destiny is giving you a title when you buy a house on Valentine Place. In the book previous to that, a book called *Operation Memory,* there's a poem called "Cambridge, 1972." And there was a poem entitled "New York City, 1974" in the same volume. And I know that in writing those two poems, I was writing about a time and place. And I wouldn't say it was nostalgia; it was more history. It seemed that the place was somehow definitive.

I think that in my own writing, the idea of a place—its name, its particular culture, the language that's spoken there, the dialect—seems to me to be a part of reality that I must like. Because I so often turn to it. There must be a dozen poems in *The Daily Mirror* that begin with New York City.

What value is there in establishing a setting early in a poem?

It's one of those things you do instinctively, without thinking about it, until someone notices the pattern and asks you about it. If a lyric poem is almost definitively an encounter of the individual poet with the cosmos, you might well want to begin by noting the coordinates of your existence.

You mentioned your place in Ithaca. Are you the same poet there as you are in New York City?

I think if you're a New Yorker as I am, you bring it with you wherever you go. You walk faster than most people. You get more impatient when you're driving a car and reach an intersection. You also have a certain energy level that can be triggered off with the right amount of coffee, and in New York I have a lot of professional commitments beyond writing that I don't quite have in Ithaca. When I'm there, the chances are I can devote a certain number of hours a day to sitting in front of a computer and putting words together. So I tend to be very reclusive when I'm there. The beauty of the landscape and my own garden give me much pleasure. There's a glorious lake. There's a great farmer's market. There are great things there. But I tend to spend huge chunks of time in my study, taking advantage of my library, my books, my papers, and the gift of having the time to spend writing.

April 9

I woke up not in Paris
that's the first thing that went wrong
after the pleasure of a week
of speaking French badly
also the smoke detector went off
when I made coffee,
and my telephone lacks a dial tone
so I know I'm back in the greatest city
with my incomparable view of garbage
in the alley out the window with sun
a bright white on red brick turning yellow
and just enough blue to imply a sky
high enough and far enough away
to stand for all that's mind (mine)

—*David Lehman*

The City So Nice They Named It Twice

Of the rich variety of cultural advantages available to New York City residents, it's quite clear to me that the one that really matters the most is the freedom everyone feels to blow his or her car horn.

Sure, the ballet and all that bullshit are great. The Guggenheim. Yankee Stadium. Papaya King. But all of that is really available in any city with more than fifty thousand people. It is with the car horn that New Yorkers carve their niche. The horn honking is constant. In an hour sitting in my car on the Upper West Side, horns blare continuously. The complex and beautiful language mostly seems to pass along this message: "I have become bored with the view of your car. I wish for you to pull over and let me pass along so I may wait in traffic behind someone in a different color Toyota."

New York is a remarkable place. About half the people I know think it's the greatest city in the world. The bagels alone sway most of my pals. Many of them go to New York three times a year. They see some art. They get matinee tickets to either *Phantom* or an off-Broadway play where actors dress like kitchen implements and revolt against the Eastern Bloc–styled drawer they live in. They eat a pretzel the size of a Christmas turkey and then take the train back to Pittsburgh or Baltimore.

I love Times Square. I love the sidewalk in front of MTV. I love Central Park when it's not crowded. I love 30 Rock. I love looking out the windows of my hotel and thinking, "Holy shit! Look at all the tourists." I love the neighborhoods where locals sit on stoops and chat across the street with the neighbors. I love Riverside Park, narrow and bustling, but lovely for being jammed between the high rises and the Hudson Parkway.

It's exciting and busy and, for many, the only place in the world where all of the senses can be stimulated simultaneously. I see its beauty; I see its allure. But once we finished our interview this afternoon, we hustled across the George Washington Bridge, and before too long we were two beers and two big plates of food into a languorous and funny evening at the Longhorn Steakhouse in Parsippany, New Jersey—for my money, the greatest city in the world.

Lucie Brock-Broido
New York, New York

Lucie lives in comfortable decadence on the Upper West Side, quite near Columbia University, where she teaches. She welcomes me into her apartment, and the luxurious red of the chairs and wall hangings suffocates me. Sweet William, a Maine Coon cat, scampers away as I arrive, but he gets used to me quickly and is a major part of the interview, sometimes fielding questions for Lucie, sometimes just batting his powerful front paws at some of the wires and cords that keep my recorders and cameras running.

Although Lucie's been at Columbia for ten years (she directs the program here, as she did a decade ago at Harvard), this is the first year she's not spent part of the time in her much loved "castle" in Cambridge, Massachusetts. She misses Cambridge because for years that is where she's written all of her dense and beautiful lyric poetry. She's rented her place out and, on two occasions, has made the drive up just to sit in the driveway. She picks up mail from her boarder but turns down the opportunity to go inside.

We drink powerful coffee and chat away a lot of a winter afternoon. She talks with great fondness about her students, about their poetry. And she talks forcefully about how important it is for her to help them in any way. She went to Columbia years ago as a student, so she knows what her students face, and she's a partner to them as they work.

She's a rare beauty, a rare talent; and when afternoon moves to early evening, I feel forlorn to know that I'll be leaving soon.

~ ~ ~ ~ ~ ~

What's your relationship like with New York City?

I've been here exactly ten years. But I was also here in graduate school in 1979, and I had a distinctly unfriendly relationship with it then, a very dark one. Since then, I've lived in five different places, all for poetry reasons. The first time I left here I went to Pittsburgh, Provincetown, Virginia, Boston, and to Cambridge. And Cambridge was my dream—has always been my dream. I made that up when I was small and thought, "This is where I want to spend my life." And I do indeed have a house there. It's like a little castle, and it's the only place I write. It's an 1840s workman's cottage that was blown up into this bright, light, three-story place with stained glass and many skylights and a loft.

All hand-carved wood everywhere. It's extravagant, sexy, luscious, and has a wonderful fireplace in the room in which I write.

I came back to New York City with huge reluctance, not wanting anything to do with New York because it's not where I write. I came thinking it would be a drive-by occasion because I was offered this job at Columbia, where I had been a student but where I knew they devoured their own and spat them out. But, lo, I find myself now a decade later, tenured, crazy about my job. No other job I want other than the one I have. But I still am not smitten with this city, though my life is here now. I have incredible ambivalence. I honor this city. There's lots of glitter here, but there's also more real life than anywhere else I've ever known.

And I was here on 9/11. Had just gotten down from Cambridge, had driven here. Woke up here on that morning. And on that day, my relationship—as many people's did—changed. I began to honor the city even more. I was very proud of the way people treated one another, and I noticed it for months and months afterward. I felt less scared. I felt less hostilely sardined in the subways. I felt an empathy for the city and its denizens.

I consider myself irrevocably northern. Just because of weather. Everyone has loathed this present, wicked cold snap; I've been in heaven. I think it's the greatest thing. I can't get north enough. It's not political. It's not cultural. It's not artistic. Cold weather is a religion.

I know that you only write in Cambridge, but is there a place, a landscape of some kind, that you carry with you, that feeds your poetry?

I have always known that when I was writing I have actually been in one particular place in my mind's eye. And that is the city of Haworth. It's Brontë country. It's in Yorkshire and is the home of *Wuthering Heights* and the parsonage where the Brontë siblings grew up. And I've known since I was fifteen and read *Wuthering Heights* that that landscape was home to me.

About ten or twelve years ago, on New Year's Day, I went—desperately ill with a flu—and took an overnight flight to London. I was hell-bent on getting myself to Haworth to the parsonage, going out on the moors to pick heather and bring it home.

I went to great pains to pick this heather! It was a five-thousand-dollar plucking and worth every cent—and worth all the coughing and flu and fever to go get it. I read before I returned what you can and can't bring back, and you can't bring back any living thing other than yourself. So like the young man who smuggled the hashish in the film *Midnight Express,* I taped the heather to my body. I had it on my person. I had some in my purse. I had a big story for customs. Was I going to smoke it? But I had to have that heather. And I got it home safely, and

I keep it dried in my basement in Cambridge. Somehow in my kingdom, that's what helps me write. A student of mine called it "ur-manna," the secret stuff you get from the earth that lets you write.

How does that landscape work for you? Are there triggers or elements that prove to be starting points for your work?

The cold in general triggers electricity and warmth in me, which triggers yearning. I have to be yearning to write, which is why I keep it so encased, so specific, so un-daily, so rare. It has to be pent up.

Gloom in nature is a magnificence to me. The autumn causes for me whatever carnal lust that most people feel in spring. When the crocus heads come up, I want to go to Greenland or Newfoundland. The little flowers depress me. I'm going to sound like the Addams family *(laughs)*. Something deep inside is touched that says, "This is not renewal of life." It's not a "good" thing, that kind of greenness or budding.

I was born and raised in Pittsburgh, through and through. I decided on the map to imagine the state of Massachusetts. I knew John F. Kennedy was from there. And I knew New England was the supercenter of autumn in America. I've always loved all things autumnal. Autumnal holidays are beautiful to me. The light changes then. The light that I adore is—the French expression is—the "hour between dog and wolf." The dusk, when you can't distinguish between the dog and wolf. It's not the *night* I'm after. That play of shadows in between, on the verge.

There's the weather, the cold, the light.

All of this lends an extravagant darkness to my work that is depressing *(laughs)*, what the poet and critic Stephen Burt, in his essay on the new "elliptical poets," calls "desperate extravagance."

Michael S. Harper
Providence, Rhode Island

A poet's office is every bit as personal and idiosyncratic as a poet's home. So I'm embarrassed to admit that this morning, while setting up in one of Michael Harper's offices on the campus of Brown University, I can't stop myself from exclaiming, "Your office is exquisitely messy!"

If I could have added context to all of this, Harper would have known something of the terrible mess of my own workspaces—at home, at work, even in Winnie Cooper. But I really am a little astonished. Envelopes, manuscripts, books, and files pile on every flat surface, at least six inches high on the desk. It overwhelms me. Harper tells me he has other offices on the same floor that—as I see when we visit later—are ordered and neat. But in this leave year, Harper has let his own office go a bit. After my comment, Harper grins and says, "I work at it, man. That is to say, I don't waste any time thinking about it." And during my visit, he has occasion to pull out a handful of things, a student's book, a book by one of his old pals; and his hands always go right to them.

I should have known better, because Harper's heart is that of a true jazz artist. I should have seen through what I saw as messy to what is really there, augmented chords, flatted fifths, a gigantic hand making that minor seventh.

We turn to the project at hand, and I am swept away and overwhelmed at Harper's storytelling. He's the champ. His tales are terrific, enjoyable, vital, and—in the end—astonishing in message and resonance.

~ ~ ~ ~ ~ ~

You've lived a lot of places, but where do you think you're from?

I'm a kid born in Brooklyn. I was born in the same house my mother was born in and delivered by the same man. So when people start lecturing me—which often happens, people who are not New Yorkers and who are living on East Sixty-third Street—and start dictating to me, I just look at them in amazement. The presumption is that they're natives. Well, we're all interlopers. This whole idea of "it belongs to you" is crazy.

You haven't lived there for a long time now, not since you were a boy. What is your relationship with New York City now?

I lost Brooklyn when I was thirteen. It wasn't my choice to leave. My parents decided they were leaving. It's a complicated question when you talk to a minority even though I'm native-born.

I was taught to read before I started school; my mother taught me how to read. I was a child of the Depression. We managed to survive it. I know what hard times are like because I know what my parents sacrificed in order to do whatever they did. When we left New York, I was thirteen years old, and you know how strategic that is. I had just finished my first eight grades, and I had just taken my exams to get into the best schools in New York. And then I was going to another place, learning another neighborhood; and poetry is all about one's neighborhood. And particularly one's psychic neighborhood, where one lives in one's head.

I spent a lot of time not only in various neighborhoods but on the ground and the ferries, the whole matrix of New York City. I started riding the subways of New York without my parents' knowledge when I was five years old. That was 1943. It was wartime. It took them three years to catch me. And I haven't really written about that except I lived it that way.

This was at a time when a young person could travel anywhere in the city and an adult would make sure—if you got lost, you could walk up to anyone and say, "I'm lost"—that you got to where you wanted to go. It was that kind of civic community. And there were eight million people living in the city, but that didn't stop them from being responsible.

Of course, there's enormous loss. Not to mention the mix of ethnicities and language. And as I get older, I notice how rigid class is and how permanent race is. It's important that you move over to accommodate people who might or might not be just like you. And you can do this by eating their food. Isn't it a wonderful thing to eat Chinese food or Puerto Rican food? *(Laughs.)* That's what being in the city means. That kind of immersion, beginning with your taste buds, gives you a tolerance for a range, for living in the world.

So you finished school and college in California. What was the transition like for you as a city kid when you went to Iowa?

I was a student of Christopher Isherwood's at L.A. State College. I met him in 1959. My other teachers were Wirt Williams, a novelist, whose first novel was praised by Hemingway, and Henri Coulette, a classmate of Donald Justice. Isherwood, an expatriate novelist from UK and a Cambridge University dropout, didn't believe in writing programs. When I said I wanted to go to Iowa to beat the draft and to stay out of the Army, he recommended me. He just went on and wrote a letter. It was a whim. But isn't it a wonderful whim?

They used to call Iowa—and the Iowa Workshop—the Athens of the Midwest. And I used to think, "A cornfield, Holy Christ." I was a bicoastal kid. You know that famous cartoon from the *New Yorker*? You come to the Hudson River, and the next thing you know you're in San Francisco and the Pacific Ocean; and there ain't nothing in between,  right? *(Laughs.)* Well, that's the way it was then.

If I hadn't had a lot of initiative of my own, I'd have never gone to Iowa. Of course, as a minority—I was the only black person there—you had all sorts of peripheral problems as well. Where are you going to live? And they had a lot of discrimination in housing, unless you were an athlete. Paul Engle *(the founder director of the Writers' Workshop)* tried to send me to Mrs. Lemme, a black woman who owned buildings and rented rooms to black performers on the road. Her husband owned the local shoeshine shop. I was too green to know that I'd have been infinitely better treated in her house. But what did I know at twenty-two?

You've journeyed around, and it seems as if you've settled here in Rhode Island. Has there been a plan to all of this?

I think of my own life and how whimsical it was. I didn't think I was going to stay here at Brown for thirty years or more. And I didn't think I'd be at a university like this. My aunt's husband was a Brown graduate in 1935. He was a medical doctor. He went to Case Western Reserve and spent the rest of his life taking care of poor people. But he came here. His father was a redcap, worked on the trains and did the Northeast corridor and stopped in Providence, and probably said to his son, "Brown University's a pretty school."

I didn't want to come to Providence. Providence is New England, number one, and an eccentric place to live in to begin with. If you haven't lived here five or six generations, you might as well just forget it. You're going to be an outsider and just get comfortable with that.

C. D. Wright

Barrington, Rhode Island

C. D. Wright's work is a miracle to me. For as long as I've been reading her, I've wanted to get inside her work and pull it apart, finding the secret invisible threads that hold it all together. Unlike my own work, which remains fraught with the narrative tools left over from my start as a fiction writer, Wright's work succeeds so beautifully because of what she leaves out.

The work is still dense, consuming. But her best work, her most vital work is free of unnecessary connective devices. The poetry is evocative. The reader is left to construct part of the poetic world and is therefore asked to be a better reader.

I can never stop myself from trying to sum things up, to reveal a tidy ending, to screw my courage up to deliver a last line that is the key to the puzzle above. Wright's work cascades. It's alternately shimmering and stony. Each word, phrase, absolutely integral to the final piece. No excessive movement or braying.

In the planning for this visit, C.D. was unsure that she had much to say about place—it's already in her work. Many poets I've met on this trip have wanted to hold back part of their process or their art. None of us—entirely—knows what the secret ingredient is. For some, it's the transfer of scattered lines out of a notebook onto a computer screen that is magical. For others, it's that trance we sometimes find as we channel the work from some unknown location. All through these months I've discovered forbidden zones, places where poets won't let themselves travel with me alongside.

Born in the Ozarks of Arkansas, she has two distinct homes—that place and now this place in Rhode Island, a state she calls her adopted home. In her poems and essays, she's mined much of the landscape of both. Not overtly, not merely as accoutrements to some other tale, but as the metaphorical underpinning of the poems themselves. It's easy to see place in something like "The Ozark Odes," but it's tougher (more rewarding) to find it in something like the book-length poem Deepstep Come Shining.

So it is with the weight of all that that I arrive at her home just blocks from Narragansett Bay, south and east of Providence, Rhode Island. The two-story home is red, with a matching barn, on a gigantic sweeping lot that has a growing wall of bamboo to one of the side streets. She lives here with her husband (the poet Forest Gander, who planted the bamboo and cares for it) and her son (Brecht). Brecht eats a giant bowl of cereal while C.D. and I talk nearby in the muted living room.

~ ~ ~ ~ ~ ~

Your collaborative book One Big Self *is an amazing look at the prisons of Louisiana. How has that place affected you?*

I think it's a long-term impact. It's still mulching. It took a long time to do the project, a long time to bring it into being. The photographer with whom I work (Deborah Luster) is still printing from the project. We've been discussing for the past seven months what we're going to do next. It still has some relationship to violence in America. The pervasiveness of violence, the way it is "embedded"—to use the Pentagon's term—in the culture, makes it impossible to stop addressing.

Did you write about that place immediately, or did it take a while to figure out what you had to say?

It's pretty fertile material. And it's a whole shadow world, so there's a lot to explore. I spent a lot of time reading, watching films, corresponding, visiting the prisons. It was a whole surround of information, and it took a long time to digest. But figuring out what was relevant to the project and what stayed the course of the project, as well as what deepened and furthered it and what was just clutter—this took time. How to give compelling shape to the material is the issue.

While your work—which is stunning and lyrical—may not strike a reader as being full of the natural world, are there any natural world elements that impact you more than others?

I don't feel disconnected from the natural world, but I also don't feel disconnected from the city—which is not all artifice after all. My temperament goes back and forth between the urban and rural. I'm certainly grounded in rural, and I've never seen any reason to leave my ground behind. To some extent, my patch is portable. I live in a raging suburb here, but in my eyes it's an acre of Arkansas. Otherwise I wouldn't be in this town. After people, trees are the most important life forms for me, even more than critter life—my own hound excepted of course.

You have a quote in an issue of Southern Review *from about ten years ago about the division between urban life and rural life. You say that it's the "only serious border left to us." Are there starting points for your poetry in this divide?*

I don't know what the starting points are, the end points for that matter. Internally, I think the noise of the city is the music of the city. Trying to understand the thinginess and the headiness of the city can contribute mightily to your own work. In the country, I wouldn't say it's the silence, but more the awareness of a world without voices that weighs in. Obviously, the city is also a landscape as much as it is a site of acceleration.

Do you think that poets have an obligation to write about—or to capture— the places of their lives? I ask this because certainly your early work seems to be interested in capturing Arkansas.

My place of origin does not always have a visible or audible part to play in the poem at hand. Formatively, it has a place in my character and my art. That part, I think I have internalized by now.

I think poets have an inclination to write about the crises of their lives and their times. Place matters, but no poet is obliged to write about a place. Maybe their place is their shelter from the forces. And the forces generally can't be avoided in the writing.

In "69 Hidebound Opinions," you say that "Going home is an overwhelming inarticulate experience." Is there ever a point in a writer's life when going home can result in a more articulate experience?

I would have to modify that comment now. Your first geography does not necessarily conjure the same welter of feelings and experiences every time you make contact. The inability to articulate may in fact go in hand with the lack of necessity to do so. You may somatize your "motherland" to the degree that the affected areas are elsewhere, and those areas are what need to be examined.

from The Ozark Odes

RENT HOUSE

O the hours I lay on the bed
looking at the knotted pine
in the added-on room
where he kept his old Corona,
the poet with the big lips—
where we slept together.

ARKANSAS TOWNS

Acorn
Back Gate
Bald Knob
Ben Hur
Biggers
Blue Ball
Congo
Delight
Ebony
Eros
Fifty-Six
Figure Five
Flippin
Four Sisters
Goshen
Greasy Corner
Havana
Hector
Hogeye
Ink
Jenny Lind
Little Flock
Marked Tree
Mist

Monkey Run
Moscow
Nail
Okay
Ozone
Rag Town
Ratio
Seaton Dump
Self
Snowball
Snow Lake
Sweet Home
Three Brothers
Three Folks
Twist
Urbanette
Whisp
Yellville
Zent

LAKE RETURN

Where the sharp rock on shore
give way to the hairy rock in the shallows,
we enlisted in the rise and fall of love.
His seed broadcast like short, sweet grass.
Nothing came up there.

DRY COUNTY BAR

Bourbon not fit to put on a sore. No women enter;
their men collect in every kind of weather
with no shirts on whatsoever.

CAFE AT THE JUNCTION

The way she sees him
how the rain doesn't let up

4-ever blue and vigilant
as a clock in a corner

peeling the label from his bottle
hungry but not touching food

as she turns down the wet lane
where oaks vault the road

THE BOYFRIEND

wakes in darkness of morning
and visits the water

lowering his glad body
onto a flat rock

the spiders rearrange
themselves underneath

LAKE RETURN

Why I come here: need for a bottom, something to refer to;
where all things visible and invisible commence to swarm.

                                        —C. D. Wright

Mark Wunderlich
Provincetown, Massachusetts

Provincetown is at the end of the world, the tip of Cape Cod, a tiny windswept collection of B&Bs and fudge shops. We get there a day early, so see the entire town—pretty clapboard houses on the water, bigger places out toward the point. We see four lighthouses, stand on frigid beaches (with tufts of snow mixed in with the wet winter sand), talk to couples with dogs wet from the surf. We even see two guys emerge from the Atlantic side hauling surfboards, dressed like sea lions in matching black scuba suits.

It is peaceful, but it is also midwinter. From May until September this place is teeming with tourists. So even though it is dreary today, we roll with Winnie Cooper along narrow roads that reach out to the promontory.

By the time we head out to find Mark Wunderlich's apartment, the sun is out, and Provincetown is bathed in light. Mark and I go into his bright apartment, filled—I must say—with some nutty touches: some kind of skinned rug, a large animal head adorned with beads and baubles, some kind of circa 1950s couch that might be something very hip that I'm too much of a boor to know about, and a fishing rod against one wall with eyelets the size of a pocket watch.

We sit across a table, and, as always, I give some kind of overview of why on earth my wife and I are doing what we're doing. We talk about a poet I've seen recently whom Mark knows well, and we share some stories.

Provincetown has a long history of supporting artists and writers. Mark knows this firsthand, having won two fellowships with Provincetown's Fine Arts Work Center over the years. After the last one he just stayed and likely would remain except for the continuing skyrocketing cost of living. He and his partner have just bought an old stone house in the Hudson River Valley and will be moving soon. It will be a bittersweet departure; but many of their friends have been relocating there as well, so it will be a welcome and warm place.

~~~~~

How have the places of your life played a role in your poetry?

I've lived in so many places in my adult life that some of that gets a little murky. It seems I can't write about a place until I leave it. The

232

one place that is omnipresent—that is always there and has the most impact—has been the small town I grew up in Wisconsin, which was this very small town. And I didn't even grow up in town; I grew up on a small farm outside of it. The town was called Fountain City, and it's on the Mississippi. It's kind of geographically, spiritually, psychically, historically isolated. There were neighbors who didn't have electricity, who cooked on a wood stove. They talked about their cat being charmed by a snake. This old farmer, Bill Wendt, was the only person I'd ever known who was chased by a pack of dogs. They kept newspapers on their kitchen floor to keep their linoleum good. That kind of a place and those kinds of characters were throughout that region.

Since leaving there, I've lived in Los Angeles, San Francisco, for many years in New York. And I've traveled a lot. But I still can't get over that notion of being country.

When you left there and went to college in a city, then on to New York, what sort of shifts did you feel?

I went to Madison, Wisconsin, where I went to college, and suddenly I saw this whole urbane world opening up. There were people who were like me; I had peers. That was tremendously exciting. I continued to live in cities for a long time.

It was difficult living in New York and carving out a life as a writer. There is such opportunity to be out in the city, and I remember creating a little space for myself in my apartment, where I would retreat and go to work, and then go out into the city and have this life of a young person in New York. Which I loved. I adored the city. For the first three years I just walked around with my mouth open, looking up. I was astonished. It felt like the center of the universe.

The AIDS crisis was in full bloom. It was full blown in New York. And the city was in bad shape in the early '90s. You saw young men in wheelchairs, on crutches, who were incredibly emaciated. It felt very dire. There was this revolving black market at night, where men would find things—either stolen goods or stuff picked out of the trash—and set things up on the sidewalk at night. It moved around, depending on where the cops would chase them off. And they would sell these things at night on the sidewalk, including used syringes, tourniquets, used crack pipes. You would just walk these blocks and look at these things that had been pulled from the garbage or stolen from someone's apartment. These things would be sold every night on the street, in this act of desperation and incredible ingenuity. The city was so exciting, but also so endangered. And for the first time in my life I realized I was expendable or part of a group of people who were seen that way, just because of the geography of where I lived and because of the life I was choosing.

Despite your professed love of cities, you have really made a home here in Provincetown, this tiny, quirky, and beautiful spot. What is it about this place for you?

I love Provincetown; and when I first began reading poems, I'd look on the back of these books by poets I was reading and read about Stanley Kunitz or Mark Doty or Marge Piercy. I would see their names, and they all lived in Provincetown, Massachusetts. This was when I was in Wisconsin, and I thought, "It must be paradise there; it must be the most amazing place in the world." And I found it on the map and saw that it was on the end of that great curl of Cape Cod. As a midwesterner, the East Coast just seemed so exotic.

It's a great community. In the summer everyone comes here. It's exhausting. In the winter it provides me a kind of isolation that I like. It's small-town living, with a sophisticated edge to it. I have great friends here—writers and artists. And it's remarkably beautiful.

Do you think poets have an obligation or a responsibility to write about the places of their lives?

I personally am drawn to writing about these different locations. I like to ground all of my poems; I like to know where I am. Or I like my readers to understand where the speaker is situated. The main reason I read poems is to feel accompanied. I've turned to poems in times of great loneliness or sadness, as I think a lot of people have done. But I also just like them because it feels like a kind of intimacy—a very one-sided intimacy. When I read a poem, I feel like I'm being spoken to by that one person and it was meant for me alone. And that is a great experience to have for a reader. As a writer, what I want to do is write the kind of poems I'd like to read. I think that's what we're trying to do. Part of that making someone feel accompanied is to give the poem a location, to not have it be a talking head or disembodied voice. There are poems that operate on those kinds of rules that I love, but it isn't what I want to do. It seems like the logical first step for me, as a poet, to do that for a reader, to render a place.

Elevation

The weather is freezing, and we've gone as far north and east as we are able. Time is crushing us, and we have to get back to the middle of the country for a western route that will take us all the way to Utah on the last leg of the trip. We start across Pennsylvania in one shot, stopping once to get gas and once to make the latest in an inexhaustible supply of sandwiches. Later, I find myself spent, but still pushing along the Pennsylvania Turnpike at 11:30 at night. My wife has given out and is asleep, beautifully, in the passenger seat.

Somewhere just outside of Harrisburg, we start climbing. Endless switchbacks. There's a three-quarter moon, yellow to orange, right ahead of me; and the traffic is light.

The switchbacks continue, and the climb is steady. Somehow—and this is not normal—Winnie Cooper is running like a small sedan. The accelerator is responsive; its nimbleness amazes me.

A Harley-Davidson, its distinctive rat-a-tat-tat sound coming first, passes me. The guy has a black helmet with "Tommy" stenciled on the back. He begins to pull away, but I give it some gas and follow along behind him. We're doing 60 mph for the first couple of miles. We occasionally come behind two or three semis struggling up the hills. I keep thinking that we'll level off, hit a valley, something, but the incline is steady.

Eighty miles from Pittsburgh I notice I'm up to 70 mph. The pavement is glassy smooth, and the moon gives a little light. But it's still a highway near midnight, so it's dark everywhere else. We bend left and right, up the switchbacks. I keep thinking, "What the hell is the elevation here? How high are we going?"

Two semis have to weave from the slow lane in front of me. Tommy, the bike guy, is still ahead. The slow lane has narrowed because of construction barriers. The semis are in front of me; I ease off the gas and watch my speedometer start to fall. This is more normal. Winnie is brave, has a V-10, but rarely goes north of 50 mph on hills like these.

Off to the right, up another climb, I see Tommy's taillight as he pulls away. I tap my steering wheel awhile, and I take a drink of water out of a bottle next to me. It takes about five miles for me to pass the semis; but when the road flattens temporarily, I really get rolling. I hit 75 mph, and the road is empty.

I have my window open, and the wind is rushing through here like I'm on a roller coaster. I see Tommy's light ahead of me. In a few minutes I'm behind him, and we settle in together. We bank the long, slow corners, he a second ahead of me or so, and we use both lanes—the left lane for bends that way and the right lane when we cut back.

He's aware of me—he couldn't not be—but he senses I'm not passing. We climb higher and impossibly higher. As we pass about the fifty-mile mark, we haven't seen another car in five minutes. I look down once and blink. My speedometer says 80 mph, and the sound of both engines is nearly deafening, the echoes slapping back from the rocks that crowd both sides of the turnpike.

Higher still. Impossible, I think. The moon hangs ahead of us, the only light save our own, and we're headed up another switchback when I hear Tommy's engine misfire a time or two. Altitude. The gas mixture on the big bike is off a hair, not noticeable anywhere else but here.

He drops to seventy, and I stay behind him. When two semis appear ahead of us on the right, Tommy pulls into the slow lane and points an index finger, motioning me to go on ahead. He eases his throttle back as he nears what appears to be a level spot of highway.

I go past, not waving, not looking, just pushing on. I eat up the two semis and am now on a giant sloping downhill. In a dream of some kind, I see the speedometer flicker back and forth on either side of 85 mph. The hum of the engine and the roar of the wind are exhilarating. It's the best I've felt about anything in a year, maybe five years. That's a horrible and sad thing to say, and my life is full of incredible blessings. But tonight is extraordinary. It's one of the best nights of my life. I love driving, I guess. Highways. I love the feeling of going somewhere. There are few things as beautiful as the rushing of the wheels.

My love of place, of new places, has to have a genesis. There has to be a reason why a night like this brings me such happiness. My folks worked for a long time in the hotel industry, and we would move every few years. About the time I'd find a friend in one town, we'd move on to the next. I learned not to put posters up on the walls of my bedrooms or to get too attached to my teachers. And as I got older and left for college, I realized that I never gave a shit about any place that was called home. That's twenty-five years ago, and I'm still moving, still running. I'm going someplace else. Anyplace. Anywhere.

And suddenly, there's Tommy again. I can see his single headlight coming up. We're on a flat when he pulls even with me. We're more than an hour into this event. I can see the lights of Pittsburgh in the distance; and though part of me wants to keep pushing along under this moon, I'm tired, sleepy, and ready for rest.

I think about Tommy. He looks to be my age or a bit older. On a Sunday night like this, I think he is going home, home to someplace where someone is waiting for him. I look over at my wife; her name is Beth. Beth since I was nineteen years old and Beth for all of my life. I would drive to the end of the world if I knew she were waiting.

It's one in the morning. Another day and another place.

Just before an exit, Tommy goes by, the Harley pouring through the night like sand.

I pull into the parking lot of a giant Wal-Mart that is closed for the evening. As always, a handful of other motor homes are here, scattered loosely in the furthest regions of the parking lot. I pull in under a soft yellow light and wake my wife up. I don't tell her anything but "We're here. We're stopping for the night."

James Cummins
Cincinnati, Ohio

It's our second trip into Ohio, but not this part of Ohio. As Nikki Giovanni pointed out to me, Cincinnati sits at the tip of Appalachia and is a southern city. Like Nashville and Louisville coming up, its geographic and cultural locations are inconsistent. We're at roughly the same latitude as Denver or Kansas City, but this is as much the South as Memphis, Tennessee, or Jackson, Mississippi.

We're here to see Jim Cummins. Cummins, in addition to teaching poetry and literature at the University of Cincinnati, is the curator of the Elliston Poetry Collection, housed in a quiet spot on the sixth floor of UC's main library. The room is set up for readings, so we have a ton of chairs to choose from.

A lot of Jim's work is really all about a psychological landscape. In fact, I've been eager to see how what he has to say about place will fit with the more traditional sense of that word.

But as soon as we begin to talk, it's clear that his work is about place, maybe more internal, but driven and shaped by external, too. He talks about the writing of one of his books, Portrait in a Spoon, *and about how the writing of that book took place in the basement of his house, late at night, after he'd read his daughter to sleep. He'd grope his way down into the shabby basement and "wrestle" the poetry to life. In a dirty town, in a small house, he found refuge in the basement, and the poems found their way to him.*

Jim is an excellent host and mapmaker. While we're talking, he scribbles some maps for us to follow later, one that will lead us to the giant brown Ohio River and one to the streets of his much beloved Hamilton Avenue neighborhood.

~ ~ ~ ~ ~ ~

How has living in Cincinnati impacted you and your work?
This place has impacted me completely. I'd like to live in a beautiful place; who wouldn't? But I wouldn't really; do you know what I mean? I went out to Iowa for graduate school. This was back in the early '70s. Things were tight economically; I had very few publications. I had no chances for teaching jobs particularly, and I took this job.

I love teaching, but I remember the night I came back. I drove along River Road and looked at these buildings, these buildings I wanted to

239

escape. Because Cincinnati, on one level, is the city of the dead. Not only is it a very conservative city, but it's a city that people never get out of. I refer to it as a reverse Brigadoon; every hundred years someone gets out. (*Laughs.*)

So I knew that was what I was going to have to fight. I saw it for years. People would come here, and they'd die because they couldn't face the abyss. Because the abyss was themselves, and you have to fight it. So that night, driving along River Road in the middle of the night, looking at all the dead faces in those houses and I thought, "Holy shit, I was so happy in Iowa."

This place was a place both to escape from, and also it was the repository of me, of what I was and did. It was cold and implacable. For me, Cincinnati was full of great, silent spaces, at the other side of which you could hear other people having fun. So when I came back here from Iowa, my heart just sank through to my feet. I was sick in my stomach for a whole year until I reacclimated. It's deadly here in certain ways, almost on a toxic level. But on the other hand, I'm grateful for lots of things that are here. My daughters. And a life that I'm grateful to have.

But this was going to be my home, and I had to fight through that level of it. It never stops, because it's not a lonely place, but it is a solitary one. People are solitary here. It's a German town; they have German ways. They lock up their houses at eight o'clock. They're behind their locked doors, in their little places, doing whatever they do. So that solitude sort of descends on you when you come to live here. It's been a very shaping factor.

Now, in my middle age, I have deep, deep affection for the city and the state. With my eyes open, though. I mean this place is not perfect, but it's that interaction between it and me, that fight that I've needed to maintain myself, the fight that shaped me.

Consequently, when you talk about how place shapes you, I think my poetry is about psychological landscapes. Even when I went to Europe for a year, I had to be in a neighborhood. I had to be someplace that is something vis-à-vis something else, the vantage point on someplace else. I like to travel, but I don't have the wanderlust. I really like to see the same people each day; I like to see them turn. I like to see us all grow old together. I like to see how life works, and I feel you see that best by staying in one place.

I finished high school here, I went to college here; and so, a lot of those powerful experiences are set in this space, along this river that I love—the Ohio—among these buildings, in this kind of solitudinous space. In my next book I want to give voice to exactly that, where I begin and where it begins and ends. This amazing place.

Before he died, Jim Wright came back here to read. He would never leave New York City because he thought of Ohio as the land of the dead.

But for every Ohio poet, there are three or four who have mattered, and Jim Wright is one.

Wright's terror in this place and classification of this place as the land of the dead is something I'm completely in sympathy with. But I want to be the weed that grows out of that, because you're dealt what you're dealt. The demons that Wright couldn't defeat here. But I have come, not to love this landscape, but to be part of it and have an edgy and strong relationship with it.

Spring Comes to Hamilton Avenue

In spring the pear trees blossom
on Hamilton Avenue
and for a week or two
the young black kids with nowhere to go
sell their dope to each other
under resplendence.

For a week or two
the "Blue Jay" is a bright eye,
and the old beaks who gather there
to sort neighborhood gossip
remember their own.

Ray is gone now, the self-proclaimed
"Mayor of Northside,"
but there are several Rays left
warming on benches
under the white and blowing trees;

and this morning, across the street,
Bill steps out from the clutter
of his hardware store,
tilts a red cup to his lips,
then smiles around
with a general benignity
under the white flowers.

So much pain in the world—
so brilliant its occasional release!
A bus moves by slowly,
an old woman at a wedding;
a girl stands up on her bike—

how I loathe the ones
who say we've fallen
from some glory;
how I loathe their god.

—James Cummins

Frederick Smock
Louisville, Kentucky

We leave urban Cincinnati behind and almost immediately find ourselves in lush and hilly Kentucky. We make our way to Louisville and snake through surprisingly narrow and crowded city streets to Frederick Smock's home, a second-floor apartment in a house from the 1920s that sits just blocks south of Cave Hill Cemetery, a sweeping and gigantic mid-nineteenth-century graveyard where Smock's grandparents rest.

Smock welcomes me into his writing room, a placid, Spartan, and perfect space. A tiny wooden desk sits in one corner next to a large wood-framed window (a dozen panes). In front of the desk is a rolling wooden chair with two overstuffed pillows. It's the kind of chair one could sit at for a while. The small writing surface is lit by a nine-inch lamp. A few small volumes crowd one side; in the middle is a stack of stapled pages.

The adjoining right-hand wall has a single 48-inch-tall bookshelf. It's full but not overfull. The back wall, facing the window, facing the desk, features a tiny end table and a big red futon.

The room is quiet and still, and the peaceful space has taken me in. Smock's voice is even, and his motions are muted, tiny. He sips occasionally from a coffee cup. Sometimes his hands clasp. Before we chat, he takes me down a hallway to show me his studio. On one wall are about a dozen canvases (for a gallery show, his second ever). He admits freely he's an amateur, but his passion for it is pretty clear. The canvases are all landscapes, each packed with color, most with heavy, dark skies, far-off buildings, the occasional tree in the foreground. They are like a dozen versions of one image, each slightly different. He's working it out, placing and replacing the elements. I'd like to stick around and see the final canvas, where he gets everything where he wants it.

~ ~ ~ ~ ~ ~

There was a great piece in Louisville Magazine *about you growing up in your grandmother's house. You used to lie on the roof of the garage, overseeing the backyard, the alley, and all the life that teemed in that neighborhood. How has that place fed your work over the years?*

That's a big question, and the answer is "Lots of ways." As I delve into it, one of the things it suggests to me is an awareness of surroundings and space. There are people who go through life just unaware of the rooms they live in, the buildings that surround them. I think that's why we have so much awful architecture in this country. People just don't pay attention. But I've always been very alert to my surroundings, very aware of wanting my surroundings to reflect not only myself but to allow me to keep hold of part of my personality.

That house also, because it was a house of women—a mother, a grandmother, a great-aunt, and then all these widows and nuns—and they all took care of me. They helped create a sense of warmth about place.

What is your relationship like with Kentucky?

It used to be a love-hate relationship *(laughs)*. Being a Kentucky native—a Louisville native—I lost a few years in college wanting to be a New York poet, thinking that's where it was happening. Even though I had grown up reading Kentucky writers and had met Jessie Stuart on a number of occasions when he came into town—and loved him as a child. As I got a little older, I began to think that wasn't cool. I wanted to be from anywhere but Kentucky. So that was not productive. Then I began to make my peace with it when I began to discover some other Kentucky poets, poets whose voices really were more like my own. I became friends with Richard Taylor, Wendell Berry, James Baker Hall, and some others, who through their books—and later through their friendships—sort of mentored me and let me know it was okay to be from this place. And now I love it.

How does place work for you in your work? Does it provide context, foundation, metaphor?

For me, it's often a place to begin. There's an exercise I do with my students where I ask them to draw a sort of blueprint of the house they grew up in and place a few things they remember around the house. And then, using those things, write a sentence about each of them, finally turning those sentences into a sort of poem of reminiscence. For me, the physical place—especially as it lives in memory—is an avenue into emotion and idea. It's a doorway through which you can apprehend those other things. Without that, I think I'd find it a lot harder to find my way to emotion, epiphany, whatever it is that's going to happen in a poem. The best poem is almost always the one that is unplanned. You're fretful throughout, thinking, "This one's going to crap out like they usually do." *(Laughs.)* But then something wonderful and unexpected happens and part of the answer is place is an avenue to get to these other things.

You edited American Voice *for many years, a magazine that published a very diverse group of writers. Did you ever get the sense while you were putting that magazine together that you were really learning something about the places from where these writers come?*

Oh yes. I was very aware of Kentucky being a place away from the centers of publishing. To do an international literary anthology from Kentucky was kind of goofy. Sallie Bingham and I even marginalized ourselves at the beginning. We thought of calling our journal *The Other Voices.* We were at dinner one night in New York with Frank McShane, who taught at Columbia, and he said, "You ought to locate it more centrally; call it the *American Voice,* something like that." And so we did. It was an obvious suggestion.

It was very important to be open to all of the writing that was going on around and not finding voice in the more mainstream press—regional voices, women, writers of color. These are people who were not being published as much as they are now. And we had some inspiration. When Thomas Jefferson was plotting out the new territories, he drew the new Greenwich meridian right through Louisville. It was going to be the Greenwich of the West. And Thomas Merton said Kentucky was the center of the universe. Of course, I think he had in mind the Bardstown area with the distilleries and the monasteries, because he liked his bourbon.

We were very aware of being a center in our own way, but a center that was away from what people *thought* of as the center. We always published Kentucky writers alongside those of national and international renown, so they would see their work side by side with people who had won the Nobel Prize for Literature. And think, "I do belong on this sphere."

Heron

The blue heron has come to Franklin County.
That is, to the topmost branches of a dead
cypress beside a pond on my friend Richard
Taylor's farm. We hiked up there with the dogs
the other day; even the blind dog came along.
We clambered over slave walls, through
high grass, to the top of the hill. The pond
shone like the eye of a cathedral dome and
we stood round it, almost touching the heavens.
There the tree, her nest big as a sombrero.
The valleys lay below us, checkered in greens,
palisades of the Elkhorn rose up in the east,
the skies led away to far blue horizons.
Somewhere out there, heron was unfolding her
long pale wings. We had it on good authority.
The *New York Times* did an article on her,
and the blind dog kept looking in the same direction.

—*Frederick Smock*

Mark Jarman
Nashville, Tennessee

In a torrential rain we make our way south through Kentucky toward Nashville, a clean and prosperous city full of arts, tourists, and— apparently—a lot of other motor homes. We set up Winnie Cooper in pitch darkness, while standing in a muddy bog at the extreme end of a gigantic RV park near the Grand Ole Opry. As lightning crackles overhead, we sleep fitfully and then awake early with the sounds of other travelers trying to extricate themselves from deep ruts we've all caused by parking willy-nilly on any flat spot we could find.

After extricating ourselves from our swampy overnight home, we drive in brilliant sunshine toward the southern suburbs and then find—at one end of a pretty and long tree-lined road—Mark Jarman's house. It's right out of the '60s, split level, slanted roof, set way back on a large lot, surrounded by a wide variety of hardwood trees, a giant Y-shaped cherry right in front.

Jarman meets me at a big glass door and takes me in on the main floor. Light pours in from the back of the house, where I can see through to the backyard. It used to be horse pasture, he tells me. There are some houses back down there in the valley now, but you can just see their roofs. Jarman's backyard is heavily wooded, filled with birds and bird feeders, a few stray tree limbs from the giants that were here on this wonderful spot long before the house.

Jarman sits with his back to a four-sided fireplace, and I sit opposite him at a big wooden dining table. I have a real sincere love for Jarman's beautiful, nostalgic, and haunting poems. In person, he's quiet, serene, getting over a cold, but focused and alert to my questions.

~ ~ ~ ~ ~ ~

You've lived in some vastly different spots. Do you think that the places of your life have had an impact on the poet you've become?

I think they've had a significant impact. I think of myself in some ways as a poet of place who's been uprooted for the past twenty-five years, and yet I've lived longer in the mid-South than I've lived anywhere else. One of the reasons place has been important to me is that when I was very young, my father moved us from Southern California—my mother and father were Southern Californians, Angelenos from south central L.A.—and transplanted us to Scotland, where he served a little church in a linoleum factory town on the Firth of Forth. The landscape couldn't have been more different.

To go from Southern California, where spring and summer were the two seasons, to Scotland, a bleak, cold, damp other world—albeit starkly beautiful—where the language was different in many ways, where the culture was different, the daily life was different, was a shock. It gave me a strong sense of what it meant to be in one place or the other.

When we were finished living in Scotland, we came back to Southern California. That experience, too, was a kind of rupture because by the time I left Scotland I felt attached to it. So to come back to the United States to another strikingly different place also had a profound effect. I now have a sense that my poems often begin either on the shore of the North Sea or the Pacific.

Since living in the South over the last twenty-five years, I've become very attached to this terrain as well. I don't feel like—I'm obviously not—a native, although I was born in eastern Kentucky. I have a book-length poem called *Iris,* and part one is set in western Kentucky, where I taught for a few years. It could be thought of as my love poem to this part of the South—the hills, hollows, red oaks, fields of corn and tobacco, hidden streams, and limestone outcroppings.

Do you think of place as something that grounds a poem, or is it more complex than that?

I think it's a grounding influence. Is the poem going to have some literal reality to which it is attached? Or is it going to exist on a rarified plane of abstractions and floating signifiers? To me, Charles Wright is the great poet who exemplifies the answers to those questions. If he didn't have his places—Italy, eastern Tennessee, Montana, the Blue Ridge—to anchor him, his poems would just float away. He needs them. And since he refuses to construct a narrative through his poems, he needs to have this other thing to hold them in place and also to make them available to a reader. Place is one of the anchors a poem needs; the other is either subject or narrative, in order to hang on to the world and not just exist in a sort of Platonic realm.

You have a number of poems that feel really rooted in a sort of historical place, warmly nostalgic poems like one called "The Supremes." Do you think of your past as a place to write about?

When I think of that place, since I lived there in the '60s, I can see its relation to many historical events. "The Supremes" is also about race. I have a poem called "Ground Swell," in which I write about surfing with a boy who attended my church, who was killed in Vietnam, whose funeral my father performed. Remembering him in that place gave me an understanding of a larger world—you know that sense of the local and the universal. All of the markers of the universal occur in a local place. That's why I often return to that place, to reattach myself to history. Nevertheless, there is a vein of nostalgia that runs through my work; I can't help it. It's a feeling of homesickness. I've gotten over it a bit. It's inevitable that you do. It puzzles me sometimes that I no longer have that yearning need to live there again, even though whenever I am in Southern California, I feel a connection to the place I have never felt in the South.

Are there certain elements from the natural world that serve as triggers for your poetry?

That's a great question because I do have them. Seeing waves or wave formations, whether they're actual waves out in the sea that I get to be among or that I remember, or wind passing through red oaks, rain passing through the hollow below our house. When I recognized how important they were to me, I began to make them a deliberate sign that would run through my poems. Then there are kinds of weather in this part of the world that will remind me of weather in other places. It's so ephemeral and weird, but there are days here that seem like days in Southern California. If I get a smell of coal smoke—not wood smoke—that will take me back to that thin, acrid, otherworldly feeling of morning in Scotland. Those kinds of things.

Here, as you can see, I've got about sixty hardwood trees. And I have an ambivalent relationship with them. They're wonderful, but they're also an impending responsibility because they're getting old. Every year one or two of them dies, sometimes rather dramatically, as in they fall over *(laughs)*. Except for the time in Scotland, where the season was always dreary, gray, and holding, with a brief spring and briefer summer, seasonal change was not something I grew up with. Living in this part of the world, there are four distinct seasons—boy, they come on time. Vernal equinox, spring is here. Autumnal equinox, summer is over. Winter solstice, it's time to be cold. My response to it is not a native response. I'm still a visitor to this place and observing it.

Nashville Moon

The moon is such a good thing to come back to,
Like the good dream in which a long lost friend
Returns from death and is once more your friend
And, though you have forgotten him, forgives you.
Of course, among the stars and before dawn,
The reason that the moon seems so alive,
When it is truly, deeply not alive,
Is moonlight, and the face that it puts on.

The moon sets at the dead end of our street,
Above a house where someone wrote a song,
Above graves where some people have been buried
Over a hundred years. Right down the street,
It shines like it belongs in an old song
That might wake people who have long been buried.

I laid it out, how A would beat its wings
And set off tidal forces against B,
Which with a spasm would repel toward C
The waves that D would organize in rings,
Letting them spread, until I tugged the strings
That pulled them all together perfectly.
And everything would end up beautifully.
That would be that. And that would settle things.

And then my friend, a kindly Rabelaisian,
Aware that I thought this was in the can,
Took a drag, a drink, shook earth with a cough,
And asked if I knew how to make God laugh.
Dazed by my brilliance, I didn't get the question.
He paused for breath, then whispered, "Have a plan."

—Mark Jarman

Carl Phillips
St. Louis, Missouri

St. Louis is a city in all respects of the word. Big-time sports—the baseball stadium rises up suddenly right in the middle of the central business district—industry, commerce, tourism. The gleaming silver arch is visible for miles as you arrive. Billboards outside of town advertise—in nearly equal numbers—casinos and churches.

Parts of the city west of the big river reveal a diverse populace. Gentrified neighborhoods with coffee shops, bookstores, and cobbled walkways butt up against neighborhoods that look as though they didn't survive the bust of the '70s. You see empty storefronts, burned-out houses, empty, weed-strewn fields, and every kind of trash—from half a pool table to truck tires—discarded alongside streets with appealing names like Euclid and LaClede.

But even at its worst, it's vibrant and bustling. Street vendors are set up for a big Saturday. I see people selling everything from flowers to barbecue. There's one optimistic fellow sitting in a lawn chair selling—what appears to be—about a hundred bar stools.

At a local grocery store, people gather at the front doors, some going in with empty baskets, talking to friends coming out with full ones. A sort of bare and dismal park is livened up by twenty kids working one giant Chinese kite, two older teenagers watching, actually almost rolling on the grass laughing, as the kite veers out of control and lands on the sidewalk, string sawed off by a "Drug-Free, Gun-Free" metal sign.

Carl Phillips's home hides on a gorgeous tree-lined street in the shadow of the 150-foot-high giant green dome of the Cathedral Basilica of St. Louis. The house dates to the turn of the last century, and its front is dominated by a giant magnolia tree. Inside, the house has high ceilings, hardwood floors—with occasional and surprising marble slab inlays. Carl's study is on the second floor, full of light from giant bay windows that open into the backyard.

Carl and I sit in the front living room; he's on the "dog's" couch, I'm in a big chair. Max, the milder of the two dogs, is barking at me. Barking doesn't cover it. As he barks, I can see the muscles in his legs and back tense. His mouth flies open, the teeth, nice and white and present. If Carl were not so calm, I'd imagine that I would just look like a great big doggie treat.

~ ~ ~ ~ ~ ~

How has place impacted your poetry?

For me, maybe it's less a matter of place than of placelessness. I grew up on air force bases, moving around nearly every single year until I was in high school. Sometimes I think that's the reason I ended up being a writer: I could create a sort of world to carry around with me.

On one hand, I like to think of myself as being from Massachusetts. I went to high school there, and college, and taught there for a while. But as of this fall, I've been in St. Louis for ten years, and I realize I can't really choose, at this point, which place I call home—or I don't want to choose. I live on Cape Cod in the summer, and I find that's good for a certain amount of time, and then I really miss being in St. Louis again; and vice versa. Maybe it's been built into me not to be able to live in any one place permanently. As for how that affects the writing, it may be why the poems aren't about a particular place usually, but about questing within and beyond place, never being quite able to sit still, as if restiveness equals what it means to be alive.

So I think that's where place figures into the work. It might also explain why I write the way I write, the often sinuous syntax. I think it's a way of stalling, never quite staying in one place, stalling getting there—as soon as you arrive, you plummet off in another direction.

My poems changed a great deal once I moved to the Midwest. When my first book came out, the reviews described the work as urban poetry. I'm sure that getting together with my partner, Doug Macomber, had a big part in the work's changes. He's a landscape photographer; so when we came to the Midwest, we spent a lot of time going out to the countryside, just sort of tracking the light at sunset. Just staring for hours. In his case, staring and waiting for the right shot. In my case, well, wondering what to make of another field, another sky. That's how I came to love the Midwest. For a long while, I'd been constantly looking for the ocean, missing it. I needed to be away, in the very different landscape of the Midwest, to learn the difference between searching and seeing, in this case seeing those bits of the world in front of me. As a result, the poems are as likely now to feature a Midwest landscape as a marine one.

You talk about the midwestern landscape, but St. Louis is clearly a city. What is there about living in a city and this neighborhood in particular?

I love the diversity here, the racial diversity, the sexual diversity— this is, among other things, a decidedly gay-lesbian neighborhood, which means that it's also the neighborhood for the independent bookstore, coffee shops, and a lot of art galleries. It also means that Doug and I are no longer the exotic couple that we were just a few miles across town, where we lived before—which is refreshing.

So it means a lot to me to be in a city and yet to have the small neighborhood feel that exists here as well.

It also seems fitting that I would live two doors down from the Basilica. Every day, every hour, you hear the bells up until the six o'clock culmination. Somehow I feel as if I'm living through the canonical hours with the clergy at some secular level. My big models, after all, are (George) Herbert and (Gerard Manley) Hopkins, in terms of how to fuse secular and sacred longing in a poem. At one and the same time, I resist organized religion and am intrigued by it. So it seems perfect to live in the shadow of the Basilica, without spending a lot of time entering the building itself, and yet living a life not unconnected with the daily routine there. In the morning, I look out the window and can see, all at once, a fleet of nuns passing, some teenage girls jogging past the nuns, a gay couple holding hands, and a homeless person making the morning rounds—it's a heady mix, which is something one gets, of course, in a city.

You split your time between here and Massachusetts—summers on Cape Cod, the rest of the year teaching at Washington University. Do you write here and in Massachusetts?

I think I write the same amount there as here. In Massachusetts the solitude does help. I spend a lot of hours doing what looks like nothing, staring off into space. Here, the hecticness of life at the university and in a city in general creates a pressure that's been oddly productive. I'm more likely to write what I think of as a finished poem here in St. Louis. It's as if some part of me realizes that there is less time available here, so when I do have time to write, I can't afford to waste it. Whereas I'll often leave from the Cape at the end of summer and think I've written a lot of poems, but it'll turn out that only a few of those are worth keeping.

Different kinds of poems sometimes emerge from the two different environments. The first poem I wrote here in St. Louis was triggered by a story in the news about a gay man who'd been killed by a straight man pretending to want to pick the other man up for sex; he'd led him into the woods, killed him, cut off his penis. It seemed weird and ritualistic and frightening, and made me wonder what kind of a place I'd come to. But it led to a poem in *From the Devotions,* about that urge to follow someone in the name of desire and how that desire can blind one to other very real dangers.

The title poem of *From the Devotions,* on the other hand, was inspired by incidents at Herring Cove Beach in Provincetown. I kept seeing men lying on blankets with little piles of stones beside them. It turned out that the pile represented a dead friend or dead lover. I was fascinated by this way of maintaining devotion and wanting to have something that stood for the past relationships. And at the same time, these men were very much aware of other men going by, so they were open to new adventure. That's what started me thinking about devotion and the nature of it and especially how to reconcile devotion to the dead with the impulses of the living. Both poems are concerned with the same impulse, with desire and its place, but they come at these issues from very different angles. I feel that some of this must have to do with the different perspective that comes from being in a different place.

Driveway

We stop at the home of some dear friends for a night and a fabulous dinner. We even bring in a dessert that my wife makes in Winnie Cooper's tiny stove. We drink wine and show some photos from the trip and hear about our friends and all they've been up to for the past year. They spent a week in Ireland recently and have just obtained two new puppies, but mostly they want to know about us. Where did we like it the best? Where are we going to go after the trip? What is the book about? Are we ever going to get jobs again?

We spend hours on a backyard patio, eating, laughing, and catching up; and then they take us inside, show us our room. It's a giant guest bedroom done up in yellows and whites. There's a stack of towels on one chair. It smells like potpourri. Even the lights are dimmed. We close the door, get undressed and into bed. We lie there for a while talking about the next day, the next highway.

When it's clear we're not going to get to sleep, we sneak out of the room, down the hallway, pet one of the puppies who is still awake, and softly escape out the front door. We open Winnie Cooper, leaving it completely dark, and slip into our own bed. We feel foolish. We get on a giggle streak that makes my eyes water and my belly hurt. But in a few minutes we're dead asleep. I don't hear a thing until a kid on a bike whacks the side of the motor home with a newspaper the next morning.

Scott Cairns
Columbia, Missouri

A college campus makes me simply drunk with happiness. My wife drops me near the parking lot of a new building going up at the University of Missouri, and I am swallowed up by teeming groups of college students escaping at fifty minutes past the hour. Four lanes of traffic come to a dead stop as hundreds of book-bagged and terribly thin, attractive, fresh-faced students stroll across College Street toward unseen dorms, apartments, or elsewhere. Two kids play footbag as they walk. One girl flips off her sandals right in the crosswalk, punches them into a purse, and never loses a beat in her cell-phone conversation.

I walk around longer than I might normally, just to soak all of it in. Young men with sleeveless shirts and earrings. Young women with earrings and sleeveless dresses. I peer in through the windows to the library, and it looks like a college catalog admissions brochure: three students huddle around a gleaming computer, one older student pointing a younger student the way to the stacks, the restrooms, the elevator, whatever. A professorial woman beams out at me as I look in.

Scott Cairns is waiting in his Tate Hall office for me. He's recently moved offices, so he's still in the honeymoon phase, shuffling books from case to case, looking for just the right angle for the desk.

He's a genial guy, as interested in me and my questions as he is in answering them well. We talk about his background in Washington State, a place I love as well. We talk about his early work, which he identifies as being the most place oriented, but we get around eventually to the spiritual.

Cairns has written for years as a part of a quest (my word) to come to an understanding of the presence (his word) of God. He finds glimpses of meaning while writing, and each poem helps him fill in the great unknowns in his search.

Together we wonder if spiritual landscape fits the overall theme of this book project. And while we ponder it, Cairns talks a bit about the physical landscape of his youth—the mist and the mountains and the rocky beaches of the Pacific Northwest. In those places, overgrown, thick, heavy, and seemingly always shrouded in vapor, he found his way. How like that is his work as a man?

258

~ ~ ~ ~ ~ ~

How has place impacted your poetry?

I grew up in Tacoma, Washington, and spent most of my summers on the coast, or the peninsula, or in the Cascades. So beaches figure in. Old-growth timber figures in my imagination. And rainforest. Mountains. All of these are laden with special weight in my imagination. And whether or not that pressure ever translates into a particular text for a particular reader is probably beside the point.

Although certain textures of the places I've lived in the meantime—Virginia, Utah, Texas, Missouri—have certainly surfaced in poems, I think the landscape of the imagination is fairly established, pretty much dominant. Since I left my home in Washington State in 1978, it's been an imagined landscape rather than the one immediately before me that provides most of the pressure.

But I go back to Washington, camp there with the family, ride the ferries, slog through the underbrush; and those visits keep the vividness of that place available, its particularities and its general feel. Which is to say, those visits keep me haunted by that place, those misty, high mountain ranges, especially when the clouds and the sky are very close.

I haven't been thinking about literal places so much, because circumstances have moved me away from the literal place that has kept such a hold on me. In the interim, I think I've had recourse to texts as substitute places. So a (Wallace) Stevens poem like "The Idea of Order at Key West" becomes, in a sense, my beach. And I continue to write poems off of that poem, as a way to embrace at once both the textual beach of the moment and my beach of the imagination.

Do you see a connection between the landscape of your youth and the landscape of your more spiritual poems?

Yes, because when I say that the landscape of my youth haunts me, that's indistinguishable in my mind to the sensation I experience in regard to the presence. Those evergreens and mists comprise a landscape that's currently available to me; yet when I'm in it, I feel a sacred aspect to the place before me, as if the apparent is the beginning of an enormity that is, say, less apparent, suggested. And I suppose I'm just figuring this out now, but that dynamic is very much like the way I feel about poetry. Poetry is an opportunity to articulate a presence that I suspect, but wouldn't expect to exhaust. I think these sensations—regarding the sacred place and regarding the poem—are complementary, if not identical.

One poem of mine, "Mr. Stevens Observes the Beach," was one of my recent attempts to write about a place that was right in front of me.

And even there, the poem's success lies in evoking, in performing what I'd call an apprehension of the ineffable. Stevens didn't overtly show up in the poem until later drafts. When we lived in Virginia Beach, we lived about a block and half from the Chesapeake. The beach there started to bring back the beach of my youth. It was a completely different scene, but I wanted to talk about that odd return, my sense that the prior scene was also present in the current one—you know about my God obsession, right? By their nature, beaches tend to evoke, to perform the marginal space between what you know and what you don't. They're emblematic for me of that powerful interstice.

So, while the immediate place I'm living isn't something that I've deliberately attended to, it's inevitably having an effect. Just as in worship, for instance, the literal attitude of your body has a lot to do with the attitude of your prayer, your spirit. It took me thirty years to figure that out. So I do think the attitude of one's physical location, physical body, is always going to inflect the psyche, the heart.

Is there anything physical about the journey you've been making through the spiritual landscape?

One of the first texts that started me off toward the Christian East was a book called *The Sayings of the Desert Fathers*. Those desert fathers were, for the most part, ascetics who literally lived in desert places. So we're talking a genuinely barren landscape, where there is, nonetheless, this well—this inexhaustible welling of the presence—that is glimpsed, perhaps, because other distractions are subdued. So these fathers subdued a lot of the distractions that you and I toil with, the cacophony that we suffer. They found a way to dim, to quell somewhat, the constant din of human commerce, and so were able to apprehend a lushness even there, even in the desert. And I guess that's what I'm hooked by, the idea of the kingdom of God, which is every bit as available as any other place. By the way, I'm not one of your Gnostic-apocalyptic Christians who believe that we have to destroy the world in order to attain the kingdom of God. It's a tilt of the head, a tilt of the heart. A leaning in to what is constant and present and inviting.

Honoring a place, wherever that place is, is just a matter of paying attention. And suddenly you have this apprehension of an inexhaustible fullness around us. I get glimpses of that sometimes, glimpses that alert me to its reality. It doesn't happen all the time. Just a little taste to keep me going.

Mud Trail

I'd been walking the mud trail, the mud
leaping out the sides of my boots for hours.
I was thinking I was alone, surrounded
only by the high reach of douglas fir
and cedar. I think it was a change
in the air I noticed first, a warmer,
heavier scent of animal, I was
alone in a small clearing,
then I was not alone and was
surrounded by a hundred elk rising,
or a single elk rising a hundred
times. And the forest was a moving river
of elk, none of them hurrying away, but all
slowly feeling ahead, and beginning
their journey to the east, a hundred times
the same journey.
                    Miles from there,
they would rest, bed down among
huckleberry and salal, all of them
pulling in their hundred sets of hooves, lowering
a hundred velvetted heads, waiting
for whatever sign or word that calls them
all together to rise again.

                                        —*Scott Cairns*

Elizabeth Dodd
Manhattan, Kansas

The sun is going down in Manhattan, a modest and hilly midwestern college town that is laid out along the Kansas River. We park in a church parking lot, and I walk over to Elizabeth Dodd's place with my bag of equipment. She lives near her academic home, Kansas State, and she's just home from class when I arrive. The sun peeks through a stand of trees, and we sit on a screened porch in her backyard. Cars go by, but the town seems awfully distant.

Like many academics, Dodd is where she is partly because of a job. Born in Colorado, raised in Appalachia, she finds herself in the prairie of central Kansas, a striking and beautiful landscape somewhat at odds with the region's stereotypes. Her own work has been informed by all of the places I've mentioned, but Kansas figures prominently in her book Archetypal Light. *While we talk, she reads portions of it; and as she does, I close my eyes and see the prairie on fire with millions of tiny red plants and see the trees of the poems take human form.*

~ ~ ~ ~ ~ ~

A number of the poets I've spoken to have acknowledged how important the natural world and its elements are to their work. Are there features of the natural world that influence your work?

The first great landscapes of my life were the mountain landscapes of Colorado and the hill landscapes of Appalachia. When I moved here, to tallgrass prairie in Kansas, I felt enormous loss and vulnerability. There was no cover. I mean, I have trees in this yard, but from here to Topeka there's nothing as far as woodlands are concerned. There's all this grass out there and the horizon opening on and on, the sense of two vast horizontals, between which we walk as upright, vertical forms. I felt quite at sea out here in the tallgrass prairie. And it took three or four years for this landscape to enter my psyche.

So now I feel that there are really three landscapes that play in my emotional life, that play in my aesthetic life. But, of course, one travels. One of the great things about the academic world is that you can take off in the summer. And any place can be interesting; and if you're there long enough, you start to notice what's significant about it, what's beautiful about it, what's wounded about it. I've recently begun to spend time in the backcountry of the northern Cascades, where my brother lives. He

is an environmental activist
and an excellent backpacking
companion, and we have
taken three really wonderful
trips into the wilderness and
into areas that he is working
to save. He's taken me to
camp underneath fir trees
that are truly old growth, five,
six, or seven hundred years
old. Some of my most recent
poems have been coming out
of this experience.

*One element that this book is dealing with is regionalism. Some of the
poets I've met are adamant about being classified as regionalists. They
really feel that they are from some place and that their work represents
and captures that place, so they want to claim it. But not everyone feels
that way. Is there anything about Colorado or Appalachia that you still
feel beholden to?*

Oh, of course. In literary history, regionalism was often a pejorative,
a lesser subset of realism. But it sounds to me as though people are
reclaiming it. I certainly have heard critics do that, and you're reporting
that poets are as well. But in literary history regionalism was a form
of limitation. It was a diminutive, and it suggested something of
narrowness, something of cramp.

But, I certainly don't experience a relationship with any kind of
a locale in that way. Even so, now that I am here in the middle of my
life and I do feel that I have these three important landscapes, I don't
think I can say that I'm a regional writer. I think I'm a writer to whom
landscape and physical locale matter enormously. If I ever am writing
as a regional writer, I would suppose it's as someone from Appalachia,
from having a childhood there, a kind of past that you never leave. But
I've lived on the Great Plains, the prairies, for fourteen years, and I do
write a fair amount about that. I love the light and the openness.

*Is there work of yours in particular that you'd say has come about
primarily because of place?*

Yes. My second book, *Archetypal Light,* is the clearer example. A
lot of these poems were written out of a period in my life when I was
trying to come to feel at home in a prairie landscape, when emotionally
I was feeling marooned in that kind of space. And once I began to feel
at home here, a lot of these poems celebrate that. The book really is a
very celebratory collection. It is an attempt to think about the aesthetics

of existence, the beauty of language, the ache of landscape, a sense of deep time.

Every spring the ranchers burn the prairie, getting ready for the rejuvenation of the grasses. We're in range country; this is cattle country. One night I was out on some prairie that is owned by the Nature Conservancy and administered by the Division of Biology here at Kansas State University. It's called the Konza Prairie. It's the most stunning place. It's 8,500 acres. Two hundred bison. We were up on one of those high flat-top hills, after dark, listening for birds, watching the sky. I was coming down, passed this great tree, an oak tree, sort of spreading out. And I just suddenly realized that I was in a savannah. And I had never thought of this. I thought, "I'm a hominid," because that's what hominids did; they walked everywhere. They walked out of Africa, and some of them, it seems, walked back. They went everywhere. And there I was walking down this narrow grassland trail. So I got a very profound sense of deep time and was interested for a while in some reading I was doing about Paleolithic time in the short-grass prairie, farther west from here, and some of the volcanic activity that was going on then. And all of these ideas began to adhere; and instead of having verticality and the lift of trees or the lift of mountains as an aesthetic touchstone, I was thinking about the horizontal, that horizontal line. Here, the hills are flat on top, as if someone has brushed the top of them with a hand. There's that great expanse of skyline.

In terms of how it's affected my work, it's always seemed to me that *how* we live is one of the great subjects of poetry. It's how we are who we are. And for me, that means the material life in landscape, the physical life in landscape, at least as much as it means personal interrelationships among human beings.

If you look up "place" in the *Oxford English Dictionary*, you'll find the list of meanings is just enormous. But here are some that are quite pertinent to what we're discussing: "A particular part of space, of defined or undefined extent, but of definite situation. Sometimes applied to a region or a part of the earth's surface."

That language suggests an ability both to focus right where the feet are placed and to pull back in order to gain a sense of context, of the largeness of possibility. That is, all the other places we might be if we weren't here. If we think about it, being present, being here is often highlighted, illuminated, with recognition of fragility. We are fragile, of course, mortal and mutable in ways that the places we love are not; yet, in the modern era of ecological disaster and environmental devastation, we know that the larger, enduring landscape is now vulnerable in ways it wasn't, even a century ago.

Sonnet, Almost

In the near canyon wall
the rock wren wrests
architectural presence, chest-
high in the sandstone's dry, pale
potential that opens, diurnal,
under post-solstice sunlight shifting
in the south, to all
the world utters, birdsong or cliff ringed
with the music that fills
(if you listen) each aperture left
when rock or root fell,
leaving this brightening cleft
we now find, mouth turned to the world
saying "here is my heart, yes, take hold."

—Elizabeth Dodd

Jonathan Holden

Manhattan, Kansas

Holden is a wryly funny man, who is quick with a hearty laugh. We sit in a spacious and beautiful living room in his home in Manhattan and talk easily about all manner of things, my favorite being a story about some girls heckling him for being too skinny when he was young. He turns to me and recalls their jeer, "Skinny Man, Skinny Man," bringing back the memory with real pleasure and maybe the smallest amount of leftover tragedy.

He sits on a padded loveseat that is draped with a white afghan. He is indeed still skinny, dressed in slacks and a nice sweater. He brings up Wordsworth a couple of times, and we both recall the same line, "emotion recollected in tranquility." And to be sure I know he's not just an academic, he recalls his great love for the actress Kim Novak and the powerful impact she had on him when he saw her years ago in the film, Picnic, *with William Holden.*

He enjoys the questions about place but lets me know that there's only so much he'll say about it. As I've discovered before, poets keep close some of those things most important to their writing, and I sense I'm intruding.

Instead, Holden gets up and shows me a gigantic wooden deck that stretches out to the side of the house. I tell Holden how much I like it, and he tells me he does, too, but he regrets how often it has to be resealed. He hires someone to do it and thinks he probably pays too much. The dollar amount sounds high to me, but I think to myself there's not much of a chance I'd do it for any less. The point is it's a nice spot to sit and read or just listen to the birds or the traffic. "Now that's a nice place," he says, winking at me.

~ ~ ~ ~ ~ ~

How do you think the places of your life have impacted your writing?

Well, what is the cliché? "Good writing shows." And so, if one is going to show an experience, then one has to be in a place and show the landscape of the experience. And I always took that very literally.

One of my better poems is called "Names of the Rapids," and it's about being on a river; and I was definitely in a place there. And the landscape is dramatic, and, of course—in my opinion—all poems are sort of a narrative or stories. So there has to be a drama to the narrative,

266

otherwise there's no story. One's looking around in one's life for events which have some believable drama in them. Otherwise you have nothing to talk about.

The question of subject matter is a major question with me, always has been. I made a sort of aesthetic decision, one might say, as a critic, that I would begin writing about subject matter as being important to poems, rather than form. Content is more important than form. So it's a kind of antimodernist view of mine about subject matter.

What about the elements of the natural world? Are they just markers in a poem, or do they amount to more than that?

It depends on the poem. We've all studied the French Symbolists; and in *symboliste* poetry they can come to symbolize some things, and in other modes of poetry they don't. I don't know. Every single poem is sui generis; it's a world unto itself. Some poems have certain kinds of requirements, and others have different kinds of requirements.

Do you take any inspiration from the natural world?

Like sunsets and beauty and stuff like that? In "Names of the Rapids" I describe pretty dramatic events that happened. And all good poems have to have some drama in them. Are you going to hype the drama up or not? And I say, hype nothing up. But as Ezra Pound said so famously, "The natural fact is always the adequate symbol." One doesn't hype.

Where do you go, either in a physical or metaphysical sense, to get the material for your poems?

Basically, the way I work is a Wordsworthian way of working, and it's all memory. And one has vivid experiences in real life, and after a certain amount of time you can write about them. Less time or more time, it depends.

I think Wordsworth was the first great modern poet. And that's the way we all still work. All the writers that I know work that way.

Virtually all the poetry I write is from memories. And exactly as Wordsworth describes in the preface to the *Lyrical Ballads,* one goes back and remembers a scene, and it begins to galvanize you; and you get a bit of adrenalin and then the energy goes into the word as you remember vividly. That's the way I've always done it.

Have there been certain places that have resonated with you long after you were there, places maybe that were so evocative that you found yourself writing about them later?

Well, there are certain women, if a woman is a place. But I can't go any further. *(Laughs.)*

Pigs

We spend a long spirit-killing day on I-70, headed west. In western
Kansas we start to see snow again. We get $100 worth of gas, and while
I pump it, the wind tears through me. It's 28 degrees. We have another
300 miles to get to Denver, but I'm just fried. I begin thinking, "What
in the world have we done?" We pull out of the gas station, and we eat
up the flat land in tiny chunks. The message is, I guess, the travel is
not always fun. My wife takes over the driving, and I go in the back
and collapse on the couch, pulling notes and tapes from the trip out of
several large boxes. I'm trying to work, putting things in order, but as I
look at the madly arranged and out-of-control collection of information,
I begin thinking, "What in the world have *I* done?"

It is not the first time I've wondered what all of this means. What
kind of book will this be? Who else besides me wants to know this
stuff? In the beginning I knew we'd have to go to the poets and look for
answers there, but there are moments like this when I feel lost. I get
a delicious idea to just open the side windows and let the papers blow
out into the prairie landscape. That would be fitting, or ironic, or maybe
just plain dumb.

When I feel the motor home slowing down, I'm initially angry. Jesus,
we just stopped a little while ago. I knock something over and then
nearly tumble into the cab as Winnie Cooper comes to a short stop.

I'm trying to think of something horrible to say to the inconsiderate
driver when I see why we've stopped. Any roadside sign out here is a
welcome break from the flatness, but this one is a beauty. It's all black,
about twenty feet across, low to the ground, four stubby yellow flags
flying on top. Crude white letters spell out "FIVE LEGGED LIVE STEER.
LIVE RATTLESNAKES. PET THE BABY PIGS. NEXT EXIT."

My wife smiles at me. I figure the papers can be dealt with later on.
I give her the okay, and soon we are surrounded by pigs.

Bin Ramke
Denver, Colorado

After a cold night on the outskirts, we find our way to the University of Denver, where I'm scheduled to meet with Bin Ramke, a terrific poet and editor, whose work I've loved for years. Aside from his own poetry, he's widely revered for his work as the editor for Denver Quarterly *and the* University of Georgia Contemporary Poetry Series. *His choices for both venues are always impeccable—clear, lyrical work of a wide variety, always challenging, always opening.*

For the past few years, in addition to his duties here in Denver, Ramke has taught as a visiting writer in Chicago at the Art Institute, and he talks about the interesting dynamic that created. Fall semesters in Chicago— with endless museums and ever-present public transportation—and then spring and summers in Denver, a more sprawling city, where cars and highways fill every conceivable space in between the mountains.

I go inside his building, and Ramke greets me warmly in the hallway outside his office. His desk is crowded with books and papers. Behind him the wall groans with a floor-to-ceiling bookcase. It's all neat, but the room is full. He picks up a collection of poems off the chair and motions for me to sit. The book is the newest offering from his poetry series, and he asks if I've seen it.

We talk a bit about the trip, and he asks after some of his pals whom I've seen. He sees the camera and the recorders come out, and he feigns nervousness for a moment. His manner is quiet and serene. When I talk, he listens intently; when he speaks, it's slowly with articulation and a little élan. He looks past me suddenly, as if remembering, "Where's your wife?" I tell him we found a temporary spot in a parking lot nearby, and she's likely reading the newspaper or walking around campus. "Do you think she'd like to come in?" he says, but then stops himself. "She'd probably rather see the campus than hear me," he says with a laugh.

~ ~ ~ ~ ~ ~

After a childhood in the South and a decade as an adult in Georgia, you came to Colorado. What was that change of location like for you?

It was a big deal, and there's no denying that place had a lot to do with it. The question is "What does place mean?" In a certain sense it meant for me in that particular move a more urban setting.

269

The first big issue for me was that this felt like a city. My whole development goes from a childhood in Orange, Texas, which probably still has a population of around twenty-five thousand, and then Columbus, Georgia, which at the time I didn't really appreciate. It really was a community, next to Fort Benning, Georgia, and this amazing set of cultures that sometimes came into conflict or collusion.

I do like Denver very much, love much about the people here, the experiences. But Denver has a very curious relation to race. It's a very white city. There are important racial issues here. It's not a racist city, but its racial consciousness is curiously oversimplified. Growing up in the South and living in Georgia, one of the things I noticed about Denver was the lack of cultural diversity. It was available, but you had to look for it.

What about the more obvious physical differences in the landscape?
The landscape here has always been curious to me. The mountains feel like a barrier, whereas water has always felt like a connection. I didn't really live near any ocean in Georgia, but Florida wasn't that far away. And there were rivers everywhere.

This part of the West feels isolated to me. And it's a curious thing about the West as I've come to understand it. People react to the identical kind of elements—some see it as freeing. You can get in your vehicle and drive for miles. But that necessity to get in your vehicle and go many miles to get anywhere feels isolating to me.

You spend part of each year in Chicago teaching at the Art Institute. How is that city experience different from this one or your time in Georgia?
One of the curious things about spending fall semesters in Chicago is having real public transportation. It feels so liberating. I can jump on a train or a bus. I feel like I can move around. It's more of a city than Denver. And that is partly because public transportation is available. I have the kind of access to things there that would never be available to me personally and individually here in Denver. I thought of museums very differently after having spent time in Chicago. Instead of it being a place where the detritus of rich people's lives was collected *(laughs)*, it became quite the opposite: a place where the poorest among us could go see things that, in other circumstances, were held back only for the privileged.

The theme is access to something. It's curious because back in Georgia I had greater access to actual personal lives, in a much wider range. I'm thinking in part of classes, the children of both the owners of the mills—mills that go back to the Civil War—and then the children of the workers. There was a disparaging term that was used—lintheads. I can remember having an early morning class, and I had a student in the class who had lint in his hair because he came to class right from his shift at the mill. Where I teach now is a private university, although not all my students are children of the privileged and wealthy.

Cities provide another kind of contact and a wider connection to an intellectual community.

What is there, do you think, that connects poetry to place?

I suppose people will tend to think of the connection of poetry and place through imagery, through geographical and geological imagery. I've tended to use the fact that our geology is so much more visible here in the West. It's magnificent. You can take a little drive and see millions of years in rock formation and rock strata. That's a highly significant part of the effect of place. In the last three books that I've done, there's a huge use of the *Oxford English Dictionary,* and the *OED* is based on a kind of geology of the language. You can dig through and see the originary uses of language. I'm fascinated, drunk with that stuff. I see that as paralleling my awareness of a kind of past that becomes visible in certain ways in the landscape. It occurs to me that the softer—geologically softer—South, as opposed to this harder geological region of the West, is somehow connected. The past is extremely present in the South, but it's also decomposing and turning into something else. But here, that past of the mountains is visible and much more resistant to seasonal changes. There's a way that my own work has wanted to show much longer historical and geographic reverberations.

As an editor, do you get a sense of where poetry lives in America and maybe what it says about America?

Poetry seems to not have a public place in the national consciousness of any significance, and yet, seeing all of this work that comes from everywhere, it's clear that poetry has an enormously significant vital place. People feel this desire to write it, and huge numbers of people do. Thousands of manuscripts come in. There's been a consistent flow of material that comes from everywhere in the country.

We're a country that has this desire to see itself as something singular and unified. We want to wave a big flag and say we are well defined. But simultaneously we recognize that we are not. We are made up of hugely diverse groups and individuals. There's a weird desperation that comes out of that. And because Americans have traveled so much and since they don't have a strong ancestral identity, I see evidence of some strange yearning to belong to a certain place. I'm not advocating a return to something or a kind of nostalgia. Even if we needed to, we couldn't.

Kenneth Brewer
Logan, Utah

The trip out of Colorado into Utah is winding. An hour or so from Logan, right near the border, we pull into the Hometown Diner, a place that advertises their famous raspberry shake and that is completely run—it seems—by fourteen-year-olds. Missy takes our order, and someone else starts the food cooking. Once the burgers are ready, Missy brings them and then retreats behind the counter. She rests her elbow on the counter, places her chin on her hand, and stares out the window at the empty road.

The town—Garden City—is picturesque, clean, and snug against a brilliant blue lake. We can see deer across the road munching on the grass and a gigantic mountain pushed against us from the west. I want to say to Missy, "What a great town. You must love it here."

But as Missy stares out the window, I think of myself at that age and sense she is like I was—waiting for the end of the shift, the end of high school, and the start of her life somewhere away from here.

We leave a big tip, get back on the road, and wind around for another hour before we emerge into Logan. We are surrounded by deep green valleys, pastures, horses, cows, beautiful farmhouses, all ringed by snowcapped mountains.

Logan itself, the home to Utah State, is gorgeous. Neat houses spill up and down long, sloping valleys. Downtown is neat and closed up tight on a Sunday morning. Families travel wide white sidewalks on the way to one of several churches, the most stunning, the Logan Mormon Tabernacle.

Ken Brewer—a most gentle and genial host—and I have a long friendly chat in his comfortable living room. A westerner since the early 1960s, he delights in debunking for me some of the more romantic myths. He's a realist and loves to show the places of his life in clear, unvarnished colors.

~ ~ ~ ~ ~ ~

How have the places of your life influenced the work you do as a poet?

Dramatically. I grew up in Indianapolis, the thirteenth largest city in the country. The neighborhood was very important. It was the east side of Indianapolis. We were two blocks east of the railroad tracks. On the other side of the railroad tracks the neighborhood changed. On the west side, all the kids went to Tech High School, which was enormous. It was not a college prep school. It had all the auto shop, mechanic, and home economics classes. A really big school, a whole city block campus. I went to Howe High School, which was a college prep school. Those two blocks changed my life.

I left home as soon as high school was over and went to New Mexico. That move to Silver City, New Mexico, which is twenty minutes from the Gila Wilderness, was an incredible change in place.

The New Mexico landscape was very important to me. I had to learn an entirely new landscape—desert flora and fauna. And the weather was different—dry heat, a different kind of lightning and thunder. Different rain and the rare snowstorms that didn't stay on the ground for weeks and eventually turn black.

Then I came here to the Cache Valley in 1968. This is a different landscape, an alpine landscape. This is a high valley here. All of those things have been important, although I don't write about place per se. It's still an important setting and symbol for the people and creatures that I write about.

What has the West meant to you as a writer?

Vision. I use that in a literal and figurative way. Vision in the sense that you can see so far. I didn't start writing poetry until I was in New Mexico. I'm a more oral poet, and I think that's a western thing. And I think there's a sense of tone that goes along with that. It seems to me that western writers have a different tone.

Sometimes the endings of poems have an ironic twist, a sardonic tone. And I don't see that in western writing. That's a part of that vision. Not only that sense of being able to see so much farther, but also that sense of vision of what your connection with the world is all about.

In Indianapolis I was around people all the time. Concrete. I think my vision of my place in the world would have been different if I'd stayed there. Coming west really opened my feeling of connection with the world.

Do you think poets have a responsibility to capture something of the places of their lives? Are you responsible to the West in any way?

I want to argue about the West. Not that I think it's my responsibility to do that. I've slowly come to understand the West, and it's not the West that I knew as a kid. I suspect it's not at all what people east of the Mississippi think of, at least not politically.

And I'm not very romantic in my writing or understanding of place. I want to be as realistic as possible. A couple of things tweak me. I don't care much for the missionaries who come from the East. I run into a lot of people from the East who think they're bringing culture to the West. I've got news for them. We've got plenty, thank you. We get these people who come in here, and they think they're doing us a great favor bringing themselves and their culture to us. Invariably they talk about how terrible it is here, and I'm saying, "I write; I read!"

And then this romantic image of the West, this old cowboy image. That's been so romanticized, and there are still some western writers who continue that image of the West. It's not at all realistic. It was never true. From what I've studied, the typical gunfight—the face-down, the quick-draw—hardly ever happened, if ever. Most of the killings were back shootings or accidents. It's hard to shoot somebody with those pistols, especially the way they show it in the movies.

I'm not too sure about the singing cowboy either. I grew up a Roy Rogers fan, Gene Autry. I liked them both. I had a Roy Rogers lamp, Roy and Trigger. Trigger's in that upright position. That was my bedroom lamp. I don't know about singing cowboys. I guess there might have been a few. *(Laughs.)*

And then images about the sense of respect for the place and the land. I think that gets a little distorted. There might have been some people who had great respect for the land as they were discovering it, but discovery seems to me a pretty brutal experience for everyone involved. I don't think discovering the West was this idealistic event.

The realistic images of the discovery of the West are not that clean. Patricia Limerick did a wonderful book called *Legacy of Conquest*. She gives a pretty realistic description of that westward movement. Even the language of that was "conquering." It was brutal stuff. It was not romantic. So when I try to write about the West, I want to write realistically and take some of the edge off that romanticism.

Paisley Rekdal
Salt Lake City, Utah

Rekdal and I spend part of a sunny morning in the front room of her spectacular and sunny home on a hillside overlooking Salt Lake City. She sits on a giant sofa, and I'm across the room in a large chair.

I was turned on to Rekdal several months ago by a colleague of hers, and I've fallen for her work. She loves the West, the inhospitable quality of it that she discovered years ago when she first moved to Wyoming. Now in Salt Lake City—still a small, somewhat hidden, and awfully misunderstood place to many big-city folks—she finds just enough of a mix of things: good restaurants, the towering mountains.

She tells me about her house, about a hundred years old, two stories with an attic. She's been here only six months, but she's already had to deal with sixty pounds of peaches off the trees in the front yard. She's painted the interior already, making it hers. She has her space for working, a private area, which she dedicates to writing and nothing else (taxes are done in another room). She's started a garden. She's been here less than a year, but the place she's made is homey and comfortable.

~ ~ ~ ~ ~ ~

I know you loved Wyoming. You've only been here in Salt Lake City for part of a year. What's your relationship like with Utah so far?

It's easier. I'm a little disappointed at how easy it is because one of the attractions of the West is how difficult the geography is and how difficult it is to feel at home.

It's depressing in that sense because I moved to Utah, and it's not really the West. Or at least my idea of what the West is. Like any other place, there are strip malls here and the Banana Republic, foreign food, foreign films. The problem with America is that all the towns are looking the same. Still, it's stunning and gorgeous, and there's such an outdoor ethic. It doesn't seem to be the kind of special or isolated place that Wyoming is. Part of me is happy about that, and part of me is not.

What was it about Wyoming that struck you so hard? I know that it had quite an impact on you.

As soon as I got off the plane and saw it. That did it. The plains with these low hills, and there was so much space. It was an instant connection. I've grown up in urban environments, and I think that what attracted me to the West is that you are forced to think of your connection to the natural environment, not simply see it as an amusement of some kind. The West, because of the space, because of the water issues, because of the isolation, forces you to consider what your relationship is with the land. It's changed the way I see myself. It's like having a new identity.

Growing up in Washington State there were all these trees, these lush gardens, and parks. And then I came to this place that was absolutely denuded. One time while hiking, I had to fight the impulse to just crawl across this one meadow because the sky was so oppressive. That sense of being physically overwhelmed was intoxicating. I was trying to negotiate what it was like to live in a place that didn't want me in it. It's absolutely inhospitable, arid, and unyielding.

What surprises me is that the environment had a huge impact on me as a person, but as far as I can see, it hasn't obviously affected my work as a poet. There are poets that I think reflect the West very well in their work. James Galvin is one. His poems are these spare, pared-back pieces that seem to accept white space, the openness of an image or a line. He doesn't rush to fill in logical or semantic gaps in his poems like I do and like many poets I deeply admire might. I read Galvin many years before moving to Laramie, and I have to admit that his work didn't make much emotional sense to me. Only after moving to Wyoming, less than forty miles from the place Galvin himself ranched and worked and wrote, did his poems really begin to take shape for me.

The lyrics I am most interested in are less essentially cerebral, more plot or narrative based. This may actually have something to do with the West, since the region seems to attract so many fiction writers: prose is highly regarded here, especially environmental nonfiction. In Wyoming, there were maybe five poets I met or heard of or interacted with, as opposed to dozens of fiction writers. Utah has a different mix, and that mostly has to do with the program at the University of Utah, its long-standing reputation in poetry, due to Larry Levis and Mark Strand. I think people are most strongly invested in prose writers who deal with the environment, the ones who recognize this weird and intimate connection western communities have with their landscapes. I think its why Gretel Erlich and Terry Tempest Williams and Mark Spragg and James Galvin and Rick Bass have done so well here. And perhaps I'm responding to a kind of low-level peer pressure in writing more accessible, fiction-friendly poems.

Do you think poets have any obligation or responsibility to capture something about the places of their lives?

No. I *feel* a responsibility, but that's a very personal thing. I feel for me that nothing is really real until I finish writing it. It gives you this idea that "It's okay to die now because I got this down, and this down, and this down." There's a record. But that ties me down to particulars of my own existence and doesn't free the imagination. It can become a sort of obsessive note taking toward death.

I recently wrote two poems that explicitly address place: one about Ireland, where I lived for a year over a decade ago, and one about Wyoming. My attempt to write poems about place have usually been attempts to capture a particular feeling or series of events, and in this way I've been consistently frustrated. Mostly, in fact, I don't write poems specifically about place at all. I think what's allowed me to write these two recent poems is the decision to bring radically different anecdotes-narratives into the poem, to animate the landscape with a perspective that isn't that of a tourist or visitor. In "The Invention of the Kaleidoscope," for instance, there's the story of Sir David Brewster, who invented the kaleidoscope, the story of a breakup with an Irish boyfriend (who is really a hodgepodge of a whole bunch of exes), and, of course, the landscape of Ireland. In "Ode," a poem about Wyoming, I refer to national politics, a car crash, a Greyhound bus ride, the idea of failure. Wyoming simply becomes the animating force behind all this.

I'm thinking of poets who wrote about place or poets who traveled extensively and wrote what I think are successful poems about that experience. The best one is Elizabeth Bishop, but the poems of hers I most respond to aren't actually poems about a particular, real place so much as poems that question the need to travel at all and, in that, question our very belief in the ability to capture a place. What really differentiates towns or countries or nations but our imagination of them? Imagination might be the place in which we really live, and so to write anything at all is thus to "capture place."

Ode

And now the silver, ripping sound of white on white, the satin,
light snow torn
under wheels, car bang metally grenading, and the wood poles,
whipping, loom—

I have always wanted to sing a song of praise

for the unscathed: myself
stepping from the fractured car whose black axle's one inch
from gone; slim pole slicing cable

up to sheet metal, seat foam, corduroy
(*like butter,* the mechanic will later
tell me, poking a stiff finger through the cloth),
to pierce the exact point

I was supposed to sit, stopping
because praise begins where pain
transfigures itself,
stoppered by a deeper kind of joy: so I
transfigure myself from driver

to survivor, the blessed Lazarine failure

bolting up and opening her eyes.
And here are the thousand wrecks
from a life configured in snow before me: myself,
at five, pulled from the burning car seat;
at twelve, bleeding from the scalp
after the car throws me from my bike; at fourteen,
tumbling over the slick hood rushing;

sockets of windows with glass
bashed out into a translucent, toothy ring; lights
and bumpers clipped clean off; tires burst; deer
gravitationally hurled through my windshield; brakes
given out and worse,

the icy loop de loops
on roads, the trucker's 16 fat wheels squealing—

All the ways technology should have killed me

and didn't.
Praise for my death-hungry luck!
And all the manner in which I've failed it—
marriage lost,

buried in the blanks of white space, my solitude
at the Greyhound station
knowing no one to retrieve me,
carless among the others pressed tight
to their own disaster or boredom—
unbearably young mothers,

drifters, boy soldiers
shoulder to shoulder with the insane, weaving
the same thread of conversation back and forth
between ourselves. How

could this happen to me
at this age, at this stage, how
did I not notice, and will you put this seat up?
and will you lend me this quarter? and will you
call me a cab when we get back home?

The young man in the seat before me, head
full of zigzagging tight braids says,
Sure you can dig up that ballot box in Florida
and while you're at it look up all the bones
buried in the Everglades, repeats it

for the amusement of the woman across from him,
who knows a presidential failure like she knows herself,
and when we pass my accident on the road points
and whistles, snickers: *Bet you no one walked away from that one.*

For this, and for all these things: praise

to the white plains of Wyoming, highway coiled
like a length of rime-colored rope; to snow
broiling in the sunlight so that the landscape
takes on a nuclear glow, so bright

we have to shield our eyes from it. Praise
for myself playing at morbidity
because I thought I had a right to it

as if flesh had to follow spirit
to such a pure depth the bones themselves
could not rest but must be broken, nerves
singed then ripped out, the heart clench madly in its chest.
As if

I had nothing
except this white earth, this
smashed car to praise

what I knew before and know
even better now, the hills
cold as a hip bone and tufted with ice. Praise
to my youth and to my age, praise

to ambition and small-mindedness,
the kind I recognize and the kind
I am soon to recognize; praise

to self-hatred for it keeps me alive, and praise
for the splinters of delight that can pierce it.
Praise for wood pole, praise for glass.
Praise for muscle, praise for bone.

The sky is bright as a bowl on a nurse's table today.

And the sun gleams into it as our bus slides by,
the light of us a wash of gold illuminating
bodies lost, bodies regained; gleaming

like my heart here, on this earth,
bloody and still beating.

—*Paisley Rekdal*

Wherein the Author Considers the End

It's a couple of months after the end of the trip, and I sit here in supreme quiet in a house full of boxes, still waiting and still wondering, "Where next?" After more than eight months on the road, we are living in the pleasant burg of Bella Vista, Arkansas, the home to our furniture, my wife's parents, and this small house we bought last summer. But it's not home. We're not staying here.

After the last interview in Salt Lake City, we found ourselves staring at a map with no more routes. There were no more poets on the list, and no more stops to make. We had nowhere to be. We charted a long, circuitous route back to the center of the country, delaying the inevitable return to some kind of normal life.

In southeast Utah are two gigantic national parks, Canyonlands and Arches, and we put them on the schedule. Like normal tourists, we loaded up the Pepsi and the cameras and went for what seemed another sightseeing obligation. You know what I mean? You end up in Tourniquet, Wyoming, and someone says, "You gotta see the rock shaped like a '57 Eldorado." So you go. You shoot nine pictures of it. You touch it. You buy a postcard and a T-shirt, then start looking for a place to get a burger.

But as we rolled into Arches, we were greeted with towering sandstone spires that reached to the sky, gigantic slabs of red rock, some razor thin, that all crowded the snaking road that leads through the park. It was stunning and humbling.

We spent most of two full days seeing what we could, hiking across gritty canyons—which sometimes led right to sudden and beautiful grassy pastures—to see sandstone arches. In the northern section of Canyonlands, we looked down sheer cliffs that fall hundreds of feet and look over hundred-mile views. We pulled lawn chairs up as close to the edge as we could and had lunch.

As one day wound down, we found a rock outcropping over the Green River valley and sat on the stone, cross-legged in complete silence. I thought a lot about the journey, the places we'd seen. I looked for deep reverential meaning in it all. Why here now? What's this place about? Why do I get to see it?

I thought about the tremendous toll that the trip was taking on me, the long hours, fitful nights, the writing, interviewing, transcribing, keeping everything running, the equipment, the upkeep on Winnie Cooper, the miles that stretch every day into fuzzy horizons, the travel that just blurs towns and states and people together. I thought about the months that had passed. And most of all I thought about my poor wife, who stood by me right from the beginning when the book idea was born.

We sat there on this outcropping, and once I looked over at her. The entire and absolute weight of the universe was on me. And she smiled. We were miles away from anything, staring down the sheer cliff face. I wondered if she had an answer, a secret, a path out of here and onward. I wondered if she was just thinking about pushing my fat ass off the ledge.

Now, miles and months away, I find myself writing madly. The travel has been a goldmine for my imagination, and sometimes I sit on our porch—a waterfall crashing below me—and on my laptop tap lines that pour undiluted out of me and the places I have seen. I write the desert, the mountains, the plains, and the rocky coast; and people we met along the way are on every page. I'm getting it all down.

Once we got off the road for good, we cleaned out Winnie Cooper, and the want ad went in the paper the next day: "2004 Winnebago, V-10, queen bed, satellite dish. Saw a billion stars. Price negotiable."

With nearly twenty thousand miles of perspective pressing on me, I've realized that the notion of stopping, of settling in one perfect place is not my dream after all. When we began this journey, I imagined that one night we'd cross the threshold of a new town somewhere. We'd roll in through a town square, spot a kid eating an ice cream cone, drive up to a house with a porch, and we'd be home.

That's not how it's worked out.

The place for me, at least, is a moving target. The place for me is always a little further down the road.

Once, months ago, we were majestically lost somewhere in America. We had taken too many chances with my casual navigational strategies, and we were rolling down a high-numbered highway directly back to the last place where we thought we knew where we were.

And there was no panic. There were things to do, of course, a place to be. A poet waiting somewhere.

But what can you do? Instead of going to pieces, I just turned the radio up when I heard a song we've always loved. I reached over and grabbed the map off of the dash and tossed that thing somewhere in the back. Beth laughed and I did, too. I reached across and touched her hand, we sang this song, and just pointed our vehicle down whatever road it was we were on.

This was the place. It wasn't on any map.

Gas Giants

I was born
in the shadow of a highway,
and I grew up
in the back of my daddy's car.
I fell in love with the Nevada roadside,
lying, sleeping,
while my daddy drove.

On every highway
that I ever wandered,
are the burned out shells of miles gone by.
Weeds growing up through metal
to remind us
that we all run out of gas
sometime.

Bury me
in the grass, darling.
Bury me somewhere
where my daddy cannot see.
Bury me in a gas giant.
With my hands upon the wheel.

—*W. T. Pfefferle*

Index